THE STORY OF THE CHURCH

REVISED AND EXPANDED

THE STORY OF
THE CHURCH

Alfred McBride, O. PRAEM.

ST. ANTHONY MESSENGER PRESS
Cincinnati, Ohio

Rescript
In accord with the *Code of Canon Law*, I hereby grant my permission to publish
The Story of the Church: Revised Edition.
Reverend Joseph R. Binzer
Vicar General
Archdiocese of Cincinnati
Cincinnati, Ohio
January 14, 2009

Permission to Publish is a declaration that a book or pamphlet is considered to be free of doctrinal or moral error. It is not implied that those who have granted the Permission to Publish agree with the contents, opinions or statements expressed.

Scripture citations are taken from the *New Revised Standard Version Bible,* copyright ©1989 by the Division of Christian Education of the National Council of the churches of Christ in the U.S.A. and used by permission. Excerpts from *The Agony and the Ecstasy,* by Irving Stone, copyright ©1961 by Doubleday, a division of Random House, Inc., are used by permission of Doubleday, a division of Random House, Inc. Excerpts from *Conjectures Of A Guilty Bystander,* by Thomas Merton, copyright ©1966 by The Abbey of Gethsemani, are used by permission of Doubleday, a division of Random House, Inc. Excerpts from *The Collected Poems Of Thomas Merton,* by Thomas Merton, copyright ©1946 by New Directions Publishing Corporation, ©1977 by The Trustees of the Merton Legacy Trust, are reprinted by permission of New Directions Publishing Corporation. Excerpts from *The Seven Storey Mountain,* by Thomas Merton, copyright ©1948 by Houghton Mifflin Harcourt Publishing Company and renewed ©1976 by the Trustees of The Merton Legacy Trust, are reprinted by permission of the publisher. Excerpts from *The Long Loneliness,* by Dorothy Day, illustrated by Fritz Eichenberg, copyright ©1952 by Harper & Row, Publishers, Inc., renewed ©1980 by Tamar Teresa Hennessy, are reprinted by permission of HarperCollins Publishers.

Cover and book design by Mark Sullivan
Cover image © Shutterstock/Pavel K

Library of Congress Cataloging-in-Publication Data
McBride, Alfred.
The story of the church / Alfred McBride.
    p. cm.
Includes bibliographical references (p.   ) and index.
ISBN 978-0-86716-876-1 (pbk. : alk. paper) 1. Catholic Church—History. 2. Church history.
I. Title.
BX945.3.M38 2009
282.09—dc22
                                        2009001204

ISBN 978-0-86716-876-1
Copyright ©2009, Alfred McBride, O.Praem. All rights reserved.

Published by St. Anthony Messenger Press
28 W. Liberty St.
Cincinnati, OH 45202
www.SAMPBooks.org

Printed in the United States of America.

Printed on acid-free paper.

09 10 11 12 13 5 4 3 2 1

CONTENTS

INTRODUCTION

. . . .

"Will I see before I die the church of God as in days of old, when the apostles spread their nets to take not gold or silver, but the souls of men and women?" It has been almost a thousand years since Saint Bernard of Clairvaux asked that question, yet his dream of recovering apostolic innocence never dies—even when century after century yields a more sober picture of Catholic behavior. For over two thousand years the Catholic church has housed an unruly family of saints, sinners and ordinary folks. Its history is the record of a boisterous lot of people—inspiring, infuriating, sometimes frustratingly dull and often engagingly charming.

No single volume can contain the whole story of that vast history. In this book I have selected what seemed to me the key events, the peak experiences in our history, and knitted them together in as reasonable a sequence as I could to give a sense of continuity.

This book is history from a human perspective. I believe that straight narrative history tends to distance the reader from the event. Therefore I have chosen to present thirty key events of the church's history largely in fictional form: short stories, mini-dramas, interviews, diaries, letters and dialogues. In this way I hope to bring the personal element to life again and let the message of the past assume greater relevance for our own day.

Each event is placed into historical context through sidebars, and there are questions for reflection and sections that help connect the topic under discussion to current events in the church. A timeline at the beginning of each section relates the secular events of that era to the religious happenings.

Why Study Church History?

The best reasons I can offer to study church history are the lessons I have learned from the study.

First of all, it seems to me that history does repeat itself. I know that the context makes this repetition less than obvious and that there is never an exact recurrence of any event. But there are, nonetheless, startling parallels. Fourth-century Catholics resisted moving liturgical celebrations from houses to basilicas, just as twentieth-century Catholics raised eyebrows at the "innovation" of home liturgies. The pacifist tendencies of second-century Christians are reappearing in the thinking of some twenty-first–century Catholics—even bishops!

At the same time, we are not bound to repeat past mistakes. Heresy-hunting has a long and dishonorable record among us, whether the dissenters are fourth-century Arians, twelfth-century Cathari, sixteenth-century Protestants, eighteenth-century political liberals or twenty-first–century theological liberals. Our history in this area is sadly repetitive. We must always disagree with opinions and judgments that seem contrary to orthodoxy, but is it really necessary to oppress those with whom we are not in accord? Today, with the Vatican II documents on religious freedom and ecumenism, we at least have policies of dialogue and tolerance that would have served us well in ages past.

The second lesson I have learned is that a crisis ignored is a crisis postponed. When an institution fails to adapt to historical change, it faces a crisis.

The sixteenth-century church refused to face the rise of nationalism and the emergence of an educated elite that would not tolerate papal interference or the moneygrubbing associated with the questionable approach to indulgences. This failure to adapt led to the crisis of the Reformation.

A similar failure occurred in the eighteenth and nineteenth centuries when it became clear that monarchy was a dying institution. Altar clung to throne and both tumbled in the chaos of various revolutions.

Crisis does not go away. Eventually, at Vatican II, the church caught up with the emergence of democratic structures and began to adapt.

Which leads to my third lesson: The church is remarkably durable and resilient. Despite its failures to adapt and its proverbial resistance to change, despite encountering body blows that have felled empires, the church is still around. Ultimately the church does come to terms with change, even if it takes a long time to do so.

Some might argue that adaptation needs to go slowly so that the church can assess the positive and negative aspects of change, prudently keep the valuable and jettison the useless. What about those who are hurt by unreasonable delay? Ah, yes, but look at those who would be devastated by undue haste. This too is our history, an unresolvable argument between innately conservative and liberal temperaments. Nonetheless, the church is still here and still very much alive.

The study of church history offers natural evidence for the church's durability and continuity and supports our supernatural belief that Jesus abides with us always. It is our faith that he will not let the gates of hell prevail against us, that he has sent the Holy Spirit to dwell in our midst.

Thus church history is, in the final analysis, sacred history—a continuation of the salvation history begun with Abraham. It is a record of a people called to faith and aided by grace, a people who have sinned shamelessly and loved God with abandon. I trust that, above all, this is the lesson you will learn in reading and studying this history of the church.

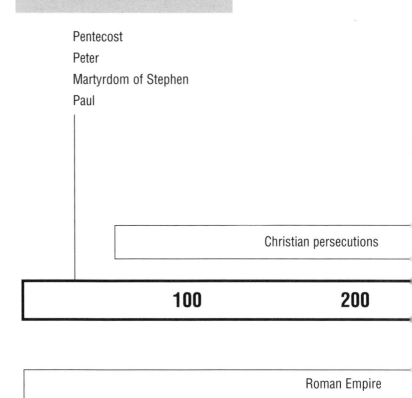

EVENTS IN THE CHURCH

Pentecost
Peter
Martyrdom of Stephen
Paul

Christian persecutions

100   200

Roman Empire

EVENTS IN SOCIETY

part one: EARLY CHURCH

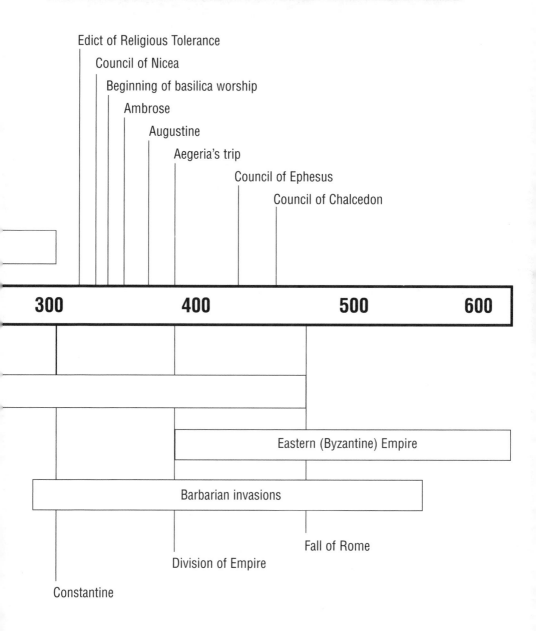

Edict of Religious Tolerance

Council of Nicea

Beginning of basilica worship

Ambrose

Augustine

Aegeria's trip

Council of Ephesus

Council of Chalcedon

300   **400**   **500**   **600**

Eastern (Byzantine) Empire

Barbarian invasions

Fall of Rome

Division of Empire

Constantine

CHAPTER ONE

. . . .

THE CHURCH BEGINS

> [Y]ou are Peter, and on
> this rock I will build
> my church.
> (Matthew 16:18)

. . . .

PETER STIRS THE CROWDS IN PENTECOST SQUARE
(c. 30-33)

The Greek traveler stood bewildered in the Jerusalem crowd. What was happening? All about him Jews from many nations milled excitedly and pointed to a group in the center of the square.

The traveler had heard that the Jerusalem holidays were exciting, but he was not prepared for this. The crowd was electrified. What was that group up to? He tried to weave his way closer.

"You are drunk!" someone shouted at the group.

The traveler heard one of them, the big man with the gray-streaked hair, respond: "We are not drunk. We are stunned with joy because we have had an experience like Israel had at Sinai."

The Greek traveler wondered what he meant by that.

"Why not own up," heckled another. "You've been to the wine bottle once too often."

Then the big man raised his hand for silence. The crowd fell quiet.

"Do not judge by appearances," he began. "Listen to our words. At Sinai,

3

Saint Peter
For the Old
Testament back-
ground to Peter's
remarks about Sinai,
see Exodus 19:3–6.
. . . .

Pentecost
Pentecost—
the fiftieth day—
was a time in
Judaism to visit the
temple in Jerusalem.
The city was teeming
with visitors when
the Holy Spirit
arrived.
. . . .

God called Israel to be a community of faith. God called our ancestors there to be a holy nation. That meant they should form a community that would worship God and live a worthy life. God also summoned them to be the light of nations, that is, to be a missionary witness helping all people to know God."

"I think I can agree with your first point," ventured a Pharisee in the crowd, "but I don't really believe God wanted us to be missionaries."

"My friend, you have forgotten the meaning of the story of Jonah," the big man remarked. "He was a preacher told by God to go on a missionary trip to Nineveh. Recall that Jonah resisted the call at first until God overcame him. Jonah was an example of how Israel, too, resisted the call."

"Who is that man?" the traveler asked of no one in particular.

"His name is Peter," a tradesman replied.

"He is their leader," said a woman nearby.

A young woman in the crowd, moved by Peter's sincerity, asked, "How is it you were speaking in a language we all could understand when you burst upon us here in the square? How did you manage to unify all of us who speak so many different tongues?"

"Perhaps I can explain this best to you," Peter answered, "by comparing this to the old story of the Tower of Babel. That was a tower of human pride that resulted in a breakdown in communications. The people at Babel could not understand each other.

"Our Master, Jesus, asked us to spend time in prayer to await his Holy Spirit. We followed his word and meditated for nine days in the Upper

Room. Into that tower of prayer this day came the Holy Spirit, whose greatest work is to bring all people to unity in Christ. At Babel, people babbled. Here we speak a message that will unify people in mind and heart."

"Is that why you said you've had an experience like that which Israel had at Sinai?" asked an elderly man.

"Exactly," replied Peter. "The difference is that what happened at Sinai was but a shadow of the promise and reality that has happened here today. It is because of Jesus, who died and rose for us, that it has happened. Because of him and his Spirit, we really can be a community of faith and a light for the nations."

"How can we have this experience?"

"Is there any hope for us?"

"Go on, tell us more."

"As I look out over the vast crowd in this square," answered Peter, "I think of a world full of dead bones. I know that my comrades and I must go into this valley of the dead and bring life. Don't you remember the story of Ezekiel and the dry bones?"

[God] said to me, "Mortal, can these bones live?" I answered, "Lord GOD, you know." Then he said to me: "Prophesy to these bones, and say to them: O dry bones, hear the word of the LORD... I will cause breath to enter you, and you shall live. I will lay sinews on you, and will cause flesh to come upon you, and cover you with skin, ...and you shall live; and you shall know that I am the LORD"(Ezekiel 37: 3–6).

The traveler listened to Peter's voice as it carried over the square. It is like a wind, he thought, bearing good news to the world.

On that Pentecost day, Peter asked the people to repent, to change their way of life, to seek a new life in Christ. And they did respond. The Holy Spirit of Jesus moved into the valley of dry bones and brought three thousand to life.

A new church began!

"Your young men shall see visions and your old men shall dream dreams," Peter exclaimed.

That's what happened. The young let loose a flood of heart-expanding ideals across the earth. The old suddenly realized that their dreams of a happier tomorrow were no longer foolish thoughts, but a reality come true.

LOOKING BACK

. . . .

The Church Begins

The apostles were gathered together in Jerusalem for the observance of the Jewish feast of weeks (Shavuot), celebrated at the completion of Palestine's seven-week grain harvest season in early summer. This season began with the feast of the Passover when the Jews celebrated their historic escape from Egypt.

This harvest festival of fifty days climaxed in the offering of the sheaf of the first fruits to God. At first an agricultural feast, Judaism gradually transformed it into a historical feast with a spiritual meaning. It commemorated for the Jews the revelation of God on Mount Sinai, the giving of the law. By the time of the apostles, this Jewish feast had come to be called Pentecost, the Greek word for "fiftieth," for this was the fiftieth day after the Passover.

It is profoundly significant that on the occasion of this festival, which combined the celebration of the harvest and the memorial day of God's manifestation to the chosen people, a new manifestation of God was made in the dynamic power of the Holy Spirit. As the old covenant was commemorated in the Passover and completed on Mount Sinai, so the new covenant was commemorated in the Christian Pasch and completed on the festival of Pentecost, when the Holy Spirit came upon the disciples.

At this time a new power broke into their lives, manifested in various ways: ecstatic utterance in unintelligible speech ("speaking with tongues"), the power to prophesy, the ability to discern God's manifestation in life. Great enthusiasm and belief urged these followers of Christ to action, giving them the strength to do and effect what apparently was previously beyond them. A new life was born in them.

The evangelist Luke makes Pentecost the birthday of the universal church. Peter's discourse (Acts 2:14-41) is the first promulgation of the gospel. The gift of tongues for Pentecost is symbolic. The new church will unify humankind in the one body of Christ.

CONNECTING TO OUR TIMES

. . . .

Share Your Faith With Others

On December 8, 1975, Pope Paul VI published his *Apostolic Exhortation on Evangelization in the Modern World*. He wrote, "The tenth anniversary of the closing of the Second Vatican Council seems a fitting occasion for this exhortation. Its teaching can be summed up in this single objective: to ensure that the church of the twentieth century may emerge ever better equipped to proclaim the Gospel to the people of this century" (#2).

Peter's first sermon at Pentecost was a call to conversion to faith in Jesus and initiation into his church through baptism. Both Paul VI and John Paul II continue Peter's ministry of evangelization for our own times. They challenge each of us to share our faith with others. Studies show that Catholics are bashful about doing this. Only two percent of Catholics are willing to witness their faith to others and invite them to faith in Jesus and communion with the church. Contrast this with evangelical Protestant Christians, who are far more enthusiastic about sharing their faith.

The New Testament church grew because the apostles and disciples responded to the graces of the Holy Spirit and gladly proclaimed Jesus in word and deed, in faith and love. It has been said, "The only thing we take with us in death is what we gave away in life." Let us give the treasure of our faith especially to those who are seekers for truth, joy and authentic self-fulfillment.

FOR REFLECTION AND DISCUSSION

. . . .

1. Peter converted three thousand people to Christ on Pentecost. There are eighty million unchurched people in the United States. What can we learn from this story of Peter to motivate and help us evangelize the unchurched?
2. The gifts of the Spirit, outlined in the Pentecost story (Acts 2), are spelled out in greater detail in 1 Corinthians 12—14. Read those chapters and discuss personal applications to your life.

3. Discuss the seven gifts of the Holy Spirit (wisdom, understanding, counsel, piety, knowledge, fortitude and fear of the Lord) and how they are as important today as in the age of the apostles.

4. Members of the charismatic renewal prize the gift of tongues—a gift very prominent in the Pentecost narrative. What is the relative value of such a gift in comparison to love and service? (Read 1 Corinthians 14.)

5. Confirmation is a personal Pentecost for each one of us. What has it meant, practically speaking, in your life?

6. Prophets have always attributed much of their insight and personal courage to the presence of the Spirit in their lives. Who are some modern prophets who seem to be filled with God's Spirit? If you were to act prophetically, what might you be prompted to do?

. . . .

CHAPTER TWO

FIRST-CENTURY ADJUSTMENTS

> I pray that the sharing
> of your faith may
> become effective when
> you perceive all the
> good that we may do
> for Christ.
>
> —Philemon 1: 6

. . . .

PAUL THE TROUBLESHOOTER
(c. 52)

"What is going on down in Jerusalem?" Paul of Tarsus was always easily annoyed, but now he was furious. The Christians in Jerusalem were setting up entrance requirements for church membership that Paul judged to be absolutely wrong.

"Think of it," said Paul to some of his Galatian friends. "They want to force the old rules onto gentile candidates for the church. They're demanding that gentiles agree to be circumcised before entering the church and, when they become Christians, to abide by the Jewish dietary laws, such as not eating pork."

"From what you've told us, Paul," said one of his friends, "they're missing the point of what Christ required of those who would join the church."

"Exactly," replied Paul. "Jesus was interested in a new way of life, not ancient religious customs. He invited people to embrace a new life and to celebrate this decision with baptism and the Breaking of the Bread."

"It's strange," remarked another friend, "how they've forgotten that Abraham, the father of all people of faith, was not circumcised, nor did he observe the dietary laws."

"Of course," said Paul, "Abraham pleased God by his faith and his good life. The Jerusalem group is making a mistake by forcing these old practices of piety on the newcomers."

"It's easy to see how that would happen," replied an old man in the group. "Those venerable religious practices have meant so much to the Jewish people."

"True enough," Paul went on, "but we must show them that these things are not essential to the religion Jesus taught. I'm going down to Jerusalem immediately to stop this development. Let the newcomers develop their own practices of piety to suit their mentality."

Paul did go down, and he won the day. (Read the story as told in Acts 15:1–21 and Galatians 2:1–21.)

This was but one of the many problems Paul faced. It is important to recall that Paul's concern for the problems of his people grew out of his idea of Christian love. "If I speak in the tongues of mortals and of angels, but do not have love, I am a noisy gong or a clanging cymbal.... If I give away all my possessions, and if I hand over my body so that I may boast, but do not have love, I gain nothing" (1 Corinthians 13:1, 3).

It is the love of Christ that urges Paul on. Each human problem with which he deals in his letters is an example of how this love can be made real in daily life.

Had Paul written a modern newspaper question-and-answer column, he might have given advice in this way:

"Dear Paul": A First-Century Advice Column

Q. I am a Christian homemaker, and I am concerned about the contaminated meat [meat previously offered to idols] that I find at the meat counter. Can I in good conscience buy such meat for my family?

A. Don't worry, the meat really isn't contaminated because the gods in question do not exist. Still, if you think you would scandalize a fellow Christian by buying and eating it, you might, for that person's sake, decide to pass it up for a time.

Q. Our house liturgies have degenerated beyond belief. During the supper part of the liturgy, people are dividing into cliques. The rich eat expensive dinners and some of them get drunk. The poor often go hungry. How can we possibly call this the meal of friendship?

A. If anything could be called sacrilegious, it is what you describe. The people who do what you say are ridiculing the Eucharist. All those who eat the bread and drink the cup had better examine their behavior and improve. Otherwise they will incur God's judgment on themselves.

Q. Lately, we've been experiencing an abuse of the gift of tongues. The "tongue-speakers" prattle on endlessly. We have no interpreters in our congregation. At least if we understood what the tongue-speakers were talking about,

After his conversion to Christianity, Paul spent much time explaining his change of heart in the synagogues of Damascus. Then he passed some years in meditation in the Arabian desert. Thereafter he went to Jerusalem, where Barnabas, a gentile convert, convinced the apostles of Paul's good intentions. From Jerusalem Paul began his mission to the gentiles and Greek-speaking Jews. Eventually he became the apostle to the non-Jewish world, the answer-man and chief adviser on the new religion.

Gospel Audiences

Our lesson demonstrates how Paul responded to the pastoral problems of his day. More broadly, we should understand that New Testament books were directed to specific audiences with their needs and interests in mind. We can see this best in the gospel audiences, the local churches.

The church of Matthew's Gospel was originally composed of Jewish Christians, but gentile Christians had come to predominate. His Gospel treats the fundamental question of how obedience to God's will can be expressed in the new age created by the death and resurrection of Jesus.

Mark's Gospel speaks to gentile Christians unfamiliar with Jewish customs. The author shows them how to have Christian courage in the face of persecution.

Luke does not know the details of Palestinian geography. This suggests that Luke was not a Palestinian and that he wrote for a non-Palestinian audience largely made up of non-Palestinian Christians.

According to the introductions in the New American Bible, *John's Gospel is more than history. The narrative serves his theological purposes. He writes to an audience experiencing the division between the church and synagogue. He extols the equality of women. The Samaritan woman is a prototype of a missionary. The first witness of the Resurrection is a woman.*

Paul's preaching of Christ was not Good News for everyone. He spent two years in Ephesus, where his ministry began to take a toll on the local silversmiths, who had enjoyed success selling miniatures of the Temple of Artemis to pagan worshipers. The silversmiths' protest in support of their jobs and the temple (Acts 19:23–41) became a near riot. City officials had to intervene. Paul, realizing that his presence was a liability for the Christian community, moved on to Macedonia.

. . . .

we might be able to tolerate it. As it is, the whole thing is more a nuisance than a gift of God.

A. I couldn't agree more. Certainly the gift of tongues is a gift of God, but it is not exactly the most important one. Teaching, nursing and governing are far more useful gifts. Faith, hope and love are better yet. Tongue-speaking doesn't have to be a nuisance if you put a time limit on the speakers and are sure to have an interpreter. If you can't do this, then I suggest you maintain a respectful silence.

Q. I'm a widow and would like to remarry. How do you feel about that?

A. I rather wish you wouldn't, so you could spend most of your energies on the things of God.

Q. Since the end of the world, the second coming of Christ, is so near, I've quit my job. I figure there's no point in working if the end is so close. I must admit I'm having trouble with my family. Our food supplies are low.

A. I never meant my teaching on the second coming to be an excuse for idleness. You may recall that when I visited you I paid for whatever I ate and did some part-time work during my ministry with you. A real Christian does not act irresponsibly. I don't think Christ is coming to find shiftless people, let alone reward them for their idleness.

LOOKING BACK

. . . .

First-Century Adjustments

This chapter conveys some of the problems the early church faced as it tried to get off the ground. It's one thing to present the teachings of Jesus to a Palestinian culture, but what happens when you try to adapt the gospel to a very different Greco-Roman mentality?

Paul and others had to try to get the gospel across to city people—both the "man in the street" and the more sophisticated. Read his sermon to the Athenians in Acts 17:16-34.

To preach effectively to the Athenians, Paul had to know the city and its people. Here, in modern language, is how Paul might advise missionaries to familiarize themselves with the city in which they will preach:

- Walk around the city. See what's going on. Get the feel of the city and its people. Books may help, but shoe leather is better.
- Look at the "gods." What do the ads say? What's playing at the movies and theaters? What's going on at the stadiums? Who's performing at the night clubs?

Using this kind of strategy, Paul was able to present the gospel in a way that would make sense to people. The teaching of Jesus is timeless. But the presentation and application must be timely.

The introductory episode and the "Dear Paul" column take up the timely topics Paul had to face. The scriptural reference for each of the problems is given below along with some commentary:

1) *Entrance requirements:* Practically all the first Christians came from the Jewish faith. It was only natural for them to want gentile converts to agree to circumcision and the Jewish dietary laws, for these were cherished and venerable customs of piety in the Jewish community of faith. But Paul's experience taught him that these customs didn't mean much to gentiles and sometimes served as an obstacle to conversion. Paul concluded that these customs were not essential to the "new way" of Jesus and argued successfully that they not be required for gentiles. (See Acts 15:1-21 and Galatians 2:2–21.)

2) *Contaminated meat:* Note the delicacy Paul employs: "The meat is really all right, but don't scandalize your neighbor." (See 1 Corinthians 8.)

3) *House liturgies:* It would be nice to believe that the early Christians were a community of saints. Actually, they were just as subject to faults and misemphases as we are today. Paul knew how to "rap knuckles" when needed. (See 1 Corinthians 11:17–34.)

4) *Tongues:* Groups of charismatic Catholics, people trying to capture an awareness of their personal relationship with the Spirit, have sprung up throughout our country. Paul's words are of special interest to them. Read 1 Corinthians 12—14. Chapter 12 tells of the variety of gifts from the Spirit. Chapter 13 says that love is the greatest gift. Chapter 14 tells how to deal with the "gift of tongues."

5) *Remarriage of widows:* Paul is here stating an opinion, not a law. He encourages widows to spend their new free time working for the gospel. But, should they wish to marry, they are certainly free to do so. (See 1 Timothy 5.)

6) *Second coming:* The Thessalonians were treating the second coming with lazy abandon. They were literally giving up on life. Read the whole Second Letter to the Thessalonians for the full picture. Paul's corrective measures are contained in 3:6–13.

The problems taken up in this chapter required from Saint Paul the timely application of the gospel. He exercised his pastoral role in applying the principles of Christ to the daily life of Christians.

Our own time has its own set of problems (issues such as peace, celibacy and authority). These problems also demand the heat of love and the light of truth, which is the fire of the gospel. Here is our common fellowship with the first Christians, inasmuch as we follow the same teaching of Christ and try to use it to solve our own religious problems today.

CONNECTING TO OUR TIMES

. . . .

The Challenge of Inculturation

Saint Paul's response to the pastoral needs of the churches he founded and served is a model of what we would today call "inculturation." While the gospel message is the same for all nations, it needs to be adapted and applied to a particular culture and the pastoral needs of a people. For example, Christ's teaching about the indissolubility of marriage requires one approach in the United States, where divorce is a major problem, and a different one for tribal Africa, where polygamy is still practiced. The gospel goal in both cultures is the same: a stable, permanent, monogamous Christian marriage. How this is achieved in a pastoral setting requires respect for the positive aspects of different cultures as well as an appropriate way of solving the challenges they present.

New cultures and new eras of history pose new moral challenges such as nuclear war, population growth, *in vitro* fertilization, stem-cell research, cloning, world poverty and hunger, and so on. These would be the questions facing Paul today.

Finally, liturgy and prayer will take on the expressiveness of a given culture. African-American liturgies often include clapping and swaying, while Hispanic-American ones include many aspects of popular devotion, such as processions with statues of Mary and the saints. There are many beautiful mansions in our church where diverse cultures may pour out their hearts to God in ways familiar to their history and customs.

As Catholics in a multicultural church, we should have hearts open to the splendid diversity of God's people. We should be enriched by it and work patiently to solve the challenges that it presents.

FOR REFLECTION AND DISCUSSION

. . . .

1. Saint Paul is credited with bringing Christianity to the entire known world. He made several journeys to convert all to Christianity, not just Jews. Could Christianity have remained a Jewish sect as opposed to an international religion today without Paul?

2. Saint Paul spent much of his life in travels throughout the known world. He encountered many cultures and customs. Yet he seemed to welcome everyone into the church. He felt Christianity was for everyone. Do you think Christianity fits in everywhere in the world today? Do you feel welcome in a parish different from your own? Do you make visitors feel welcome in your church?

3. Read about other countries and see what customs are practiced by the Catholic church there. Would those customs fit in here?

4. Why was Paul so successful? Could someone do the same today?

PAUL'S TRAVELS

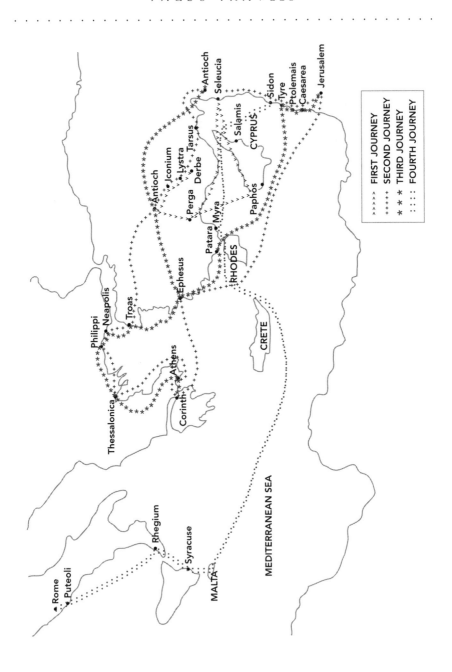

FIRST JOURNEY
SECOND JOURNEY
THIRD JOURNEY
FOURTH JOURNEY

. . . .

CHAPTER THREE

MORE THAN MARTYRDOM

> I am the wheat of God.
> I must be ground by
> the teeth of wild beasts
> to become the pure
> bread of Christ.
> —Saint Ignatius of Antioch

. . . .

Real religion is not only worth living for, it is also worth dying for. The whole history of our church is filled with stories of heroic Christians who chose martyrdom to witness their belief in Christ. Christ himself led the way as the king of martyrs. Stephen followed his master to death and became the first Christian martyr.

In the first three centuries of church life, thousands of Christians paid with their lives for their belief in Christ. Certain Roman emperors became famous for terrorizing Christians and brutalizing the church. Men like Decius, Diocletian and Nero established the ancient equivalent of the World War II death camps in stadiums where Christians faced lions instead of gas.

The roster of Christian martyrs is lengthy and impressive. Ignatius of Antioch, Cecilia, Lawrence, Agnes, Clement and Lucy are but a few of those who displayed magnificent courage in standing against those who would lure them away from their religious conviction about Jesus and his way.

Countless thousands of Christians were deprived of their civil rights, went to jail, endured torture and exile, the loss of property and the hostility of the non-Christian community because they were strong and loyal to their faith.

What made them do it? The love of Christ urged them on. What was the result? The firm planting of the church. The blood of martyrs proved to be the seed of the church.

The faith, hope and love which Jesus asks of every Christian are sometimes illustrated in acts of heroism, as in the lives of the martyrs. The training ground of such heroism, however, is the practice of these virtues in the simple things of daily life. Like people in any age, the early Christians also had to solve plain, everyday problems in the light of their religious convictions. Such is the theme of the playlet that follows.

COFFEE BREAK: ORDINARY LIFE IN THE SECOND-CENTURY CHURCH

The characters:
- Mark, a thirty-five-year-old Christian
- Maria, a newlywed and convert to Christianity
- John, a Christian father of two teenage sons

Maria: It's strange, you know, to be called an "atheist" because I don't believe in the pagan gods.

Mark: As long as we are on names, you'll be hearing them scorn us Christians as the "third race." We're neither pagan nor Jew, but a race apart.

John: I can understand it to some extent. A friend of mine once wrote me, "I feel like a stranger in my homeland."

Maria: I suppose things would be somewhat easier if we lived off by ourselves. But here we are right in the midst of city life and forced to come to terms with it. I never thought a meat counter would be a problem for me till I became a Christian. Paul's advice comforted me somewhat, but I am still uneasy about buying meat.

John: One of my secret ambitions was to be a sculptor. I love working with stone. But my Christianity would limit the opportunities for work in that profession. The profitable contracts are for statues of pagan gods. So I settled on being a tailor instead.

Maria: What did you do about schools for your sons?

John: I found a Christian tutor. The teachers at the pagan schools were teaching the myths as though they really happened. They were turning the literature class into a pagan religion class.

Mark: If you think schools are a problem for a Christian, John, you should have a week's "rest" in a city hospital. I was in for surgery last month. I tell you I couldn't help feeling nervous every time the hospital chaplain came brushing by my bed chanting a litany to one of the pagan gods.

Maria: John, you married a non-Christian, didn't you? I thought the church discouraged that.

John: That's true, Maria, but I loved her so. I thought one day she might "come around," as they say, but she remained a pagan to her death.

Mark: In any case, there's no doubt yours was a beautiful marriage. Just to move to a new topic, you should have heard our priest deliver another of his blistering sermons last Sunday against the gladiatorial combats.

John: I know from experience it's hard to resist those contests. As a young man I once agreed to attend the games to please a friend. I resolved to keep my eyes shut. But when the shouting began, my eyes popped open and I was yelling louder than the rest.

Maria: There's so much violence in our society! I met a man the other night who turned down a judgeship because, as a Christian, he would not want to pass the sentence of death.

Mark: You have the further question of war. What is a Christian to think of that?

John: Our first Christian theologian, Tertullian, said that when Christ told Peter to put down the sword, he thereby disarmed every soldier.

Mark: What would happen if we laid down our swords and the enemy was at the gate?

John: He said we should leave the outcome to God. Even if things got rough, it would only last a short time. Of course, he thought the second coming was soon to happen, so naturally the time of troubles would be short.

Maria: Do you remember when Origen gave that lecture series here last year? He forecast that when Christianity became widely accepted, it would so change the quality of society that war would vanish.

John: But in the meantime, what am I to do with my two sons who will soon be eligible for the army? I'm not inclined to recommend they serve in the

Catacombs
Early Christian martyrs were buried in caves (called catacombs) *outside the walls of the city of Rome. These underground cemeteries for many who suffered and died for Christ still remain today.*

. . . .

Origen
Like his father, who was beheaded during a persecution under the Emperor Septimius Severus (193–211), Origen (c. 185–c. 254), the great biblical scholar and speculative theologian, was ready to offer himself for martyrdom as a teenager. His mother, however, saved his life by hiding his clothes. This forced him to stay home, where instead he wrote a famous treatise on martyrdom addressed to his father in prison.

. . . .

army of a state that thinks nothing of terrorizing Christians.

Mark: On the other hand, I have Christian relatives on the northern border where skirmishes with the barbarians are common. Their young sons have joined the local militia. Every able-bodied man is needed just to assure mere survival.

John: Yes, there are no easy answers to these questions.

Maria: You know, one of the things I've missed since I've become an "atheist" is the use of makeup. I always enjoyed using eyeliner, rouge and perfume.

Mark: I hope you've thrown away your wigs, too. Our priest asked whose hair he would be blessing if he laid his hand in blessing on a wig.

John: I don't know if it's any comfort to you, Maria, but I think you're beautiful the way you are. Still, I wonder sometimes if we haven't pushed this rejection of personal adornment too far.

Mark: I'd like to talk more about this, but my wife is waiting for me at the fish market.

Maria: I must be going, too, or my husband won't have any dinner on the table tonight.

John: Good-bye for now. We'll take this up again.

LOOKING BACK

. . . .

More Than Martyrdom

During the first two centuries after Christ, the Christian people were subjected to ten major persecutions or reigns of terror. Subsequent histories of that period have tended to concentrate on the cruelty of the Roman emperors and the heroism of Christian martyrs. Little attention has been paid to the periods of repose between persecutions—the majority of the time in which Christians found themselves. They were indeed a beleaguered minority, but most discrimination was at the level of minor irritations. In other words, life did go on. "Coffee Break" describes this dimension of early Christian experience.

The following material describes the imperial policy and the public attitude of the Roman state toward Christians. But, in practice, this became a critical issue mainly during periods of active persecution.

Hostile Roman imperial policy against Christians began around 60 and continued for the next two hundred years. Nero charged Christians with anarchy and hatred of civilized society and, thus, with being political agitators. In the Roman theory of government, the state was central. Religion was a branch of the civil service and was linked with the safety of the state. It was a matter of patriotism to honor the national gods, the emperor and the state itself. To refuse to do this was considered a sacrilege, and one was accused of being a nonbeliever, an atheist.

Christians, who refused to acknowledge the gods, were at once both anarchists and atheists in the eyes of Rome. In time they became scapegoats for many of the troubles that afflicted the state. Ten major persecutions unleashed the fury of the Roman government against Christians.

As the episode "Coffee Break" indicates, it was not always easy for Christians to achieve reasonable and peaceful coexistence with Roman society. The army put young Christian men in a conflict-of-conscience situation. For those who were pacifists (not all were), the army was out of the question altogether. For those who went into the army (and many did), there was a further problem: The Roman army was especially devoted to the god Mithra; it spread his cult in their campaigns. The Christian soldier had to disassociate himself from this cult. But if he did, he was martyred.

Christian encouragement of celibacy was seen as an attack on Roman family life. Christian fasting irritated the orgy-minded, banquet-loving Romans. The Christian practice of severe restraint in dress and cosmetics offended the fashion-conscious Romans. Such habits set Christians apart from the Roman state, family and religion. Christians saw Jesus as their real leader. Rome saw them as a third race that had to be destroyed.

CONNECTING TO OUR TIMES

. . . .

Becoming a Martyr-Witness Now

Martyrdom for the Christian faith became as common in the twentieth century as it was for our brothers and sisters in the early days of the church. During World War II, Saint Maximilian Kolbe died at Auschwitz in place of a fellow prisoner who was thus able to survive the death camp and return to his family. In later years, millions of believers in Iron Curtain countries suffered in many ways for their faith. Some were deprived of higher education and satisfying employment and some endured harassment. Others were sent to gulags (concentration camps).

Our secularized society offers many challenges to believing Catholics. Consumerism, individualism and sexual permissiveness confront Catholics with a call to simplicity of life, a concern for the community and society, and sexual self-discipline. Perhaps we are not called to endure beatings, jails and executions, but we face subtler forms of opposition which require courageous living. A martyr is a witness. A martyr does more than pay lip service to Jesus. A martyr-witness practices what he or she believes.

Many persecutions have occurred in history. We have looked at the persecution of Christians by the Romans. The Nazi regime put many people to death in concentration camps during World War II. Over six million Jews perished. Many Christians suffered, too. Four million gentiles died because they resisted Nazism or simply because they were Gypsies, homosexuals, communists, or considered mentally or physically "defective."

FOR REFLECTION AND DISCUSSION

1. Many martyrs from the early church can still have an impact on our lives today. Read a short biography of an early saint and reflect on this person's courage and faith:
   - Peter
   - Paul
   - Perpetua
   - Agnes
   - Any other person that you admire.

2. Ignatius of Antioch was an early church Father. He wrote important letters which tell us of life in the early church. Why are church writings so important? Is the Bible the only important book for Christians?

3. Write a letter to explain baptism, confirmation or the Mass to a friend. Give a detailed account.

4. "Coffee Break" attempts to show the challenges to Christian practice that came from the milieu in which the early Christians lived. How do the following contemporary experiences serve as a challenge to Christian behavior today?
   - Sex and violence in films and TV
   - Lack of discipline and value orientation in schools
   - The prospect of terrorist attacks
   - High divorce rates
   - Poverty at home and in the Third World

5. Students are asked to participate in many activities in addition to getting an education. How can the following help you as you try to fit your Christian values into the modern world?
   - Habitat for Humanity
   - Pro-Life Movement
   - Amnesty International
   - Local soup kitchens
   - Big Brother/Big Sister

6. What in "Coffee Break" do you find striking about the Christians' response to problems of their time?

. . . .

CHAPTER FOUR

EARLY LITURGY

> He was revealed in
> flesh,
> vindicated in spirit,
> seen by angels,
> proclaimed among
> Gentiles,
> believed in throughout
> the world,
> taken up in glory.
> —1 Timothy 3:16

. . . .

Simple warmth and hospitality marked home worship in the early church. The home atmosphere conveyed the meaning of Eucharist as "the holy in the common." It illustrated the unity of Christians gathered in one Lord around the table. The following story about the quality of a liturgical leader catches the spirit of their effort.

COME TO THE WELCOME TABLE
(c. 200)

Claudia had finally lulled her baby to sleep when she heard her husband come in.

"How did the meeting go, Richard?"

"We elected Martin to preside over our house liturgies."

"He's a good choice. I don't know of any man in our neighborhood who can make you feel more at home. He seems to have the word *welcome* engraved on his bones. What kind of procedure did you follow?"

Richard kicked off his sandals, poured himself a glass of wine and stretched out on the couch before replying to Claudia.

"The retiring president, Julian, took charge of the meeting. He started by reading us a quotation from the First Letter to Timothy. It went something like this:

Now a bishop must be above reproach, married only once, temperate, sensible, respectable, hospitable, an apt teacher. He must manage his own household well.

"I'm sure he stressed the word *hospitable* in the reading," Claudia stressed.

"Yes, he did. He added another short reading from the ancient *Teachings of the Apostles*:

When a poor man comes to liturgy, whether from your own neighborhood or from a strange place, if he is old and weak be sure, O Bishop, with all your heart to provide a place for him, even if you must sit on the floor.

"I assume Julian gave a little speech after the readings."

"Certainly. He reminded us that since our worship takes place at home, it should naturally reflect the virtues and styles of home life. We aren't going to have big crowds like the impersonal throngs at the pagan temples."

"All the better," Claudia reiterated, "since that allows us really to know each other and be a fraternal gathering of friends."

"Precisely, Claudia, and he added that we should not overlook the value of the informality that our home setting brings to worship."

"I do enjoy the fact the we have so much conversation at our liturgies. I enjoy the discussions and get a lot out of them. Still, I wish our catechist would not refer to these discussions as the 'word service.' I think he's being too stuffy. He's spoiling a good thing."

"I'm not going to argue with you over that, Claudia, but Julian did say we must elect a man who is skilled in the art of conversation. You know how some of our discussions have been a crossfire of conflicting testimonies. Julian advised us to choose a man who knows how to help people talk to—not at— one another."

"He's right there. Our Jewish neighbors call their house liturgy the meal of *shalom,* which means a meal of peace and friendship. And we are reliving the

Icthus

From earliest times, the fish has symbolized Christ because the letters forming the Greek word icthus, *meaning "fish," are the initial letters of the Greek words: "Jesus Christ God's Son Savior." The fish is also used as a symbol of baptism because a fish can only live in water, and the Christian comes to life through the waters of baptism.*

. . . .

Last Supper, where Jesus reassured his apostles for one last time that he regarded them as his dearest friends."

"Julian feels very much the same way," Richard continued. "He reminded us that our home liturgy is one place at least where we can have one brief and shining hour of peace. He talked at length about the sense of leisure, informality and friendship as hallmarks of our gatherings."

"Was there really much difficulty in selecting Martin?"

"Not really, Claudia. We all just knew that Martin was the man. We know he will hear the command God has always given to his leaders, 'Fashion me a people.'"

Their baby awoke and began crying.

"Our son is calling, Richard. I'm delighted with the outcome of the meeting. If you see Martin before I do, give him my love. I'll see his wife tomorrow and congratulate her."

LOOKING BACK

. . . .

Early Liturgy

The early Christian "Welcome Table" has been described for us by Justin Martyr. He put into writing the first full account of Christian liturgical celebration and the duties of the liturgical president about 150. The following is an excerpt:

> ...And on that day which is called after the sun, all who are in the towns and in the country gather together for a communal celebration. And then the memoirs of the Apostles or the writings of the

Prophets are read, as long as time permits. After the reader has finished his task, the one presiding gives an address, urgently admonishing his hearers to practice these beautiful teachings in their lives. Then all stand up together and recite prayers. After the end of the prayers,...the bread and wine mixed with water are brought, and the president offers up prayers and thanksgivings, as much as in him lies. The people chime in with an Amen. Then takes place the distribution, to all attending, of the things over which the thanksgiving had been spoken, and the deacons bring a portion to the absent. Besides, those who are well-to-do give whatever they will. What is gathered is deposited with the one presiding, who therewith helps orphans and widows....[1]

Fragmentum
As Christianity continued to grow, many Christian communities needed more than one worship service. In order to preserve and symbolize unity, the practice arose in some places of sending a piece of consecrated bread (the fragmentum) *from the bishop's church as an addition to the Communion bread in the other churches of the city.*

History of the Eucharist

By the time of Christ, a custom had grown up among the Jews for fellowship groups to meet together for a sacred meal, *Chaburah*, where the things of God would be considered. It was at such a meal that Jesus celebrated with his apostles on the night before his death. For about the first twenty years after Christ, Jewish-Christians continued to worship in the temple, to pray in the synagogue, as well as to meet for the breaking of bread at the Lord's Supper. We have no idea how often they met for this meal, but it was always in a home large enough to hold the community. As time went on, Christians were

Early Eucharistic Prayers

Early documents contain these instructions on the Eucharist:

Didache. *"As far as concerns the Eucharist, give thanks in this fashion. First in respect to the cup: We give you thanks, our Father, for the holy vine of your servant David, which you made known to us through your servant Jesus; yours is the glory forever and ever!*

"Then, in respect to the broken bread: We give you thanks, our Father, for the life and knowledge that you made known to us through your servant Jesus; yours is the glory forever and ever!

"As this broken bread was scattered on the mountains and, having been gathered together, became one, so may your Church be gathered into your kingdom from the ends of the earth, for yours is the glory and power through Jesus Christ forever and ever!" (Didache, 50–150).

Hippolytus. *"And when he delivered himself to a voluntary passion, to loose death and to break asunder the bands of the devil, and to trample hell and to enlighten the righteous and to set up the boundary stone and to manifest the resurrection, he took a loaf and gave thanks and spoke, 'Take, eat, this is my body which is given for you' Likewise also the cup and said, 'This is my blood which is poured out for you. As often as you do this, you make my commemoration.'*

"Remembering therefore his death and resurrection, we offer to you the loaf and the cup and give thanks to you and do you priestly service" (Hippolytus, Church Order, 31, 11:21, c. 236).

. . . .

excluded from the synagogues, but they continued to develop a form of worship modeled on the Jewish synagogue service: a reading from Scripture with interpretation, preaching, prayer and praise. As in the synagogue, anyone, even a boy of twelve, could be called on to read and interpret. The assembly was presided over by an apostle, a prophet or a member specially gifted by the Holy Spirit, who preached after the Scripture reading and invited other members to demonstrate their gifts by taking part in the service.

Even as the Liturgy of the Word began to develop from the synagogue service, the Liturgy of the Eucharist emerged from the Lord's Supper. In larger population centers, private homes became inadequate, so sectional meals were tried. This contributed to a period of strain, confusion and friction in the later part of the first century and the beginning of the second. The danger of disunity and lack of deference to authority led to the adoption of the ceremonial eucharistic meal instead of the community supper.

In early worship, prayers were completely free. Then prominent leaders began to write "pattern prayers" to be used as models for worship in the various churches. Prayers grew in substance and length. Usages developed by slow degrees into rites, and rites expanded into ceremonies. Solid, standard ground was reached by the time Justin Martyr wrote the above description about 150.

It appears that, by the time of the apostles' deaths, Christian society had already developed a hierarchy of three grades who ministered to all Christians: deacons, *presbyteri* (or priests) and *episcopi* (or bishops). Each town was under a chief bishop, who soon exclusively held the title *bishop*. As a rule, the community chose the individual for each ministerial position (see 1 Timothy 3:1–13 for the criteria used), but investiture was made by the local bishop or by superior ecclesiastical authority representing the succession of the apostles. Gradually the organization of churches in a territory took place and some leading church was given authority over those in surrounding areas.

. . . .

The Feeling of Family Worship

In the years just after Vatican II, many parishes initiated liturgies in people's homes. These worship services did not replace parish church liturgies. These home liturgies generated a sense of intimacy with the Mass as well as a feeling for family and neighborhood worship. These events advanced the understanding of the renewed liturgy and helped the participants to appreciate what the new liturgy was all about. They introduced a personal, communal and human dimension to the worship experience.

While home liturgies are no longer as common as they were several decades ago, the message remains relevant. For one thing, they help us identify with the Last Supper, where the first liturgy took place in a home setting. Second, they evoke within us a family feeling for worship, one that should prevail at our parish celebrations. We gather as God's family around the Table of the Word in Scripture and the Table of the Supper of the Lord at the altar. Finally, we will come to parish liturgy with a sense of intimacy with Christ who is indeed Lord, but who is also the dear friend who speaks to us in Scripture and the homily and who draws us into his mystery at Eucharist.

A home setting invites us to family and community, to abandoning our individualistic ways and becoming concerned for one another. The same should be true of our parish liturgies. The setting is larger and more people attend, but the call to community in Christ remains the same. The shrines of Scripture and the altar remain two forms of one reality, the "welcome table," where Father, Son and Holy Spirit preside, through the ministry of the priest, to love us, bless us and give us food for the journey of life, both here and hereafter.

FOR REFLECTION AND DISCUSSION

1. What values about worship are more easily taught by a home liturgy than one in a church?

2. Our Jewish brothers and sisters retain the ritual of the Passover meal, which they celebrate at home. Why do you think they have synagogue services as well?

3. Jehovah's Witnesses gather for worship in Kingdom Halls that are kept deliberately small. Why do you think they follow such a policy?

4. How often would you want the Eucharist to be celebrated in your home?

5. Why was it natural for the first Christians to have all their Eucharists at home?

6. Prayer is an important aspect of our daily lives. In addition to the liturgy many other forms of prayer exist. Meditation is a good way to slow down in an otherwise hectic schedule. Silence is a good way to focus on prayer and God. Family prayer is a good way to bring unity to a group within the same household, even if it is just a short petition to begin the day. Thankful prayer is a good way to remember that God is always there for us. There are many other types and methods of prayer. Discuss how many can fit into our busy lives.

7. Other than a Mass, what forms of prayer are likely to be found in your home?
   - Family rosary
   - Prayer before and after meals
   - Evening prayer
   - Advent wreath
   - Lenten devotions

8. Why is it important to pray together at home and in other small groups? Would it make you uncomfortable to practice your religion in front of your friends? Why?

CHAPTER FIVE

FROM HOUSE TO BASILICA

> The Church is God's
> and it must not be
> pledged to Caesar....
> For the emperor is in
> the Church, not over
> the Church; and far
> from refusing the
> Church's help, a good
> emperor seeks it.
>
> —Saint Ambrose

WORSHIPING GOD IN GRANDEUR: A FOURTH-CENTURY CHALLENGE

"Have you heard the news, Bishop Thomas? The government is donating a local courthouse to us for use as a church."

"Yes, Deacon Philip, but I never thought I'd see the day when we would be using a basilica, of all things, as a place to worship God."

"Our young liberals are quite excited by the idea. They say it is about time we had a way of introducing pageantry and glory into the worship of God."

"That's true, Philip, but you can expect some trouble from the old guard in the church. They have been worshiping God at home all their lives. They are not going to be too thrilled by this new way of doing things."

"Some of it can hardly be avoided, Bishop. Ever since Constantine granted freedom of religion, there has been a massive increase in our church population. Sheer numbers alone demand some larger gathering place."

"I'm with you on that, Philip, but I can foresee that something beautiful will be lost if we move completely away from the old-fashioned home liturgies. Once we get into the basilica, we are going to get more formal. The old sense of intimacy and friendship will fade away. I'm sorry to say it, but the new worship will be an event in which most of the participants will be strangers to one another."

"But everybody will be united in the same belief."

"Granted, but believing the same gospel is not the same as knowing the person beside you."

"Bishop, you said something beautiful would be lost, but won't you admit something magnificent will be gained by moving to public liturgy?"

"Well, yes, Philip, that's true. In that great hall, with an immense throng before the high altar, all of us will be inclined to sense the grandeur of God. The basilica gathering will teach us about God's majesty."

"I think it will also help Christians experience themselves as part of a larger gathering. The narrow confines of a home liturgy have a way of obscuring the universal character of Christianity."

"No quarrel with that, Philip. With home liturgy, people tend to close in on their own little groups. Basilica worship should help them identify with the whole church. Remember that we, the 'light of nations,' must not hide our lamps under a bushel."

"Bishop, this move to the basilica looks like it will give a good boost to the compulsory celibacy movement."

"I can see, Philip, where it's not going to hurt the movement. As long as house liturgies were our normal practice, it was natural to pick a married man for president of worship. Basilica worship will make the 'sacred' central. And 'sacred' will mean whatever is unworldly. There is a growing feeling that an ordained man will be expected to withdraw as much as possible from worldly concerns."

"Probably house liturgies will die out within a few generations."

"I hope they don't. The home liturgy preserves something the church will always need, the feeling of personal friendship that is central to the Eucharist. I think the church is big enough for both kinds of liturgy. One highlights the value of the human. The other extols the grandeur of God.

Basilicas

Basilica *was the name for a style of Roman buildings used as courts of justice and places of public assembly. This secular architectural form played a large role in shaping the common Western view of what a church building should look like.*

Another meaning of the word basilica is a place known for its historical importance, architecture and its contribution to the growth of the faith. The "major" basilicas represent sites important from the early centuries of Christian history. There are thirty "minor" basilicas in the United States.

"Without home liturgy, we may lose the message of friendship implicit in the eucharistic celebration. Without basilica liturgy, we could lose our sense of identity with the faith of millions. Each form of worship has a role to play. God grant that our future allows for both kinds.

"There is a time for everything, a time for hearthside warmth, a time for breathtaking majesty. Our God is both friend and Lord. The two styles of liturgy, Philip, will help you and me remember that."

LOOKING BACK

. . . .

From House to Basilica

All over the Western world, the Christian population rose from an insignificant minority, to a respected minority, to a majority, to a vast majority of the whole population. Christianity's growth went through these phases at different times in different places. Communities of increasing size needed larger churches.

In the early days of the church, Christians did not consider it important to possess temples; they celebrated Eucharist wherever the community could assemble—a home, a lecture hall. The *gathering* of the faithful took precedence over the *place* where they gathered. In the second century, Gnosticism began to raise its head in the Christian communities. It claimed all material things to be evil and held material creation, including the human nature of Christ, in contempt. In order to offset this, the church had to defend material creation and the goodness of Jesus' humanity.

The effect of this emphasis could be seen in the change in Christian worship in the third century. The material element of the sacrifice, the gifts of bread and wine, was now stressed, thus developing the Offertory of the Mass. Previously, the gathering point at the liturgy had been the *cathedra* (the chair of the bishop) or the bishop himself. In the third century, the altar became the center of attention, evolving from a simple wooden table to a fixed and more elaborate table of stone.

The church and its liturgy were considerably affected by Constantine, who ended the political oppression of Christians. In 313 he issued an Edict of Tolerance that gave freedom of religion to Christians (see chapter seven). A large number of people joined the church. Bishops, especially the Bishop of Rome, were granted positions of precedence among Roman officials. The formal court ceremonials of the imperial household had an important effect on pontifical functions. The emperor and his family erected for worship in Jerusalem, Bethlehem, Constantinople and Rome great buildings after the fashion of imperial buildings, palaces and halls. The basilica became the model for churches.

Development of the liturgy continued throughout all of Christendom until about the fourth century. A definite framework used by all developed through tradition. As the Christian population grew, stricter regulations became necessary. Liturgical texts were gradually prescribed. At first these regulations came from the synods of the leading cities: Alexandria, Antioch, Byzantium and Rome. By the seventh century Rome, long

The Easter Controversy

As liturgy became standardized, so did feast days. There was disagreement for some time, however, over the date for the celebration of Easter. Some Christians in Asia Minor celebrated Easter on Passover, the fourteenth day of the Jewish month of Nisan, which usually fell on a weekday rather than Sunday, the day of the Resurrection. Victor, Bishop of Rome from 189 to 198, threatened to break off communion with those who continued this practice. In 325 the Council of Nicea decreed that Easter be celebrated on the first Sunday after the first full moon in spring, which continues to be the practice today.

the site of a rich liturgical development, had become the dominant model for Christian worship in the West. The Roman liturgy eventually became the liturgy of the whole Western church.

CONNECTING TO OUR TIMES

· ·

Liturgy Is Poetry in Motion

As we saw in our chapter on home-based liturgies, such experiences summon us to family and communal sensitivity in our worship. They also lead us to loving concern for others and a commitment to justice in our neighborhood, city, country and the world itself.

This chapter, which describes the move from house liturgies to church buildings, introduces another aspect of liturgy. If home worship reminds us of the human dimension of liturgy, church worship draws our attention to the divine side of this experience.

Liturgy is an action. It is poetry in motion. The visible side of liturgy focuses on the action of the assembly and the presider. This, of course, includes the acts of the lectors, servers, deacons, eucharistic ministers, ushers, choirs, musicians, hospitality teams and so on.

But there are invisible actions at liturgy as well. The Father is present, pouring out the blessings of creation and providence. The Son, through the ministry of the priest, is present, communicating the graces of his saving work, his paschal mystery, in the Consecration and in Communion. The Spirit is present, transforming the gifts of bread and wine into the Body and Blood of Christ, teaching us the word of God and its meaning for us. The Spirit also conveys to the assembly the power of being a community and the realization of the body of Christ. Finally, the Spirit gives to each of us the graces of being a temple of the Spirit, a child of the Father and a companion of Jesus.

The majesty of a parish liturgy, the awe evoked by ceremony and the sense of mystery unfolded in the rituals are positive ways to help us experience the divine side of what happens at liturgy. Divine love is being poured out through the Holy Spirit, who broods lovingly over the assembly in the liturgical event.

All this does much to strengthen our faith, nourish our hope and increase our love. It offers us "God-consciousness." Yet the more this happens the more we become sensitive to concerns of love and justice because those are God's concerns, too. To benefit best from liturgy we should be conscious of its human, familial, communal aspects and of the divine mystery and acts of the Trinity that occur there.

FOR REFLECTION AND DISCUSSION

1. What values about worship are more easily taught in a church Eucharist than in a home Eucharist?
2. Why did Christians of the fourth century abandon house liturgies for worship in public buildings?
3. How do the following elements offset the potential loss of personal involvement in worship in a large church?
   - Congregational singing
   - Lectors
   - Eucharistic ministers
   - Choir
   - Music ministers
   - Hospitality ministers
   - Ushers
   - Liturgical preparation committee
4. What other suggestions would you have to increase involvement of the people in church worship?
5. Why is it important to preserve a sense of the divine grandeur and awesomeness as well as God's nearness and intimacy?

. . . .

CHAPTER SIX

DEVELOPMENT OF RITUAL

> At the Last Supper, on the night he was betrayed, our Savior instituted the eucharistic sacrifice of his Body and Blood.
>
> —Saint Augustine

. . . .

AEGERIA'S TRAVEL DIARY
(c. 390)

Saturday, March 8

I had a miserable time on the boat coming from Rome. It was bad enough that the Mediterranean decided to be stormy the whole trip, but the least I could have expected was a comfortable bed. After all, I did pay for first class. I won't book passage on that line again!

Fortunately, springtime in Jerusalem more than makes up for my discomfort. The hillsides are covered with the "lilies of the field." The sun is warm but the air is dry with a slight edge of crispness to it.

I've heard so much about the famed baptismal candidate school here. Yesterday my porter was praising the talks that the candidates receive from Bishop Cyril. "That's where they hold the classes," he said, pointing to a church that boasted two large domes on the roof. "They call the church the Martyrium, or the Church of the Resurrection. It's built over Calvary and the empty tomb."

There was an announcement on our hotel bulletin board that the enrollment ceremonies begin tonight, before the First Sunday in Lent. Since I know that amounts to little more than handing in your name, I'll wait until morning to see how the candidates begin Lent.

Sunday, March 9

The church was crowded for the morning liturgy. Up near the altar I saw about two hundred people standing and looking a bit nervous.

"What's that they're standing on?" I asked my neighbor.

"They've been instructed to take off their shoes and stand barefoot on an animal skin rug," she replied.

"What's the point of all that?" I questioned.

"Well, you know very well that only slaves go in bare feet. And Bishop Cyril says that Adam wore an animal skin tunic after he sinned. It was a sign of his shame. The meaning here is that the candidates are presently slaves to sin and Satan."

Everyone grew quiet as Bishop Cyril came forward and quizzed the candidates. If I didn't know he was a bishop, I would have said he was a Bedouin tribesman. He has their bronzed skin and coal-black eyes. After he spoke to the candidates, he turned to their sponsors: "Tell me if you know any reason why I should not admit these people to baptismal school. Will you give the pledge that these are honest people who sincerely seek God? If so, I will inscribe their names in the Book of Life."

No one objected. The candidates overcame their first hurdle.

A singer came forward and chanted the Gospel story of Jesus overcoming the tempter in the desert. Then the candidates filed out and we celebrated the Eucharist.

Monday, March 24

Today I went down to the Martyrium to see what classes were like. They certainly started early enough—seven-thirty in the morning! As usual, the sexes were separated. They began, as they did each morning, with the ceremony of exorcism.

Later, in my audience with Bishop Cyril, I asked him if he seriously thought exorcism was really all that useful.

"I know you think it smacks of magic, my dear Aegeria," he replied, "and you have a point. But it won't if you see it as a ceremony that dramatizes a quiet and persistent shedding of old habits and ways that would mar the new Christian way of life."

"In that sense, I can agree with you, Bishop Cyril, but I would be happier if you said that as clearly to them as you do to me."

"Point well taken, Aegeria. I will try."

The rest of the candidates' time was taken up in studying the Scriptures, the story of the church and the meaning of the sacraments. I liked the way they took the stories of the Bible and used them to unite the whole story of human relationship to God, from Adam to Bishop Cyril. Even better, I thought, the teachers were especially good in linking up the material to the moral issues of our day.

Tuesday, April 15

The last few weeks have been full of sightseeing as both a tourist and a pilgrim, visiting the places associated with Jesus and his life. Consequently, I've had little time to write about the progress of the candidates in Bishop Cyril's school—just these scribbled notes of their activities:

> *Fifth Sunday*—Candidates receive personal copies of the Apostles' Creed and the Our Father.
> *Sixth Sunday*—Candidates receive a copy of the Gospels.
> *Holy Week*—Exams. They look worried.

Easter afternoon, April 20

Bishop Cyril and I have become quite friendly, so he made sure I had a good place to witness the long-awaited baptismal ceremony at the Easter Vigil.

Exactly at sundown, when the shades of night were falling, the candidates faced the west and shouted: "We renounce Satan!" Then they proceeded to the baptistry, an eight-sided building modeled after the Roman bath houses.

I loved the wall paintings inside the baptistry. They were mostly garden scenes depicting shepherds and sheep. One thing that puzzled me was the drawing of a deer chewing on a snake.

"An old legend says," Cyril told the assembly, "that if a deer eats a snake, he incurs an unbearable thirst. This deer will be saved by drinking from the paradise waters." Indicating the two hundred, he said, "And our new candidates...."

The candidates then stripped off their old clothes, and Cyril addressed them. "You are now, in a sense, restored to primitive innocence. Adam clothed himself because he was ashamed. You will not be ashamed before God."

Next they were rubbed down with oil. "You are anointed with oil," Cyril continued, "to tone you up for the great contest with the evil spirit, who would still try to keep you back from Christ. In the old days your ancestors believed a monster dragon lived in the sea. In the depth of this baptismal sea is the diabolical dragon against whom you must fight. We've oiled you up for the battle.

"You will descend into the pool and be completely immersed three times in the name of Father, Son and Holy Spirit. Like Jesus in the tomb, you will be buried, but you will rise again as he did."

The candidates stepped into the pool and Cyril baptized them. As they stepped out, they slipped into white robes as Cyril told them, "Wear this new white garment as a sign of your new way of life.

"You know that Roman soldiers wear a tattoo to show which general they belong to. You have heard that pagan priests brand their arms with hot needles to show which god they worship. Some of you brand cattle to let the world know they are yours.

"This sign which I trace on your forehead with holy oil is the final seal of your baptism. This is a confirmation that you belong to the Christian God now.

As Jesus bore the scars of his passion even at Easter, so you bear the sign of the cross upon you this holy night."

I liked the ceremonies. They had plenty of meaning. I was impressed by the dignity with which they were carried out. As I saw the newly baptized wearing their white robes, carrying palm branches and walking in procession to attend their first Mass and make their first Communion, I felt I was witnessing the procession of the redeemed as described in the vision of John:

> After this I looked, and there was a great multitude…robed in white, with palm branches in their hands. They cried out in a loud voice, saying,
>
> "Salvation belongs to our God
> …and to the Lamb!"(see Revelation 7:9–10)

This has been a Lent I'm not likely to forget. I must talk with my pastor about it when I get back to Rome.

LOOKING BACK

. . . .

Development of Ritual

Aegeria's diary is a picturesque presentation of the well-developed initiation ritual of fourth-century Christianity. Many of those ceremonies have endured to this day, though in less dramatic form. In their original form they were superb educational tools—nonverbal communicators in the best sense. Happily, our revised liturgy is recapturing this spirit. Let's go over the ceremonies Aegeria observed.

1) *Standing on the skins.* The candidates stood barefoot on animal skins, combining the cultural idea of "barefoot slavery" and the biblical shame of Adam and Eve. Baptism will celebrate the Christian decision to leave the bondage of a meaningless, sin-darkened life.

2) *The exorcism.* Sin lies not only in deeds but in the evil and invisible attitude of the heart. The ceremony of exorcism calls for a purification of inner attitudes.

3) *Receiving copies of the Gospels, the Creed and the Our Father.* We cannot move to the new way of life unless we have been called by God. The Gospels are the call, the Creed our yes, the Our Father our prayer of embracing friendship.

4) *Exams.* The Christian community questions those who would enter its midst to see if they are sufficiently prepared for reception. This also symbolizes the constant testing of Christian life in the years ahead.

5) *Facing west; renouncing Satan.* The east is where the sun rises with all the poetic overtones of a new day and a new beginning. The church often called for "orienting" the altar; that is, placing it so the priest faces east. Prayers frequently compared the resurrection of Christ to the rising of the sun.

Conversely, the west is where the sun sets, the region of darkness and nighttime fears. Darkness brought with it the prospect of demons (in modern cities, the prospect of crime). Hence, the night became the symbol of the power of the devil and the life of evil. Since the baptismal candidates were about to renounce Satan, it was quite natural for them to address their renunciation in the direction that symbolized night and Satan.

Illumination (*normally ritualized on the Sundays of Lent*): *The candidates formally elect Christ and the church and seek purification as they move more deeply into their faith journey, surrounded by members of the church community who encourage them. This stage concludes at the Easter Vigil, when the candidates are baptized and confirmed and celebrate their first Eucharist.*

Easter reflection: *The newborn members of the church consciously seek to assimilate the meaning of the sacraments and the church community they now experience.*

. . . .

6) *Eight-sided baptistry*. The first formal baptistries were Roman bath-houses, which were usually eight-sided buildings. Since Christians of the first four centuries were fond of symbolic meanings, it isn't surprising that they saw a spiritual meaning in the very eight sides of the building in which the ceremony was performed. They spoke of celebrating the eighth day—Easter.

Easter Sunday was not so much the first day of a new week as the day that stood above and beyond the usual groups of seven. Hence, it stood for the extraordinary and, in fact, the eternal. "Enter into the eighth day" meant joining Jesus in his Easter life. This, of course, is exactly what was happening in baptism, since the candidate was entering into the new life of grace and union with the Risen Jesus.

7) *The anointing with oil*. Greek and Roman culture abounded in what we know today as health clubs. They were as muscle-minded and sports-minded as we are. When a contest of strength was upon them and they needed to be limbered up for the struggle, it was common to give them a rubdown with oil.

What greater struggle can there be than with the power of evil that shuts off union with God? Evil must be overcome and put down. Furthermore, it is a struggle to suppress the bad habits and sins that have resulted from succumbing to evil. Hence, the oiling represented the new Christian's preparation for the battle with the forces of evil both from within and without. If an athlete needed oil to down an opponent, how much more would baptismal candidates need limbering up to contend with the spiritual enemy that kept them back from God!

8) *The triple immersion*. The great mystery of Christianity is the Trinity's self-communication. Early Christians were deeply conscious of their profound relationship with Father, Son and Spirit. In baptism the candidate was being introduced into the very life of God, and that life was mediated in a rich Trinitarian fashion.

The sacramental act insisted on a special immersion in the name of each Person of the Trinity to symbolize the union of the candidate with each and thereby urge the newborn Christian to live by the amazing richness of God's self-communication. To this day Christians are baptized with water in the name of the Father, the Son and the Spirit.

9) *The white garment*. Once again remember that we are dealing with a symbol-loving community. Even for many Americans the white suit or white

robe symbolizes goodness. The virginal bride wears white on her wedding day. The sheriff in the old Westerns was the man in the white hat. Aegeria quotes the Book of Revelation, which describes the redeemed wearing white robes in the procession that follows Christ, the true Lamb. All of these are examples of the innocence symbolized by the white garment.

10) *The sealing.* The confirming seal of God is set upon the candidate's brow. The newly baptized now join the company of the redeemed and proceed to take part for the first time in the whole Mass, receiving Communion.

CONNECTING TO OUR TIMES

How to Benefit From Our Initiation Rites

The early church wisely created a substantial initiation rite to incorporate candidates into the body of Christ. The process contained elements of ritual, community involvement and instruction. It included a number of steps whereby the candidates advanced over a period of a year to the Easter Vigil, when they received baptism, confirmation and Eucharist.

That ancient practice has been revived by our church today and richly transposed for our needs in the light of present cultural awareness and numerous valuable liturgical studies. We call this process the *Rite of Christian Initiation of Adults* (RCIA). The value of this development has deepened our appreciation of baptism, confirmation and Eucharist, which we now call the sacraments of initiation. (New converts receive all three. Those already baptized into Christian churches receive confirmation and Eucharist for the first time.)

Still, we must acknowledge that the majority of us do not go through this process. Normally we receive baptism when we are infants, Eucharist as young children and confirmation most often in early adolescence. Hence most Catholics do not *experience* these three sacraments as one rite of initiation in the same manner that adult converts to our church do. Nonetheless, these sacraments still call us to a more profound union with Jesus and our parish community and the universal church. Every Easter, we renew our baptismal promises. This is more stirring when we join our parish on Holy Saturday evening and participate in the Easter Vigil with those who are receiving these sacraments for the first time.

We should keep the date of our confirmation on our calendars and renew our pledge to be active Catholics and to be more responsive to the call of the Holy Spirit in our lives on every anniversary. Finally, we should seek ways to make our participation in the celebration of the Eucharist always more living, conscious and active. A daily time set aside for interior prayer is an excellent way to prepare for the eucharistic celebration.

In these ways we can bring alive for ourselves the sacraments of initiation and so benefit more from their intended impact on our lives.

FOR REFLECTION AND DISCUSSION

Aegeria's diary and our current RCIA raise some questions for us:

1. Why is it important to involve the church community in the baptismal process?
2. How does this "adult focus" on our faith journey affect our appreciation of the role of continuing education in the church?
3. How would this approach affect our understanding of infant baptism?
4. What do we learn from having special liturgical ceremonies accompany the stages of initiation into Christ and the church?
5. RCIA candidates have a sponsor from the parish. What is the role of the sponsor?
6. Discuss the important things that a convert should learn about the church.

· ·

CHAPTER SEVEN

FIRST-CENTURY ADJUSTMENTS

> *"In hoc signo vinces"*
> ("In this sign you shall conquer")
> —from Constantine's vision

· ·

THE CHURCH THAT CONSTANTINE FACED

Jesus Christ prophesied that the church would begin as a mustard seed, the smallest of all the seeds that would blossom into a bush large and tough enough to have birds land on its branches (see Luke 13:18–19). Just 280 years after Pentecost, the church that began as a tiny seed in Jerusalem had a major presence in most of the cities of the Roman Empire.

When Constantine became the Roman Emperor and decided in 313 to give religious freedom to Christianity he was encountering an international church with an experienced hierarchy of pope, bishops, priests and deacons. He discovered that it possessed already a centuries-old coherent theology and a cast of eloquent defenders schooled in Greek philosophy and rhetoric. Also there existed a network of hundreds of house churches stretching across the empire from Rome to North Africa to Greece and the Middle East. In these centers of worship the graces of the sacraments, especially the Eucharist, were regular sources of sanctification for a growing church.

Constantine

As a Roman emperor, Constantine was a pagan. His mother was a convert to Christianity. She is a saint today, remembered for finding what is believed to be the true cross during a pilgrimage to Jerusalem. Saint Helena is pictured with the cross in art.

As a young soldier, Constantine had a vision of the cross. He then adopted the cross as his standard. Constantine stopped the persecution of Christians in the Roman Empire by signing the Edict of Milan in 313.

. . . .

Despite periodic waves of state sponsored terror and persecutions against them, Christians stubbornly kept the faith and bred seminal thinkers who provided ideas that would have fruitful consequences for the church's survival and influence. Martyrs fed the confidence of Christians and inspired them to move forward. In sheer numbers alone they developed beyond a threatened minority to a populous presence hard to ignore by the state and armed with brilliant thinkers who defended the faith with an intelligence and conviction that appealed to the ruling classes and converted many of their members.

The books of the New Testament supply us with vivid accounts of Christian life in its earliest days. Chapters two and three of the book of Revelation describe in summary fashion the strengths and weaknesses of local churches in seven cities of Asia Minor. From the letters of Saint Paul we can gather more detailed descriptions of the issues facing the churches in major urban centers such as Thessalonica, Colossae, Philippi, Ephesus, Corinth, Rome and the cluster of towns in the province of Galatia.

Eventually, Jerusalem would arise from the ashes of destruction in AD 70 and host a famed catechetical center under its bishop, Saint Cyril. Constantine moved the center of the empire to Byzantium, a relatively minor seaport at the edge of a peninsula jutting out into the Bosporus Sea. Eleven years after he liberated Christianity he began building Constantinople in 324. The first stage was completed in 330. In years to come it grew into a brilliant metropolis and outshone all its rivals in splendor, influence and religious importance, though Rome always maintained its primacy.

By the time Constantine came to power there were centers of Christian life that had had two and a half centuries of growth, tradition and powerful religious identity. Constantine was not encountering a timid faith minority. Year after year these families and communities witnessed the gospel with ever-increasing confidence. Far from being intimidated by emperors and soldiers Christians possessed an uncanny relationship with the Risen Christ who empowered their durability and capacity to attract more and more converts. Constantine's mother, Saint Helena, was a Christian who exerted her own influence on him.

Following are four vignettes of influential Christian communities in major cities of the empire. These brief stories illustrate the dynamism of Christianity despite militant opposition.

Ephesus

Three prominent Roman cities in the Middle East became home to an expansive group of Christians. Each of these cities had populations exceeding a quarter million and was ripe for evangelizing. Conversions were slow but steady, curtailed by persecutions but growing nonetheless. For two years Saint Paul evangelized in Ephesus, a center of the worship of Diana. From apostolic times Ephesus was the site of a Christian community that was honored by Saint Paul with one of his most lyrical teachings about the centrality of Christ and the union of the Body of Christ in him.

Tradition holds that Saint John settled there and took care of Mary the mother of Jesus until

Nicea and Early Church Councils

In the history of the church, there have been twenty-one church councils. The first of these was the Council of Nicea, called to formulate a creed.

The Nicene Creed was written in two stages. The first part was written at Nicea I in 325 and the last section was added at Nicea II in 787.

Most of the early church councils were held in the eastern part of the Roman Empire. In 324 Constantine had moved the capital to the city of Byzantium, which he renamed for himself—Constantinople. The capital was moved because Rome was constantly under barbarian attack, finally "falling" in 476.

Early Heresies

Heresy is teaching a false belief. As the church Fathers were organizing the early church, some individuals as well as some groups wanted to change the beliefs of Christians.

Three heresies affecting the Christian church from the third to the eighth centuries all dealt in one way or another with Christ's humanity versus his divinity:

Arianism *taught that Christ was not divine or equal with the Father.*

Nestorianism *taught that Mary was mother of the human nature of Christ only; thus, not Mother of God.*

Monophysitism *went to the other extreme, emphasizing Christ's divinity and minimizing his humanity.*

. . . .

In defending the Eucharist against certain heretics, Saint Ignatius of Antioch wrote, "They abstain from the Eucharist and from prayer because they do not confess that the Eucharist is the flesh of our Savior Jesus Christ, flesh which suffered for our sins and which the Father in his goodness raised up again" (Letter to the Smyrneans, 6:2). *In pleading for unity in the church he emphasized the uniting role of the clergy and the Eucharist: "You are my abiding joy if your members remain united with the bishop and with his preyters and deacons…Be careful therefore to take part only in the one Eucharist: for there is only one flesh of our Lord Jesus Christ, and one cup to unite us with his blood, one altar and one bishop with the preyters and deacons who are his fellow servants"* (Letter to the Philadelphians, 1:1–2; 3:2–5). *In foreseeing his martyrdom in the Roman arena where he would be killed by wild beasts, he invoked a Eucharistic picture, "Let me be food for the wild beasts for they are my way to God. I am God's wheat and shall be ground by their teeth, so that I may become Christ's pure bread"* (Letter to the Romans, 4:1–2).

. . . .

her Assumption into heaven. It was chosen as the site for the fourth ecumenical council in 431 at which the council bishops reaffirmed the teaching of the church that Mary is the *Theotokos*, the Mother of God. The first known church dedicated to the Virgin Mary was built there.

Alexandria

Alexandria on the Egyptian coast was an immensely wealthy trading post with a yeasty mix of ethnic groups. Its prominent Jewish community was a natural starting point for Christian efforts at conversion. It became home to outstanding builders of the church in Alexandria such as Origen (185–254) who was one of the most brilliant Scripture scholars in church history. He excelled in philosophy, classical languages and the study of the Bible.

He is remembered for contrasting six translations of Scripture by placing them in parallel columns and comparing the words, phrases and sentences to determine what would be the most accurate. While he sought the literal meaning of the text, he also supported a spiritual interpretation that could uncover a moral meaning, an allegorical reading or a heavenly reference. His methods and conclusions influenced the early church and many generations later. The fathers of the church were extraordinary interpreters of Scripture and Origen ranks among the best of them.

Another key leader from Alexandria was Saint Athanasius (296–373). A theologian and bishop of the city, Athanasius attended the Council of Nicea and later became its foremost defender. He battled Arianism, a heresy that denied the divinity of Christ. He persuaded Saint Antony of the desert, whose moral authority was profound due to his much-admired desert spirituality, to come to Alexandria for a brief visit to uphold the truth about the divinity of Christ as taught in Scripture, tradition and the recent Council of Nicea. The Christian faith in Christ's divinity prevailed though the Arian heresy stubbornly lived on for several centuries.

Antioch

Situated in Syria, ancient Antioch was the first city after Jerusalem to house a Christian community and where the apostles were first called Christians (Acts 11:26). Saint Peter served as its first bishop before he went on to be the bishop of Rome. Saint Ignatius of Antioch (35–107) held the office of bishop there for forty years. He was converted to Christianity by Saint Peter and had the privilege of meeting many of the first Christians, who had migrated from Jerusalem after its destruction. He is a bridge figure between apostolic times and the next generation of Christians.

In his old age he was indicted by the Roman government for treason against the state, meaning he refused to acknowledge the Roman gods. Under armed guard he sailed to Rome over several months, visiting Christian communities along the way. During this leisurely voyage he wrote seven letters that reveal the earliest practices and doctrinal teachings about the Holy Eucharist and the tripartite aspect of holy orders: bishop, presbyter [priest] and deacon.

Rome

From the very start Rome acquired a special reverence from the Christian world, because Peter was its first bishop and Paul spent at least two years there preaching the gospel. Both men were martyred there. In the early period the Christian community in Rome was literally an underground church. They constructed catacombs as burial grounds for their dead and celebrated Eucharist around altars built over the graves of martyred saints. The Roman government did not interfere with cemeteries so the setting was safe. The government forbade Christians to have church buildings, so the faithful assembled in homes for worship services and other sacraments. The secrecy surrounding these gatherings led their enemies to accuse them of atheism, because they did not believe in the pagan gods, and cannibalism, because they "ate flesh and drank blood."

Eventually, defenders of the faith—called *apologists*—arose to explain the truth and Christian faith and worship. One of the better known apologists was Saint Justin Martyr (100–165). Trained as a philosopher in Asia Minor, he converted to Christianity and moved to Rome where he opened a school that offered what we might call adult education classes in the faith. He wrote "apologies" (defenses of the faith) to the emperor Antoninus and to the Roman Senate. Eventually the state condemned him and six companions to scourging and death.

In embracing Christianity Constantine allied himself with an empire-wide religious community that practiced strong family life, lived Christ's commandments of love of God and neighbor and observed the Ten Commandments given to Moses at Sinai. They were accustomed to respecting government except when it violated the teachings of Christ. In other words, Constantine welcomed into the Roman bloodstream dutiful citizens that could provide it with fresh vitality. "The Church would never be the same again—for better or for worse—so Constantine's conversion is certainly one of the greatest turning points in the history of the Church and the world."[1]

FOR REFLECTION AND DISCUSSION

. . . .

1. Early church councils such as Nicea, Ephesus and Chalcedon struggled for ways to express the mystery of God. They produced statements on the Holy Trinity and on the divinity and humanity of Jesus that have served us ever since. What would happen to our approach to Jesus if we saw him only as God, with nothing human about him? How would we relate to Jesus if we thought of him as God dressed up in human form?

2. How would we view Jesus if he were thought not to be the Son of God at all? Suppose he were not divine, only human. Would we pray to him? Would we think he could possibly be our Savior?

3. Why is it important to us that Jesus be really human and really divine?

4. The mystery of God induces in us sentiments of awe, reverence and modesty of expression when speaking of God (no one statement says it all). We also say that there is a mystery about the human being. What are some sentiments that arise from this approach to the human? How can we come to appreciate the uniqueness of each person?

5. Constantine considered himself a colleague of the bishops. What are some advantages and disadvantages that arise from this union of church and state? Do you think the United States' separation of church and state is better? Why or why not?

6. Constantine was the Roman emperor, yet he was very much involved with the leadership of the church. He attended councils and influenced the selection of popes, but was not baptized until he was on his deathbed in 337. Should secular leaders participate in church business? Why should the church remain independent from the government?

CHAPTER EIGHT

. . . .

THE WESTERN CHURCH AS SERVANT

> [A priest] should not
> seek anything for him-
> self, but reckon his
> neighbor's well-being
> as his own advantage.
>
> —Pope Saint Gregory
> the Great

. . . .

"FILL THE POWER VACUUM": A FIFTH-CENTURY IMPERATIVE
(c. 476)

"Frank? Why, it is you! Whenever did you get back from Rome? How are you? You look so different!"

"Hi, Laura. Yes, I just got back. I—"

"Oh, Frank, it's good to have you home again. When you were gone so long, we thought.... Well, things are so dangerous over in western Europe."

"Much more than you could ever imagine, Laura."

"We hear the whole society is crumbling."

"Yes, it's very sad, Laura, to see the West in such a mess."

"What in the world caused it all, Frank? I mean, Rome was such a strong and well-ruled empire."

"Well, you know when Constantine came here to the East a century ago, he pretty much left a power vacuum in the West. The ruling families who were left soon died out. And the new wave of barbarians, who had no respect for the world they were invading, didn't help matters."

"Is there any hope for the West, Frank? Isn't there any force or group that could help build society?"

"It's a funny thing, Laura, but there is hope. Oddly enough, the political hope of the West lies with the church. The church seems to be moving into the power vacuum. I say 'funny' because we are so accustomed here to a church that works mainly at developing new forms of liturgy and at thrashing out problems of theology. But in the West the church is now involved in such questions as what to do with schools, farms, unsafe streets, food distribution and price controls."

"Well, good for the church! I agree it seems a bit odd, doing that kind of work. But if that is the need, then the church is certainly performing a great service. How does it come to have the talent for this kind of administration?"

"Well, all during the centuries of persecution, the Christians lived in a kind of shadow society. They weren't able to take part in public life, so they lived an 'underlife' that imitated the superb administrative skills of the Roman rulers. They were like understudies waiting in the wings to take the lead if it were ever offered to them."

"Frank, do you really believe the church was planning a sort of takeover as it watched Rome fall?"

"No, no, Laura. I didn't mean that at all. Christians never consciously plotted to replace their masters. It was just a happy coincidence for the West that, at the time when people with administrative skills were needed, the church was there—able and willing to answer the need."

"I still can't imagine the church there not being all wrapped up in liturgical concerns or dogmatic

The Fall of Rome
In 395 the sons of Emperor Theodosius divided the empire between them for administrative purposes. The two divisions functioned as independent states and, since their boundaries coincided closely with the divisions based on language and culture, the separation became permanent. In the West invasion and settlement by Germanic peoples continued to weaken the power of succeeding emperors. In 476, when Odoacer the Rugian deposed Romolus Augustulus from his puppet throne, the history of the Roman Empire in the West was closed.

The barbarians sacked the city of Rome in 410 and the West was never the same again. The Huns arrived at the gates of the city of Rome in 452, only to be met by Pope Leo I, who turned them back. The popes remained in Rome throughout the 'Dark Ages' even after the government fled.

. . . .

questions. But things being what they are, I suppose it does not have the time."

"Exactly, Laura. Bishops there are more like secular governors. They worry about the price of fish, salary complaints, tax evasions, grain supplies—you name it. They get involved with the merchant marine, wills, cheating landlords and border disputes."

"One thing is for sure, Frank, a church like that is going to have a strong sense of order and organization, if for no other reason than that it will have had so much practice."

"That's right, Laura, the church in the West is moving toward an orderly system of moral teaching and church law."

"That's no surprise, Frank, for a church that deals so closely from day to day with social problems and moral behavior."

"But I have one major fear, Laura, for our brothers and sisters in the West. There can be too much of a good thing. The church has assumed the exercise of political power because there is a great need. This is in answer to the Spirit's call to be a servant to that society. But will the church give it up when the secular society is strong enough to go out on its own?"

"The church has been at it for a century now, and probably will have to wield power for at least a century more. The church is creating a new civilization. I guess my concern is based on the axiom, 'No one surrenders power willingly.' My hope is that when the time comes, the Western church will prove an exception to that rule."

"Frank, I really have to run now, but I'm having a few people over tonight, some of your old friends. Could you come? I know they would love to see you. We are all hungry for news about the West."

"I'd love to."

"Say about eight?"

"Wonderful, see you then."

LOOKING BACK

. . . .

The Western Church as Servant

The material in the above episode falls into three parts: (1) how a power vacuum occurred; (2) why and how the church could fill it; (3) the values and disadvantages of filling the power vacuum.

1) *Rome's fall.* As mentioned in chapter seven, Constantine moved to the East, an action which had its most severe effects a century later when barbarian invasions coupled with weak leadership left the West in chaos. This absence of strong leadership developed a power vacuum and the church stepped in to fill it.

2) *Church rule.* During the centuries of persecution, Christians formed a "community within a community," observing and absorbing the managerial policies of their Roman overlords. The years of experience that the Western church thus gained in administrative work influenced the kind of theology that would develop later, namely, a concern for human behavior (moral theology) and a concern for an efficient institution (canon law).

3) *Servant church.* Europe owes a remarkable debt to a church that stepped into the fourth-century chaos and helped bring to birth a new civilization. Not until the seventh century was Europe beginning to gain sufficient strength to go

Servant of the Servants
Symbolic of the church as servant was the preferred title of Pope Gregory the Great (590–604), "servant of the servants of God." He saw as the duty of the Bishop of Rome to do anything necessary to maintain the communion of churches.

. . . .

The Emperor's Advice
Theodosius ordered all of his subjects to "rally to the faith brought to the Romans by the apostle Peter."

. . . .

59

out on its own again. The church had indeed been midwife to the making of Europe.

In doing this for Europe, the church was fulfilling its role as servant of God. Just as faith calls for love and service at the individual level, so also it summons the institutional level of the Christian community to reflect the same love and service in the broader public dimension. The task may be secular but the motivation is divine, whether it is a neighbor sitting with a sick person or the organizational church administering the parceling of land to barbarians newly arrived from the North.

The Eastern Church

By contrast, the Eastern church lived within the confines of a prosperous and stable empire. This cultural situation freed the bishops to concentrate on their pastoral role in the areas of sacramental life, spirituality and theology. It afforded theologians the leisure to develop in-depth understandings of major doctrines such as the Trinity and the Incarnation and to present defenses against heretical aberrations. This explains why the great church councils of Nicea, Ephesus and Chalcedon were held in the East: not only because the heresies were more localized there, but also because the church there had the talent to deal with them.

This also accounts for the rich development of spirituality and mysticism that are characteristic of the Eastern church. There the church had the time and the freedom of several centuries of imperial support and protection. This was aided and abetted by the monasticism of the East, which was oriented much more to prayer and meditation than that of the activist farmer-monks of the West. Eastern monks were not obliged to clear wildernesses and play the frontier roles of their Western counterparts. Basically subsidized by the wealthy, they could take time to mature the mystical bent to which they had given themselves.

CONNECTING TO OUR TIMES

. . . .

A Church That Serves People Today

In this chapter we see how the church of the West ministered to the people of Europe, who faced the chaos caused by the fall of the Roman Empire and the barbarian conquests. Law and order had collapsed and basic needs like food distribution, public safety, health care and fundamental commerce required able leaders to oversee their fulfillment.

Because so many of the Catholic bishops were members of the old Roman leadership families, they were able to bring the skills of their family training to roles of administration—not only for the church's religious needs, but also for the basic human needs of a society in chaos. In doing this the church's leaders were fulfilling a command from Jesus to be "servants" of all peoples. Many bishops and popes were thus required to exercise both political and religious leadership to make this happen.

Today our church no longer needs to occupy political roles such as king, president or prime minister. But the church still is called to be a "servant" to the basic needs of people whose human dignity demands it. In the United States, for example, the Catholic church is the largest non-governmental provider of social services. Catholic charities provide services to the poor, people with AIDS, the indigent, unwed mothers and their children, those suffering from substance abuse, hungry people and many others in need.

Worldwide, the church's missionary organizations bring the gospel as well as education, health care and food to millions. In addition the church's social teachings call for "development" for the world's impoverished nations. This includes: (1) education for girls in countries where only boys are schooled; (2) new technology for farms; (3) new roads so food can be properly distributed to the hungry as well as to ports for marketing; (4) clean water programs both to avert disease and provide irrigation; (5) advanced health care and hospitals; (6) encouragement of loans from rich nations to poor ones—loans which respect the moral, cultural and spiritual values of these peoples.

Under the principles of justice and the highest regard for human dignity, the church has found a new way to practice its old role of being a "servant."

FOR REFLECTION AND DISCUSSION

. . . .

1. When the western part of the Roman Empire collapsed, the church used the administrative skills of its bishops and pastors to bring order out of chaos. These religious leaders became the secular governors and mayors of

leaderless states, cities and towns. Their work of service brought hope to a despairing world and created the basis for a new civilization.

2. One of the major reasons that the church was so successful in taking over in Europe was that the clergy were educated. Universal education is a modern phenomenon. One hundred years ago the average person did not read or write. Imagine how few were educated in the early church! What would it be like if only one in a thousand persons could read, write, count?

3. Culture in the West suffered during these years. In the East the culture flourished. This brought about a feeling of superiority in the East. How did this affect the church?

4. Should the church become involved in the secular society? How should priests, brothers and sisters relate to politics? Should they demonstrate for causes, get involved in other countries' domestic problems, or should they just do "church" duties?

CHAPTER NINE

SAINT AUGUSTINE

> You have made us for
> yourself, O Lord, and
> our heart is restless
> until it rests in you.
> —Saint Augustine

In any ranking of the ten most influential men in the history of the church, Augustine will always be included. During his seventy-six years (354–430), he witnessed the emergence of the church as a powerful force in society. He also beheld the decline of Roman political power and the waves of barbarian invasions from the North. More and more he dwelt on the otherworldly "city of God" as he observed the collapse of the "city of man." The forces that created that catastrophe finally succeeded in 476, the date historians assign to the fall of the Roman Empire.

In the following imaginary interview, a biographer questions Augustine about his life and times.

An Interview With Augustine
(c. 420)

Interviewer: Bishop Augustine, did you receive a Christian upbringing?

Augustine: My mother, Monica, was a Christian. My father, Patricius, was a pagan. It was customary to raise children in the religion of their father. Officially, I was a pagan, but my mother determined to make me a Christian. I was an independent spirit and resisted my mother's wishes.

Interviewer: Did your mother control your education?

Augustine: Mother may have been an ardent Christian, but she also believed I should have a sound classical education in the pagan schools. She saw no contradiction between her efforts toward my Christian character development and a first-class education.

Interviewer: Is it true that your mother was a battered wife?

Augustine: In my childhood days it was common for North African husbands to beat their wives. But my father never laid a hand on Monica. She knew how to control him. I heard her speak of other wives as "slave girls of their husbands." In their quarrels I watched her wait out his anger and then coolly take charge of him and even convince him how she had been right in the first place. Monica was a formidable woman.

Interviewer: Do you think your mother was overbearing to you?

Augustine: There is no doubt I thought she tried to make me a mother's boy. She insisted on following me everywhere, even when I grew into manhood. I shook her off briefly in my twenty-eighth year, when I traveled to Europe. I had to lie to do it. I still feel bad about that. You know that in my *Confessions* I tell that story and express my remorse. "Thus I lied to my mother—and what a mother." I see now more clearly that her main motive was to make me a Christian.

Interviewer: Why did you convert to Manichaeism?

Augustine: I was feeling some guilt about my moral life. I had taken a mistress and sired an illegitimate son. I sought relief in religion. I studied the Bible and was disappointed. How could anyone accept the contradiction of a vengeful Old Testament God and a New Testament merciful Christ? Worse yet, I judged the stories in the Bible to be too coarse and unreal after being immersed in the refinements of the Latin classics.

I was pleased to find that the Manichaean religion repudiated the value of the Old Testament just as I did. Not feeling very good about myself, I identified with the Manichaeans, who also held a low opinion of the goodness of human nature. I needed a religion that emphasized severe self-discipline. Manichaeism suited my ascetic bent of those days.

Interviewer: How then did you come to be a Christian?

Augustine: I think my mother had the most to do with it. I could not deny her personal influence upon me year after year. And think of those powerful prayers of hers. Of course circumstances also played a role. I am by nature a restless searcher, a questioner. I am not easily satisfied with soft responses.

I had taken a teaching position in Milan. The most celebrated speaker in the city was Bishop Ambrose. I began attending cathedral services and listening to Ambrose's persuasive sermons about the Old Testament. He cleared away many of my objections and presented me with a challenge to become a Christian.

I spent many hours with Ambrose discussing the possibility of my conversion. He advised me to study Neo-Platonist philosophy. I now see why, for my Manichaean outlook concentrated my attention on my body and on physical matters. Neo-Platonism woke me up to the values and reality of the life of the spirit.

Nevertheless, I was cautious. It took well over three years of such study and thinking to turn me around. And then it happened. I was sitting alone in my garden and relaxing from my study of the New Testament. I thought I heard a child call out playfully, "Take and read." Startled, I looked at the biblical text in front of me:

> [L]et us live honorably as in the day, not in reveling and drunkenness, not in debauchery and licentiousness, not in quarreling and jealousy. Instead, put on the Lord Jesus Christ, and make no provision for the flesh, to gratify its desires. (Romans 13:13–14)

In that moment my doubts dissolved. I was filled with light. I became a Christian.

Interviewer: You have become a celebrated

Faith in North Africa
Augustine spent his youth as a pagan. He went to study in the city of Milan in Italy, where he was converted under the inspiration of another great saint, Ambrose. Ambrose was a renowned orator, a well-known scholar and composer of many early Christian hymns.

Filling the Void
As the barbarians invaded the Roman Empire, the church and the office of the pope gained power and filled the power vacuum left when the government moved East.

Monasticism

Another movement founded in Northern Africa was that of monasticism. Saint Anthony of Egypt founded a group of monks who lived what is referred to as the "desert experience." Augustine spent time in the desert after his conversion.

. . . .

Christian theologian. What has made you so successful?

Augustine: I will leave my fame and so-called success to you and others who may care to reflect on my career. I frankly see myself less as a theologian and more as a pastor for my people. I have been bishop of this small North African diocese of Hippo for nearly thirty-five years. I view myself as a small-town pastor. I know practically everyone by name. I am involved in their weddings, funerals, family tragedies and triumphs. I am outspoken—some would say too vocal—about the public issues that affect my people.

I believe my job is to nourish the faith, hope and love of my people. You know what my sermons are like. Two to three hours of give and take with them. Yes, there is a bit of the philosopher in me. What else would you expect of the selfimportant young intellectual I once was? I love the impact when my people and I interact. They teach me as much as I teach them. In my solitude at the monastery in Hippo my writings soar because of my pastoral experience.

Interviewer: Don't you think your debates with the Donatists influenced your writings?

Augustine: Yes, I thrive on controversy. The Donatists were fair game. They were too clean, too rigid for the rest of us Christians. They never forgave the collaborationist bishops during the persecution of Diocletian. Even when those bishops were reconciled to the church, the Donatists refused to acknowledge they were real bishops or that the priests they ordained were real priests. Only the successors of the martyred bishops were genuine. To join them you had to be rebaptized.

Actually they helped me understand that the sacraments work even when administered by sinners. Not that priests should be sinful, of course. The Donatists had the problem of all religious elites. They had the self-righteousness of the self-chosen. Too pure. I could not ignore them when they drew away whole towns and cities from a proper understanding of the church.

I was not always temperate in speaking about them. I recall preaching, "The clouds roll with thunder so that the house of the Lord shall be built throughout the earth. And these frogs sit in the marsh and croak, 'We are the only Christians!'"

I still like those lines.

I argued that innocence is only one side of the church. Christians must become holy. Christians also must coexist in the same community as sinners and correct the sinners.

Interviewer: Is it true you are bitter about the way Jerome treated you?

Augustine: Unfortunately, I never met Jerome except in letters. I was young when I began writing to him. He was already an established giant in biblical studies. I admit I was arrogant then and treated him without due respect. He was quick to correct me: "You are still young. Do not challenge an old man in battles about the Bible."

I was wounded. I wrote him, "How can we engage in discussion if you have made up your mind to offend me?" When Jerome decided to bury the hatchet, writing, "Come let us play together harmlessly in the fields of the Scriptures," I was not amused.

Very seriously, I wrote back, "If you used the word *play* to imply that what we do is easy, I expect more of you. It is your duty to help those engaged in exacting study. Examining the Bible is not a matter of romping round on level ground or puffing and panting up a mountain."

No wonder Jerome ignored many of my letters. No, I am not bitter at all. I would love to have known him personally and jousted with him.

Interviewer: Why did you write *The City of God*?

Augustine: Some people think I did it to explain the sack of Rome and the other indignities the barbarians are inflicting on the empire. They are wrong. Never forget I was trained as a classical scholar in the Roman tradition. I spent over thirteen years writing *The City of God*.

That book was not one of my raging pamphlets against one or another of the heresies I have fought. I wrote it with all the self-conscious skills that Roman literary tradition demands. What prompted me? I admired the history and glory of the empire. But I also saw the propaganda and self-service, the conservatism that created a myth. That's why I wrote, "Away with the vain screen of common opinion. Away with the white-wash." I was both debunking Roman tradition and at the same time cherishing the genuine moral values I uncovered.

My audience was a small group of leisured aristocrats, trained in my tradition, puzzled by the great transition going on in culture. I gave them my interpretation of human events today. I drained the glory of Rome and projected it onto the glorious city of God. I demonstrated that the virtues of Roman heroes would only be realized in the citizens of this other city. It is in the heavenly Jerusalem that the essence of the Roman Republic will find true realization.

Interviewer: Do you think the barbarian invasions mean the end of the world?

Augustine: No, I do not. Any reader of history knows that empires rise and fall. I am not at all certain that what we see is the end of Roman dominion. Perhaps this is a political adjustment, a purification. Or maybe we are seeing the passing of an old order. I regret and mourn the death and devastation. The barbarians are preparing to invade North Africa. Soon enough we will see women raped, men slaughtered, homes burned. We have not the will nor the military might to withstand them. But the end of the world? I don't think so.

In the last ten days of his life, the Augustine who spoke and wrote hundreds of thousands of words asked that he be left alone and in silence. He ordered four psalms that dealt with penance to be copied out and posted on his sickroom walls. In prayer and quiet he died on August 28, 430.

LOOKING BACK

. . . .

Saint Augustine and Manichaeism
The belief Augustine embraced before becoming a Christian was a "materialistic dualism." It taught that the world is the end product of a battle between forces of light and darkness.

According to Manichaeism the soul was an element of light imprisoned within the darkness of the body. Manichaeans claimed to be the true Christians, preaching Christ as the one who could free the imprisoned light. Believers generally divided into two levels: the "elect" and the "hearers."

Augustine joined the "hearers" because this lower group was allowed marriage as a concession to the weakness of the flesh.

Giving New Meaning to Motherhood:
Saint Monica
As mother of Augustine, Monica possessed what we would today call a holistic vision of her maternal calling. She certainly looked after the physical needs of her son. And like any ambitious, upwardly mobile woman she spared no money or energy in seeing that her bright young boy

It is recorded that, at one point, he barricaded himself and his parishioners within a church in order to prevent an Arian takeover. Ambrose was friend and adviser to three emperors; nevertheless, he consistently fought to keep the church independent of civil power. During his career he also composed hymns and wrote commentaries on Scripture and treatises in theology.

. . . .

received an excellent classical education. She was the first to notice that her son had an exceptional mind. To assure his intellectual training she brought him to the best available teachers.

Luckily, the North Africa of her day was more than a backwater of Rome. The empire of Carthage, of which her hometown of Hippo had been a part, once rivaled Rome in political and economic power. Its descendants knew the value of education, trade, military strength and classical culture.

But Monica wanted more than a physically able, intellectually agile son. She wanted him to become a Christian and a man of faith. Her husband, Patricius, was not much help to her in this regard. She was the one who valued the Christian faith. She was both mentally and spiritually strong. When she was young, she was accused of drinking too much wine. Strong-willed already, she resolved never to let alcohol get the best of her. And it didn't.

While many African wives suffered beatings from their husbands, Monica made it clear to Patricius she would never put up with it. He learned how to contain his violence. She told her friends (with some hint of sarcasm) that "they were slave girls of their husbands. It was not for them to rise up against their lord and master." She had no intention of being a battered wife.

Monica was a woman of large emotions, easily expressed. She was furious with Augustine for taking a mistress when he was a young man. She refused to let him live at home or eat at her table. But she put great stock in her dreams and the wisdom that might come from them. She had a dream in which she met a "radiant being" who questioned her about her anger and grief. She told him about Augustine's mistress and his cynical remarks about the church. The being assured her she had little to fear: "Your son is with you." Monica took this to mean that Augustine would eventually see things her way. After that she welcomed him (and, presumably, his mistress as well) home. She grew more patient for her son's conversion.

She decided she had to be a vital presence in Augustine's adult life until God brought him to faith. When he went to Italy to pursue his career as a teacher, she followed him. He could not escape the brooding and insistent presence of his mother. He wrote, "She loved to have me with her, as is the way with all mothers, but far more than most mothers." When he sailed to Italy, he lied to his mother about it, hoping to escape her. "I lied to my mother—and such a mother!"

Monica followed him to Rome and then to Milan, where she found the remarkable Ambrose, who would be God's agent in bringing her son to Christianity. Ambrose's cultivated and faith-filled sermons appealed to the spiritually starved Augustine. Moreover, Ambrose composed music for learning the truths of faith, melodies that melted Augustine, who was always fond of music.

Augustine became a candidate for entrance into the church and took lessons about the faith. Monica loved Ambrose for the influence he had over her son. Augustine writes, "She hastened to church more zealously than ever and drank in the words of Ambrose as a fountain of water.... She loved that man as an angel of God."

Ever thinking about her son's financial as well as his faith future, she forced him to give up his mistress of fifteen years as she eyed some rich prospects to find a wife for him. What happened to the nameless mistress? No one knows, but some believe Augustine financed her entrance into a community of "virgins and widows" in Carthage.

As things turned out, Augustine was never to marry. After his entry into the church, he embraced a life of celibacy. During the first three years of his conversion he (and his mother) lived with a group of students and intellectuals in northern Italy. Finally, he and Monica resolved to go back to Africa. While they were at Ostia waiting for a ship, Monica contracted a fatal illness and died.

Before she died she told him, "Son, as far as I am concerned, nothing in this life now gives me pleasure. I do not know why I am still here, since I have no further hopes in this world. I did have one reason for wanting to live a little longer: to see you become a Christian before I died. God has lavished his gifts on me in this respect."

When she died, Augustine was so stunned by the absence of her formidable presence that he did not weep. Only several weeks later did her death really hit him.

And he released a flood of healing tears.

CONNECTING TO OUR TIMES

. . . .

What Do Conversion Stories Teach Us?

The conversion of Augustine is one of the most powerful narratives of its kind in church history, ranking in influence with that of Paul. Of course it helped that Augustine was one of history's most talented literary writers, hence the account of his conversion remains a classic and one of the best-read conversion stories ever written.

Conversion accounts such as those of Augustine, Paul, Thomas Merton, C.S. Lewis or Dorothy Day tell about their journey to Christian faith. What value do they have for us who are already Christian? We can see how they motivate seekers for truth and God to embark on a path to Catholicism. But we are already Catholics. So what can they teach us?

Conversion narratives enrich us in many ways. We may be Catholics but tend to take our faith for granted. Our eyes are clouded over with what Samuel Coleridge calls the "film of familiarity." We become jaded in the faith and fail to see its freshness and originality. We lose excitement about our religion.

Converts share with us their bouncing and unmitigated enthusiasm for Jesus and the church. For them it is all new. Their stories lend us their "eyes" so we can see afresh what we have forgotten. Someone has said that life's greatest problem is "forgetfulness of being." That is also religion's dilemma. The membership forgets how wonderful is the gift of faith.

C.S. Lewis asks us to be as "surprised by joy" as he was. Augustine charms us to fall in love again with God as he was privileged to do. Paul excites us to be so close to Jesus that we can say as he did, "For to me, living is Christ" (see Philippians 1:21). Thomas Merton invites us to a contemplative faith and a meditative life—a dimension of faith obscured by the noise of daily life. Dorothy Day inspires us to a conversion of sympathy and empathy for the poor and oppressed.

We read conversion stories to regain an enthusiasm for our religion and to stimulate our own personal conversion, which must occur again and again as we go through life's many stages and passages.

FOR REFLECTION AND DISCUSSION

· ·

1. One of the most celebrated controversies Augustine engaged in was a debate with a theological genius named Pelagius. This Pelagius argued that people were in full charge of their own moral destiny. No matter what the impact on the human condition caused by Adam's fall, human beings could choose the good from the font of their own resources. Is there something "Pelagian" about popular self-help theories such as "pulling your own strings"; "looking out for number one"; "I must take charge of myself"?

2. Augustine was profoundly impressed by the moral weakness of people and the deeply rooted character of human evil tendencies. He believed we were much more affected by Adam's fall than Pelagius would allow. People could not avoid sin without the help of grace. Augustine believed we are free, but that we need the impulse of God's grace to choose the good. We cannot save ourselves. We need the grace of Christ to motivate us and see us through. How do we experience ourselves as fully in charge and yet be responsive to God's grace? How can we avoid being fatalistic about God's role in life as well as resist the temptation to go it on our own?

3. Who are some of today's theologians? What are they saying? Do you find that today's theologians have the pastoral spirit of Augustine? Do you think it is possible for an academic theologian to be involved in parish work and still be able to do theology? Would scholarship suffer?

4. Explain in your own words what grace is, where it comes from, and so on, as if you were talking to a young child.

5. Augustine's mother, Saint Monica prayed for her son's conversion for her whole life. Why is prayer effective? What is the value of praying for others?

6. It is said that in the conversion of Augustine the pagan empire died. His becoming a Christian began the new empire which was to be Christian. How can we contribute to the Christianizing of culture today?

7. In *The City of God*, Augustine tells how this world is not as important as the world to come. How can we balance our contribution to the earthly city and the city of God?

Abbey of Cluny

Benedict's monastic rule

Alcuin and Carolingian Renaissance

500   **600**   **700**   **800**   **900**

Charlemagne
Einhard

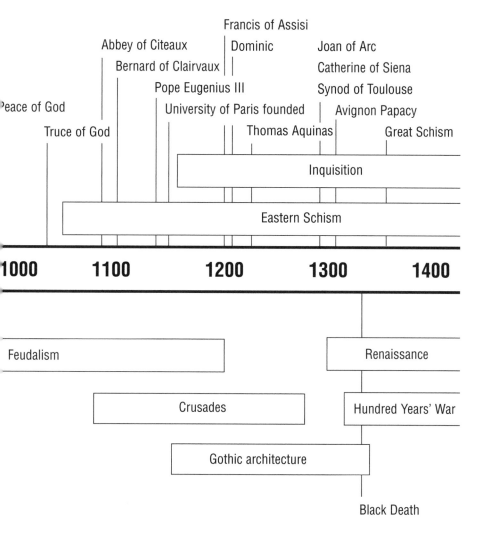

CHAPTER TEN

CHARLEMAGNE: HOW WESTERN EUROPE BECAME CHRISTIAN

> Make us eternal truths
> receive,
> And practice all that
> we believe:
> Give us thyself, that we
> may see
> The Father and the
> Son, by thee.
>
> —Charlemagne

To understand Charlemagne's achievement it is necessary to examine the movements that preceded his reign such as the fall of the Roman Empire and the historic changes that followed it. At its height the Roman Empire's boundaries were England's Hadrian's Wall in the north, the Rhine and Danube Rivers to the east, the Atlantic Ocean to the west and the Sahara Desert to the south. Constantine united the empire into western and eastern blocs and built his capitol at Constantinople.

In the years that followed, fierce barbarian invasions shattered the empire of the West and it collapsed in 476. The popes of Rome dedicated themselves to convert the barbarians and integrate them into a Christian society. This goal required an immense amount of patience, but the church over several centuries was blessed by the reign of the extraordinary Pope Gregory the Great, the Irish monks, the Benedictine Order and the kingdom of the Franks.

Charles the Great

Charlemagne was probably six feet, four inches tall. Considering that the average male height of the time was five feet, two inches, he was tall indeed.

Charlemagne made the city of Aachen in Northern Germany his capital. His father, Pepin the Short, also ruled from Aachen. The Frankish Kingdom stretched through part of modern-day Germany and France. Charlemagne was buried in the cathedral at Aachen.

Charlemagne means "Charles the Great" and he did indeed have a great reign.

. . . .

Saint Gregory the Great (540–604)

Born in Rome to a wealthy family he rose to power, becoming the prefect of the city. He surprised everyone by abandoning public life and turning the family mansion into a monastery and adopted the life of a monk. He left his solitude to serve as papal ambassador to Constantinople and after six years returned to his monastery. In 590 he was elected pope.

The Lombards, a Germanic tribe, had invaded northern Italy and tried to capture Rome. Getting no help from the Eastern empire, Pope Gregory negotiated a truce with the invaders. The civil authorities seemed helpless, so Gregory assumed the responsibility for providing food, shelter, medical care and public order for the people. In effect, he became the ruler of central Italy and began administering an area that would eventually become the Papal States. His diplomatic skills and his friendship with the Queen Theodolinda of the Lombards enabled him to begin the conversion of that tribe.

He was a born administrator and found numerous ways to improve the caliber and performance of all the bishops of the West. He wrote *Pastoral Care*, a book that outlined his vision of the bishop as a shepherd. It was translated into Greek and Anglo-Saxon and was treated as a textbook on how to be a bishop in medieval times. His other writings include homilies on the Gospels and Ezekiel as well as the *Moralia*, a commentary on Job. He was soon acclaimed with Ambrose, Jerome and Augustine as a father and doctor of the church.

He respected the rights of the great patriarchs of the East but said there are times when all bishops seek the authority of the Holy See. He wrote over 850 letters, mostly to the bishops and monks of the West commenting on their responsibilities and urging them to enforce discipline. He sent a Roman monk, Augustine, and forty others to England to convert the Angles and Saxons. In time he made Augustine the first archbishop of Canterbury.

"Saint Gregory set the papacy and the church on a path that was to make it a predominant force in shaping a new civilization out of the ruins of the old—a new political and cultural and social unity called Europe."[1] In remaking Europe a Christian world Gregory was aided by the Irish and Benedictine monks and a special relationship of the papacy with the Kingdom of the Franks.

Irish Monks

The Western Church was an urban religion with little influence over the vast expanse of rural Europe and its huge peasant population. After Saint Patrick's conversion of the Irish, who were mainly a rural, tribal people, monasteries soon flourished and served as centers of religion, life, education and culture throughout the countryside. In the sixth and seventh centuries the Irish monks became outstanding missionaries to continental Europe where they established numerous monasteries such as Jumiege in France, Saint Gall in Switzerland and Bobbio in Italy.

Their familiarity with the clan system, tribal values and rural life made it easier for them to identify with the agrarian European world. They preached and witnessed Christ in a language and style their hearers understood and embraced.

Alcuin
The learned English monk, Alcuin, served as Charlemagne's teacher and, at times, his conscience. In 778, after an uprising of Saxons in his territory, Charlemagne decreed that all Saxons, under pain of death, had to be baptized and give one-tenth of their income to the church. Alcuin expressed his disapproval of Charlemagne's methods: "A man can be drawn to the faith, but he cannot be forced. A man may be forced to receive baptism, but it does not follow that he will thereby receive the faith."

Einhard

Einhard impressed
Charlemagne with his
talent and industry.
Thus Charlemagne
placed him in charge of
the royal building
program and entrusted
him with important
diplomatic missions. In
his later years he wrote
his Vita Karoli Magni,
one of the finest
biographies to come
from the early Middle
Ages. The excerpts in
the "Portrait" are taken
from this life of
Charlemagne.

The Irish version of monasticism was based on the Egyptian model and stressed asceticism and the hermit life. The monks did not stress authority or the sense of order that European culture had inherited from its Roman days. Their charismatic method was inspiring for conversions, but another type of monastic life was needed. Saint Benedict provided the solution.

Benedictine Monks

Saint Benedict (480–550), founder of the monastery of Monte Cassino and honored father of Western monasticism, authored an ingenious Rule that created a religious life of moderation. The monks took vows of poverty, chastity and obedience in the following of Christ. The abbot applied the Rule to the life of the community in an enlightened, compassionate and flexible manner. The monks were accustomed to an orderly way of life and brought that balance of order and flexibility to the surge of nomadic tribes that flooded Europe after the fall of the empire.

The Benedictines were also enthusiastic supporters of the popes. It was Gregory the Great who saw their potential for evangelization and engaged them in being missionaries to the new world that was emerging. No one did more for the unifying effect of the papacy than these loyal monks who spread the gospel to all parts of Western Europe and created a network of organized fidelity to the Holy See. This became all the more necessary because a number of the tribes from the East had been converted to Arianism. The monks patiently turned the tide and drew them into the orbit of authentic Christianity.

The Kingdom of the Franks

Clovis ruled the Kingdom of the Franks (French) from 481–511. He was a successful warrior who drove the Roman government out of Gaul (France) and eventually conquered all of Gaul. A pagan, he married the devoutly Catholic Clotilde, who gradually converted him to the church. In a battle against the Alemanni, Clovis took a vow to become a Catholic should he win. Following his victory he was baptized along with thousands of his soldiers. He became a strong defender of Catholicism, welcomed the monks and opposed the Arians. Because of Clovis, Catholic Christianity obtained a strong presence in France which later spoke of itself as the "eldest daughter of the church."

In 753, Pope Stephen II was increasingly troubled by the military intentions of the Lombards, whom Gregory had converted, but who now wanted political control of all Italy, especially the papal lands. Stephen looked northward to the Franks and to Pepin, who had asked him to approve his seizure of the throne (which the pope did). Pope Stephen then crossed the Alps to meet Pepin and obtain his defense of the papal territory.

Pepin and Stephen met and concluded a historic agreement. Pope Stephen anointed Pepin and his two sons, Charles and Carloman, giving legitimacy to the new dynasty. Pepin in turn guaranteed the pope's rule over large territories in Italy, areas that became the Papal States. This decision set in motion the beginning of what become known as "Christendom" in which the state promoted and protected Catholicism and the church anointed the kings, a union of throne and altar that would breed tension as each side attempted to prevail over the other.

After Pepin's death, the monarchy was divided between his two sons. Carloman soon died and Charles became king of all Gaul. His first duty was to defeat the Lombards who again tried to take over Rome. He succeeded and went to Saint Peter's basilica, embraced the pope and renewed the donation of his father, confirming the pope's authority over the Papal States. For the next three decades he conquered what had once been held by ancient Rome. His empire included what today we would call France, Italy, Austria, Germany and parts of Hungary. He brought them into the Christian faith and under his political control.

Ruling a stretch of land and diverse peoples that would comprise an empire, it was only a matter of time and circumstance that Charles would be named emperor. This happened during a meeting he held Rome with Pope Leo III in the year 800. It was Christmas Day and Charles was present at Mass. Pope Leo suddenly arose, took a crown and placed it on the head of Charles. The congregation assented with, "Hail to Charles the Augustus, crowned of God, the great and peace-bringing emperor of the Romans."

What Clovis initiated as the Kingdom of the Franks, what Gregory achieved in an alliance with the Franks, what the Irish and Benedictine monks accomplished in evangelizing rural Europe is now consummated by crowning Charles as the ever remembered Charlemagne—Charles the Great!

FOR REFLECTION AND DISCUSSION

1. From the fall of the Roman Empire in 476 to the pope's crowning of Charlemagne in 800, the Western church was virtual political and religious ruler of territories under its control. With Charlemagne power was divided; the emperor took charge of secular matters and the church oversaw the spiritual realm. That neat division did not last too long. Subsequent popes and emperors intruded on each other's powers, causing strife and wars. There is a saying, "No one surrenders power willingly." Why is this so? Why would this especially be harmful for the mission of the church?

2. Charlemagne believed in the value of education. He had a personal teacher who accompanied him wherever he went, a monk named Alcuin from the city of York in Northern England. Why would an emperor need to have further education? Why would he choose a monk for his teacher? Was religion of major importance to Charlemagne?

3. Do we value religious education? At what point if any in our lives have we learned all there is to know about the faith? How can we help to educate others?

· ·

CHAPTER ELEVEN

MONKS

> He who labors as he
> prays lifts his heart to
> God with his hands.
> —Bernard of Clairvaux

· ·

The monks provided the church with a first-class contingent of missionaries for the conversion of Europe. They not only preached the gospel, they also cleared swamps, started schools, experimented with farming techniques and built monasteries around which grew towns such as York and cities such as Paris.

In scriptoriums—the monastic equivalent of research labs—they wrote out enduring copies of the books of Greece and Rome, thus preserving that heritage of human knowledge for us. They did all this in the conviction that God's Spirit willed the civilizing of the people.

Saint Benedict was the father of the monks of the West. He founded the first monastery, Monte Cassino, in the middle of the sixth century. His *Rule* has remained a monastic guide to this day.

Since even the best groups get ragged at the edge, monks faced two major reforms in the Middle Ages. The first reform came with the founding of the Abbey of Cluny in 910.

Bernard of Clairvaux
Saint Bernard of
Clairvaux (1090-1153)
*"was so famous a
preacher that he
became known as
'Doctor Mellifluous,'"*
for the words coming
from his mouth were
said to be like honey.
He had such an
extensive influence on
the thinking of his age
that he has been called
"the conscience of all
Europe." Pope
Eugenius, a friend of
Bernard's, asked him
to comment on the
pope's role as head of
the church.

William I of Aquitaine and his wife gave the monks the town, manor house, waters and revenues of Cluny so they could build a monastery. This economic windfall meant the monks could leave manual labor to the serfs. Now they could concentrate on the development of an elaborate liturgy and cultural pursuits such as the preservation of Greek and Roman classics and the conducting of schools.

The second reform began with the founding of the abbey of Citeaux in 1098. The new monks, called Cistercians, owed their thinking to Stephen Harding, author of their "Charter of Charity." The playlet that follows deals with concerns and issues of this period.

The Cistercians wanted none of the worldliness of Cluny. They wanted withdrawal from the world and a return to manual labor. They refused land grants. They took swamps and "useless" property and turned it, by their manual labor, into "golden meadows."

Their most famous monk, and the greatest churchman of the twelfth century, was Bernard of Clairvaux. But, as Bernard's letter to the pope (page 90) shows, it was still possible for a monk to have concern for events in the larger church and the world.

FROM SWAMPS TO GOLDEN MEADOWS
(c. 1115)

The characters:
- David, abbot of Cluny
- Stephen, monk of Citeaux
- Eleanor, a visitor at Cluny

The scene: Guest house at Cluny about the year 1115. The Benedictine abbey, now two hundred years old, boasted one of the largest churches in the world and a guest house big enough to accommodate forty men and thirty women.

David: Well, Stephen, how's the reform going at Citeaux?

Stephen: Quite well, thank you, Abbot David. I must say I was spoiled by life here at Cluny. I did love being at the crossroads of the world, welcoming the continual stream of visitors and lounging in the human splendor of the abbey.

David: It's strange that in less than two centuries we, who were the reforming abbey, now suffer the indignity of being told we are out of date.

Stephen: Your abbey served a great purpose. It freed hundreds of men to learn the art of prayer and to preserve the cultural heritage of the West. You achieved the impressive feat of merging religious and secular concerns in a satisfactory way for over a century and a half. You Benedictines literally reshaped the spiritual life of people all over Europe with your daughter houses.

Eleanor: Every good thing has its day. Eventually, you began to collapse under the huge weight of the possessions that mounted with each passing year. As a young girl, I visited your Benedictine Abbey of St. Alban's in England. They had a stable big enough for three hundred horses.

Stephen: You're right, Lady Eleanor, about the weight of secular responsibilities. I used to be guestmaster here. It was my job to provide clean towels, uncracked cups, silver spoons, blankets and sheets for the guests. In winter I was supplying candles and candlesticks, a fire that did not smoke and writing materials on demand.

In his letter Bernard explains that the pope is to be a man of service. He has been given the responsibility of serving others, not a position of kingly power; Bernard therefore takes the opportunity to suggest changes—although gradual—in the external trappings of papal practice. Among these are a kind of taxation of the people to support the papacy, the practice of throwing coins to the crowds during papal processions (a gesture designed to gain political favor), majestic dress and pageantry.

Bernard's counsel, presented as a "letter" to the pope, is actually drawn from a treatise, De Consideratione, written at the pope's request.

. . . .

The Monastic Ideal

As the monastic ideal spread some began to exaggerate its ascetic character. One such person was Simeon Stylites. He gained fame because he spent the last part of his life on the top of a pillar.

David: Yes, and don't forget how you had to brush away the spiders' webs and put clean straw on the floor.

Eleanor: I recall that the guestmaster checked to see whether my father removed his sword when we first arrived at the abbey. Somewhat more embarrassing, when we were leaving, he went through our baggage to see whether we had taken along any of the linen or silver of the house.

Stephen: I felt more like an innkeeper than a monk.

David: Look at my white hair—it didn't come from age. I was formerly abbot at St. Edmond's, where they had an enormous debt. It took me twelve years to pull them out of bankruptcy, but I paid for it with a prematurely white head.

Eleanor: Tell me, Stephen, why do you Cistercians insist on moving into swamps for your new houses? I know you want to get away from the distractions here, but aren't you going a bit too far?

Stephen: One easy answer, of course, is that the land is cheap. Another is that it forces us to return to the ideal of manual labor as favored by Saint Benedict. We must work to clear the marshes and lay good foundations for the buildings.

Eleanor: I suppose a common task like that does a lot to improve your community spirit.

Stephen: It seems to. I've rarely felt such a bond with my brothers as when we put our shoulders together to change the swamps into golden meadows. At least it beats chasing spiders' webs.

David: What are you going to do about prayer? I should hope you won't reject that tradition of Cluny.

Stephen: Not at all. We're just as devoted to

prayer as you are. But we are less interested in the pageantry, ceremonies and wordiness of your prayer life. We believe your way of praying is too stuffy, too formal and without meaning. It seems too much like theater. I sometimes wondered if the services were meant to please people rather than to honor God.

Eleanor: I can appreciate, Stephen, that your people have moved toward a more authentic prayer life. What bothers me, though, is the austerity of your buildings. You have no stained glass. I've heard that some of your houses forbid the image of Christ on the cross. And I believe all of your houses exclude any statuary or sculpture.

David: I worry about that too, Stephen. Our monasteries became the one place in a barbaric society where the arts flourished. Doubtless, prayer has a way of humanizing. But the arts also soften the animal and brute instincts of people.

Stephen: I know just what you mean. No one loved the soaring Gothic beauty of this abbey more than I. I know how much peace it brought me and how often it calmed the growling tensions within me.

Eleanor: Then why don't you speak up about this matter at Citeaux?

Stephen: I did, as a matter of fact. Several times I brought it up at community meetings. I even braved a showdown with Bernard himself on the matter.

David: Apparently they weren't impressed.

Stephen: True enough. But I realize that this is all part of the reaction against the excesses of Cluny. You know how reforms have a way of going to the opposite extreme.

Abelard and Heloise
A tragic love story comes from the annals of monasticism. It involved the brilliant young monk, Abelard, and his young student, Heloise. Hired by her uncle and guardian, Abelard was to tutor his young student but, by his own words, the study sessions soon involved "more kissing than teaching."

Heloise eventually became pregnant, which led to their secret marriage. After the child's birth Abelard placed his young wife in a convent near Paris. Heloise's uncle, in an act of revenge, castrated Abelard, and these ill-fated lovers spent the rest of their lives in the shadow of their love affair.

Martin of Tours

Martin of Tours added to the popularity of monasticism in the West. Born around 355, he spent most of his life in Pavia, a city in Northern Italy. At a young age Martin, going against his parents' wishes, sought to become a Christian. In an attempt to free him from Christian influence, Martin's father entered his son in the army.

While in service under Julian the Apostate, Martin was approached by a beggar seeking alms. Having no money, Martin took the cape off his back, cut it in two with his sword and gave half to the beggar. Later, in a dream, Martin saw Jesus approach him and say: "Inasmuch as you did it to one of the least of these my brethren, you did it to me."

Within two years Martin was baptized and left the army. He traveled for a while and even visited the popular and saintly Bishop Hilary of Poitiers, who became a close friend. Martin settled just outside of Poitiers and began to live the monastic life.

Because of his sanctity, the people of Tours wanted Martin as their bishop when that see became open. Some bishops protested that, as poorly and ragged as he was, the prestige of the office would be damaged. In the end, though, Martin was chosen Bishop of Tours. He did not abandon his monastic ways, however. Next to his cathedral he built a cell where he spent as much free time as possible. When demands on his time left him no peace, he moved to the outskirts of the city, where he continued to minister to the people of Tours. Martin's very life and example gave support to the monastic ideal.

. . . .

Eleanor: I sense you believe that they will get over being so strict.

Stephen: Certainly. I wouldn't be surprised that, before I die, a new flowering of the arts will be associated with the Cistercians.

David: Actually, I'm not worried about the arts. What Europe needs is some advanced thinking about agriculture, animal husbandry, milling and weaving. We need some practical breakthroughs. There's hardly been any progress since the days of Charlemagne.

Stephen: On that score, I can forecast a bright future. We are attracting some people incredibly skilled in these areas. The techniques we learned draining marshes were only a beginning.

Eleanor: And this isn't going to hurt the economy of northern Europe.

David: So the cycle may begin again. The day you make more wool than you need, you'll be at the market selling. And then you'll be right back where you started—involved again with the very world you now run away from.

Stephen: That's already come up at our community meetings. Typically, the conservative wing doesn't want to think about that. They hope to keep our reform intact, refusing to see that such a course inevitably leads back to the business world they hope to escape.

David: Well, you've done away with the extravagances that have crept in up to now. If the time comes when another reform is necessary, there will be men around to see that it's done.

Eleanor: You mentioned Bernard a little earlier. How is he doing at Clairvaux?

Stephen: He's as busy as ever. I understand he's just written a rule of life for the Knights Templar monks at Jerusalem.

David: Where did they get such a name?

Eleanor: My cousin, who's just back from the Crusades, says that they were lodged in quarters next to what they believed to be Solomon's temple. So they consider themselves "knights by the temple."

David: Stephen, did Bernard say anything special in his rule for the Templars?

Stephen: One passage did startle me: "The soldier may securely kill, kill for Christ and more securely die. He benefits himself if he dies—and Christ if he kills. To kill a malefactor is not homicide, but malicide (the killing of the bad). In the death of a pagan, the Christian is glorified because Christ is glorified." So Bernard said.

Eleanor: I know Bernard is the greatest churchman of Europe, but those words make me shudder a bit.

David: It is an unusual statement. I must think about it.

Stephen: One thing is certain. He speaks the mood of our times.

David: No quarrel with that. It catches me up short to realize that this is the mood of our times. The tower bell rings for vespers. Let us pray for our world and our people—and God's reign of peace.

BERNARD CONFRONTS HIS AGE:
A LETTER TO THE POPE
(c. 1150)

Dear Pope Eugenius,

That you have been raised to the pinnacle of honor and power is an undeniable fact. But for what purpose have you been so elevated? Here is a question that calls for your utmost consideration. It was not, as I suppose, that you might enjoy the glory of lordship.

For when the prophet Jeremiah was similarly exalted, he heard the voice of the Lord saying to him:

> See, today I appoint you over
> nations and over kingdoms,
> to pluck up and to pull down,
> to destroy and to overthrow,
> to build and to plant. (Jeremiah 1:10)

What is there here suggestive of pomp and glory? Have we not rather the imposition of toilsome administration poetically expressed in the language of agriculture?

Therefore, that you might not think too highly of yourself, bear always in mind that a duty of service has been imposed upon you, and not a dominion conferred. Surely, you are not greater than Jeremiah? And although you are perhaps equal to him in power, in merit of life he is immeasurably your superior.

Learn from him to use your position of eminence, not to show your authority, as to do the work the time demands. Learn that you have more need of a hoe than a scepter to do your job.

What is to be thought of the practice of purchasing the applause of the crowd, and paying for this with the plunder of the churches? The poor find their living sown in the streets of the wealthy. Silver coins are seen to glitter in the mud.

There is a rush from all sides. But it is not the neediest who secures the prize. Rather, he who has the advantage in bodily strength or fleetness of foot surpasses his competitors. I cannot say that this usage or better, this crying abuse, began with you. But in God's name, let it end with you.

I must go on to speak of another matter. In the midst of these depressing scenes I behold you, the supreme shepherd of the flock, advancing majestically "in gilded clothing, surrounded with variety" (Psalm 45:12–14).

Tell me, what profit does the flock derive from such magnificent pageants? If I may venture to say it, they are better calculated to provide food for the wolves than pasture for sheep.

Do you think that Saint Peter loved to surround himself with this pomp or display, or Saint Paul? No. In all things that belong to earthly magnificence, you have succeeded not Peter, but Constantine. However, I would counsel you to tolerate this splendor at least for a time, yet without falling in love with it, or regarding it as essential to your state.

Ever cordially in Christ,

Bernard

LOOKING BACK

. . . .

Monks

The life of the monks was central to the development of medieval spiritual, cultural and technical life. Their own ability to reform themselves was a sign of their dynamism and imagination. The play underlines these points:

1) *Reform for a spiritual purpose.* The Abbey of Cluny had been a reform movement in which the art of prayer, especially its liturgical form, was developed. It also was involved in copying manuscripts and salvaging the general cultural heritage of the ancients. The arts flourished and a civilizing impact was felt in Europe. But after two hundred years the abbey declined in spiritual vitality because of its wealth. The energies of abbots and monks went into keeping up the buildings, managing the large estates and dealing with vast numbers of people—tourists, businessmen and local gentry—coming in to pass the time.

Under Stephen Harding and Bernard of Clairvaux a new reform took place. It originated at the Abbey of Citeaux; hence the monks were called Cistercians. They deliberately chose secluded places for their monasteries, both to recover the spirit of manual labor and to get back to a life that allowed them to concentrate on continuous attention to God.

Like the Puritans of a later date, the Cistercians stripped their churches of all ornament—stained glass, statues, sculpture and even, in some cases, the image of Christ on the cross. Their ceremonies were severe and their life starkly simple. The purpose was to recover the spirit of prayer.

They not only succeeded in achieving monastic simplicity but also contributed technical advances in agriculture that aided the growth of Europe's economy. In time, they passed beyond their "puritan" stage and inspired a new flowering of the arts.

2) *Integration of religion and life.* Even though the Cistercians "fled the world," they fled more from its baggage than from its people. Jesus had told the apostles to travel light in order to announce the gospel; so it was with the monks. They taught people how to pray. They also taught people to recreate the earth for the sake of human concern.

3) *The Knights Templar.* This subject picks up the theme of war introduced in "Coffee Break" (see page 20). Bernard, the greatest of Cistercians, wrote the rule for the Knights, illustrating how religion and war can get mixed together and how the spirit of the times influences the rationale of even one so saintly as Bernard.

We will be seeing the phenomenon of holy war again in the episode on the Crusades (chapter fourteen). It may be helpful to keep in mind that this theme occurs again and again in religious history. In the Old Testament it is especially evident in the Book of Judges and in 1 and 2 Maccabees. Noble religious figures such as Gideon and Judas Maccabaeus killed ruthlessly for the protection of religion, the glory of God and (not to be forgotten) their own political purposes.

Popes have fought wars. Luther backed a cruel repression of the Anabaptists during the peasants' rebellion. It is impossible to render a judgment on these people from so great a distance. There is nothing to stop us from disagreeing with what they did and asserting that we do not personally believe in such behavior for ourselves.

CONNECTING TO OUR TIMES

. . . .

Nuns, Monks and Religious: Finished or Starting Over?

The small seed of monasticism planted in the early centuries of the church flowered into the male and female Benedictine and Cistercian monasteries of the Middle Ages. The seed became a garden as time went on, with the arrival of male and female Franciscans, Dominicans, Norbertines, Augustinians, Carmelites—also such exclusively male orders as the Jesuits, Redemptorists, Oratorians, Christian Brothers and many others.

Vast numbers of religious women outstripped their male counterparts in congregations such as the Ursulines, the Visitations, Mercy Sisters, St. Joseph Sisters, Sisters of Notre Dame and a bewildering number of other communities. Religious women constitute the world's largest number of Catholics committed to the religious life.

The history of religious orders and congregations has often followed the cycle spoken of by an old monk: "Diligence begets abundance. Abundance begets laxity. Laxity begets decay." The life-cycles of religious life often illustrate the bittersweet wisdom of this saying. Today, the religious life is flourishing in the developing nations, but is facing a membership crisis in Europe and North America. Sometimes the reason for this is due to what the wise old monk predicted.

But other reasons have something to do with it as well. Times of radical cultural change in the past also witnessed a temporary decline of religious life, followed by a remarkable resurgence. The arrival of print technology with Gutenberg, coupled with global expansion triggered by Columbus' discovery of America, at first shook the monasteries and convents to their foundations, only to see new orders (such as the Jesuits) founded and a second spring of religious life.

Today, the computer-driven culture, the communications revolution in information and transportation again is causing a cultural upheaval. It is reflected in the religious life as everywhere else. If history is prologue, then we can anticipate that, when the smoke clears, we will see a resurgence of religious life as well as new congregations.

Saint Bernard of Clairvaux

Bernard, a Cistercian, became a member of Citeaux. After his entrance, the monastery took on renewed life and vigor. At the suggestion of Stephen Harding, he and twelve monks founded a branch of Citeaux at Clairvaux. This foundation proved highly successful.

In investigating the life of any saint it must be remembered that saints, like anyone else, are affected by the social conditions and thoughts of their age. Bernard's advocacy of the Second Crusade and his composition of a rule for the Knights Templar (a group of soldiers formed to protect pilgrims in the Holy Land) indicate the militant nature of his Christianity. His concept of faith left little room for inactivity. He chided popes, decided agendas for councils, fought corruption at Cluny, became consultant to kings, popes, bishops— the powerful elite of his time. Regardless of how one views his zeal, one notes his profound influence upon the peoples and events of his age.

Bernard died in 1153 and was declared a saint of the church in 1174.

FOR REFLECTION AND DISCUSSION

. . . .

1. "I reprove and discipline those whom I love" (Revelation 3:19a). This biblical admonition reminds us of the link between love and constructive criticism. We see in Bernard's advice to Pope Eugenius III an application of the principle. Since Vatican II public criticism of popes and other church leaders by Catholics has increased. Discuss some of these criticisms. How valid

are they? Do you think they are delivered in the loving spirit of Revelation 3:19?

2. Is our relationship with church leaders healthier now that we feel more free to articulate such criticisms? Do we have a better church in which not only the leaders rebuke the flock, but also the flock rebukes the leaders?

3. What are some practical guidelines for public criticism of church leaders?

4. What are the opportunities and dangers in our relationships with one another for constructive and destructive criticism?

5. True or false: Most criticism and confrontation is usually made impulsively in anger or annoyance. This does more to increase confusion than to bring enlightenment. Discuss.

6. How do we avoid arrogance in criticizing others?

7. Today we normally think of monks in terms of prayer, as witnesses to contemplation. The monks of the early Middle Ages also devoted themselves to prayer. Less known is how the Benedictines—and later the Cistercians —laid a firm economic base for Europe by creating a network of cultivated land and well managed farms. These farmer monks acted as internal colonizers of Europe's frontiers, much like American pioneers pushing out into the prairies. How do today's Trappists reflect and repeat this historic tradition of the monks?

8. Explain this monastic irony: the more monks attended to social, economic and political affairs, the more their impact diminished.

9. For many people monasticism is a bygone or antiquated expression of Christianity. What is its value in this day and age?

10. In an attempt to give people an understanding of the monastic life, many communities allow people to live temporarily at a monastery. Would this possibility ever interest you? Why or why not?

11. If Bernard of Clairvaux was seen as the conscience of the church during his day, who might be seen as fulfilling this role in modern times? Mother Teresa, Pope John XXIII, Dorothy Day, Martin Luther King, Pope John Paul II or someone else?

12. Imagine you were asked by the present pope to comment on his role as head of the Catholic church. How would you respond?

. . . .

CHAPTER TWELVE

THE ARCHITECTURE OF FAITH

> Here [Chartres] is the
> Church, the Way, and
> the Life…!
> —Henry Adams

. . . .

"MEN OF CHARTRES": A CALL TO BUILD A CATHEDRAL
(c. 1145)

The town crier leaped atop a barrel in the center of the marketplace, silenced the few men gathered about him and called out to gather more. "Men of Chartres, listen. Our bishop wants us to build a cathedral. He wants it to be so magnificent that our neighbors in St. Denis will stand in awe of our work. Those men whose purity of life befits them to work on this, step forward. All those men who wish to put coins in the purse, step forward. The rest of you stand in awe of work for the glory of God."

The crowd rustled. No one would be the first to come forward. There would be days of talk and soul-searching. Only then would the guilds come forward one by one to volunteer workers.

Louis, a young stonecutter and native of Chartres, held his breath in wonder. If only I could work on it, he thought to himself. If only my work could be part of this town's praise of God.

Little did he know that soon his guild would choose him to work on the cathedral. Many like him would spend a lifetime on this work, passing the completion of it along to their children. Workers would spend years carving a small but elaborate detail high atop a spire, unseen by human eyes but done in the belief that such a deed honors God.

These cathedrals were the visible evidence of medieval faith. They were buildings that towered toward heaven to "touch" their God.

Centuries later, in our own day, we see these masterpieces and marvel at the faith which produced them.

LOOKING BACK

. . . .

Gothic Architecture

Gothic architecture is a nonverbal communication of faith. The great European cathedrals stand as an art form of faith.

The period of Gothic architecture began sometime between 1137 and 1144 with the reconstruction of the royal Abbey church of St. Denis. This particular church, the shrine of Saint Denis, the apostle of France, and also the site of several kingly coronations, represented the alliance of the church and the kings of France. It combined architectural characteristics never before brought to one building. The objective was to make it both a site of religious pilgrimage and a symbol of French patriotism.

The new spirit in architecture originating here was twofold: an emphasis on geometric planning and the quest for interior illumination. Both of these reflected religious significance. Geometric exactness and proportion resulted in harmony, which exemplified the unity of the universe as created by God. The light flooding the interior represented the divine light, the Spirit of God.

In northern Europe where sunlight is scarce, Romanesque buildings—heavy, hooded, columned—were too dark. Architects were asked to devise a building that could support huge windows to let in light. Their solution was to use the pointed arch, locked by a keystone and supported from the outside by flying buttresses. The result was a building that resembled two soaring hands, locked in prayer and pointing to God.

Once this was done, the glassmakers and the sculptors came to the forefront. The glassmakers used colored glass in order to soften the light, present a jeweled effect and offer the viewers Bible stories in living color. They were wildly successful, so much so that we are unable today to match the extraordinary coloring they achieved. This is above all true of the matchless windows of Chartres.

The sculptors brought life to stone, creating an army of saints, kings, guildsmen, angels, demons, witches and animals. Even the rainspouts on the roof shared in the world of beauty formed by the sculptors. With boundless fancy, gargoyles—wide-mouthed beasts—fed rainwater from the drainage pipes onto the ground below.

In 1145 the Gothic style moved from the rural abbey of St. Denis to the urban centers with the beginning of the construction of Chartres Cathedral under the supervision of the bishop of Chartres, a friend of the abbot of St. Denis. But Notre Dame of Paris, begun in 1163, follows the original Gothic style of St. Denis much more closely than does Chartres. Bourges and Reims were begun about 1200.

The cost of the cathedrals was met by donations from all ranks of society and from all over the country, which brought to the projects a merger of religious fervor and local civic pride.

Many of the cathedrals were dedicated to the Virgin Mary. *Notre Dame* ("Our Lady") graced the names of the major cathedrals at Paris, Chartres, Rouen, Reims and Beauvais. Jesus was the king of glory and Mary was the queen of heaven. Medieval people loved legends about our Lady, and they were delighted to see these stories depicted in stone and glass.

Friendly rivalry played a part in the building of the cathedrals. Each town wanted to have a bigger and more splendid church than the next. This rivalry reached absurdity in Beauvais, where the builders reached too high and the roof caved in. They tried several more times with the same result.

The prize for the most beautiful of all cathedrals goes to Chartres. Incredibly balanced, boasting dazzling windows and nearly ten thousand figures in its windows and statuary, it survives as a testimony of human skill and Christian faith that rarely fails to touch anyone who makes a visit to its halls. American writer Henry Adams has memorialized it in his classic work *Mont-Saint-Michel and Chartres*.

CONNECTING TO OUR TIMES

· ·

Cathedrals: Centers of Beauty and Faith

All world religions have striven to embody their faith in structures of surpassing beauty. Israel boasted of Solomon's temple. Muslims celebrate their mosques. Hindus rejoice in their shrines. Babylon prided itself on its step-like ziggurats, similar to the monuments constructed by the Aztec, Inca and Maya in South and Central America.

Christianity has created cathedrals of towering beauty. From the awesome, sixth-century Byzantine church of St. Sophia in Istanbul to the medieval Gothic cathedrals to the Romanesque and baroque basilicas, to our contemporary architectural wonders, there always arise buildings of beauty to express the exuberant faith of Christians.

In a unique way, especially for northern Europeans, the Gothic cathedral seems to have spoken most eloquently about the meaning of faith. But what is truly relevant to this discussion is the intrinsic relation of religion and beauty. Our bodies hunger for food. Our minds thirst for ideas. Our emotions reach out for affection. Our souls want faith and God.

But what seems to integrate all these hungers is our innate aesthetic craving for beauty. Keats said, "Beauty is truth, truth beauty." Philosophers often note that the one, the good, the true are all summarized in the beautiful. There is something about beauty that establishes all the hidden connections we look for when we want to make what is precious to us fit together. Love is certainly one way to do it. Another tried and true method is beauty. That is why we will always have poets, artists, musicians, sculptors, novelists, glassmakers and architects.

All their talents converge in a given cathedral—and in our parish churches. All the beauty of our worship spaces is meant to draw us to deeper faith in God.

FOR REFLECTION AND DISCUSSION

. . . .

1. It often took a century or more to finish a cathedral. What motivation do you feel a person would need in order to devote years to working on one small section of a building? Could you find the same motivation anywhere today?

2. The liturgy is the basic determining element in the construction of church buildings. Until most recent times congregational participation was at a minimum, so there was no architectural concern with bringing the congregation into the act of worship. The current emphasis on participation and community is chief among the reasons for a departure from traditional architectural styles. What is the outstanding message of modern church architecture? Does it reflect the spirit of our times? If so, what is the spirit?

3. Churches of the Middle Ages focused on the tabernacle and altar, emphasizing faith in Christ's Real Presence in the Eucharist. Many churches today have Blessed Sacrament chapels. Their worship spaces focus on the altar, the lectern and the baptismal font to show our faith journey from baptism to eucharistic celebration, which includes both Liturgy of Word and Liturgy of Sacrament. How does the present emphasis help us participate more effectively in the Mass?

4. Which type of church do you prefer for worship—Gothic or modern? Why?

5. If you were able to design a church, what would it look like? How would you express the fundamentals of Christianity through design? Is that possible?

CHAPTER THIRTEEN

FRIARS

> We must love them
> both, those whose
> opinions we share and
> those whose opinions
> we reject. For both
> have labored in the
> search for truth, and
> both have helped us in
> finding it.
> —Thomas Aquinas

The thirteenth century saw the introduction of a new kind of religious order. Its members were called friars. Unlike the monks, who confined themselves to the monastery and its surroundings, the friars went out among the people.

One religious order, the Franciscans, worked at popular preaching and did so with immense success. Their emphasis on the human side of Jesus signaled the rise of Christmas cribs, the Stations of the Cross and other dramatizations of Gospel stories.

Their founder, Francis of Assisi, with his love of gospel poverty, the beauty of nature and every person he met, is a saint who is universally appealing. Many say he is the saint who has most perfectly imitated Jesus.

A second order of friars, the Dominicans, became especially noted in the field of education and scholarship. Their most famous member is Thomas Aquinas. He was a radical theologian for his time, daring to use the thoughts of Aristotle to help explain the meaning of the gospel. Like any innovator, Thomas had a tumultuous career. But even though he battled his opponents with vigor, he did so with a sense of modesty, balance and human understanding.

The following stories are about two friars: Francis and Thomas.

FRANCIS: A TURNING POINT FOR POVERTY
(c. 1228)

"It's hard to believe, Francis, that you didn't get along well with your father when you were a young man. You seem so much at peace with yourself that I can't imagine you in conflict with anyone."

Francis, the revolutionary friar from Assisi, stopped playing his musical instrument and paused before replying.

"This peace was not always with me, Luke. I was quite wild, a leader among my friends, always anxious for adventure, always looking the part of the rich young man. But then a series of events started to make me think, and I began to sense that God was moving me to repair his house, which was in ruin. When I began to carry this out, my father became very angry with me and I began to fight with him.

"He was so totally dedicated to making money and building up the business. I hated his love of wealth, his status-seeking and his seeming indifference to anything else."

"Did you try to communicate with him, Francis?"

"Yes, Luke, I often tried to make him see that I simply had no interest in the business. I argued with him, but I always felt he wasn't really listening to me. Over and over he would say to me, 'You'll change your mind. You're just young and foolish.'"

Luke took out some food they had just begged from a farmer. He offered a chicken leg to Francis as they walked along the dusty road on the way to visit Sister Clare. Luke had been with Francis through thick and thin. He marveled at how well Francis still looked. His beard was flowing and he was brown as a nut. Francis preferred to walk barefoot. The soles of his feet had become as thick as sandals.

"What was it like, Francis, when you had the final showdown?"

"Most people thought I had lost my mind. I can't say that I blame them. It all took place at the bishop's house. My father had me summoned there to 'bring me to my senses.'

"We exchanged some very harsh words, and then my father proposed to beat me—right in the presence of the bishop. Happily, the bishop stood between us and tried to calm Father. I had reached the point where I knew words were useless. That's when the idea struck me."

"Is this the story of the stripping, Francis?"

"Luke, it wasn't as easy as it now seems in legend and story. I was convinced that I had to dramatize how I felt about the exaggerated devotion to wealth I'd seen in my own family and elsewhere in Umbria. With all the impetuosity of youth, I took off my clothes in the presence of the bishop and everyone.

"They were pretty stunned. Standing there, naked, I publicly renounced any and all inheritance that was mine by birthright."

"What did they do then, Francis?"

"At first they scarcely moved. Finally, the bishop took a cloak and put it around me. He advised my father and the other people to leave and let no more be said for the moment."

At that Luke and Francis had arrived at Clare's convent.

"Hello, Clare. Luke and I have been talking over old times."

"I'm glad to see you, Francis. Luke, I can see you're taking good care of my brother."

"He's just been telling me the story of the day he publicly embraced poverty—or, as poets have since put it, the day he married Lady Poverty."

"It still seems unbelievable," said Clare, "even after all these years. You and the brothers have done so much to touch the consciences of people who clutch their money and land and possessions."

"I wish," said Francis, "that all people could know the freedom I experience. Jesus told his apostles to travel light. Perhaps I cannot expect everyone to do this, but at least I want my friars to be an example of this in the community."

Clare replied, "As you know, Francis, there is already a movement among the friars away from your ideal. They admire your ideal, but they say it is now impractical."

"Society itself," said Luke, "does not seem as willing to support you as it did in the early days. I've heard people argue that they could put up with a dozen people like you, Francis. But a thousand of you is a different matter. How will we all survive by only begging for the day?"

Franciscan Order

Shortly after its founding in 1209 the Franciscan Order was divided over how closely Francis' guidelines concerning poverty should be followed. This eventually led to the formation of three separate Franciscan bodies.

Observants (O.F.M.). In the early fourteenth century, decline in religious life and observance led many friars to call for a return to a stricter observance of the rule. Due to associations with the heretical Franciscan Spiritualist movement, however, these aspirations were suppressed. But the reform would not die, and at the Council of Constance in 1414 they were granted church recognition and the right to pick their own vicar-general. Efforts for reunion with the Conventuals failed and in 1517 they separated to carry out a ministry that tended to be itinerant in nature.

Conventuals (O.F.M. CONV.). Due to the rapid growth of the order, with its pressing needs for houses of study and other necessities for the exercise of ministry, one group of friars petitioned Rome for a declaration concerning the obligation of poverty. In 1230, Pope Gregory IX declared the right of the friars to possess property in common under the ownership of the Holy See. Shortly thereafter the churches under their guidance were identified as conventual churches (hence the name) in contrast to collegiate and parish churches. After Trent, the Conventuals were allowed to own property in the name of the order as distinct from the Holy See. They officially broke with the Observants in 1517 by decision of Leo X and were seen as living out a more moderate expression of Francis' ideals.

Capuchins (O.F.M. CAP). This reform movement began in Italy in 1525 when the Observant friar Matteo da Bascio received permission from Pope Clement VII to follow the rule "to the letter." They were allowed to wear beards and adopted a habit with the long, pointed hood. They became so identified with this particular hood that they were called capuccino by the children in the streets; hence their name, Capuchin. Though esteemed for their work in social welfare and charity, they tended to emphasize a contemplative way of life.

This topic always visibly annoyed Francis. Losing his usual calm, he paced angrily back and forth on the brick pavement. He saw change coming and he didn't like it.

Only the day before he had fought with Cardinal Ugolino, the official protector of his order, over the prelate's solution to the problem. Great sums of money were beginning to pour into the friars' treasury. Ugolino said the church would assume the ownership of the money. The friars would have the custody of it.

This meant the end of the life of simplicity that Francis insisted should be the ideal. But the Ugolino proposal did win the day, thus changing the vision that Francis wanted to keep alive in the church.

"You have no idea," said Francis to his friends, "how critical evangelical poverty is for curbing greed in the people and in the church. An economic investment leads to an emotional investment. Then one mixes with the other until nothing can be clearly seen. I still say with my Lord and Master, 'Travel light!'"

Clare was in perfect sympathy with Francis. Knowing how disappointing the Ugolino decision was to Francis, she tried to cheer him up by directing the conversation to another aspect of poverty.

"Francis," she said, "you have found the way of poverty to be a source of great happiness to yourself, but I notice you have no dislike of the world."

"For me, Clare, that's the proper way to feel about poverty. Those who followed the Cynic philosophy practiced poverty, but in such a tight way. They decided not to own anything, so that they could never feel bad if what they possessed were taken away."

"That's playing games. That's based on a suspicion about other people. It says in advance that people can't be trusted. I wasn't interested in a peace of mind produced by that kind of poverty."

"But then there is the special kind of poverty practiced by the early Christians," said Luke, "in which they toughened themselves up for martyrdom. Had that any appeal to you, Francis? Did you think of the discipline of poverty as a means to fight off evil temptations?"

"No, Luke, that never entered my mind. Ever since I was a boy, I've passionately loved this world and all its people. Inside me, I knew my love affair with the world would flower when I was freed from any clutching after it. I

Thomas Aquinas
*One of the greatest
events in the course of
Christian history was
Thomas' writing of the
Summa Theologica.
This theological work,
used now by Catholic
and Protestant scholars
alike, continues to be
influential even seven
hundred years after its
publication. The
Summa was never fully
completed, however.
Three months before
his death, Thomas had
a mystical experience
after which he said,
"All that I have
hitherto written seems
to me nothing but
straw compared to
what has been revealed
to me." Thomas wrote
no more before his
death in 1274.*

. . . .

could exult in the birds of the air, the sun in the heavens, the lilies of the field and the people of the land only when I could lay no special claim to any of them."

Luke went on to say, "Francis, do you believe that everyone could follow your ideal?"

"I wouldn't be human, Luke, if I didn't want everyone to embrace evangelical poverty, because I want everybody to have the happiness and peace it has brought me.

"This has caused conflict for me. First with my father and now with the brotherhood. I have been reconciled to my father. I must learn to accept the path the friars wish to walk. Obviously not everyone can espouse Lady Poverty. For those who can, something beautiful is gained both for themselves and for the world."

"I see the poetry in your message," said Clare, "but I sense you also have a very practical reason in mind."

"The immensely practical result," said Francis, "is that the church will not forget its mission to the poor. If the church should become wrapped up in economic investments, it would have little time for the poor and be blind to their needs.

"The very money it collects would be used to perpetuate the church instead of being used to raise all to their human dignity. I want Franciscan poverty to keep the social conscience of the church alive."

With an amen to these words of Francis, Clare bade good night. Each went to sleep that evening pondering the message of Francis—wondering indeed how well the Christian people would be able to sustain his vision.

THOMAS: AT THE UNIVERSITY OF PARIS
(c. 1292)

"Pardon me, sir," said Eric, a touring merchant from Norway, "but could you direct me to the university?"

"Yes," replied Reginald, secretary to Professor Thomas Aquinas. "I happen to be going that way myself. Are you a stranger in town?"

"I'm from Norway, and am here on business. I've always been fascinated by stories about the universities, and now I'd like a firsthand look."

"In that case," said Reginald, "I'd be happy to answer any of your questions and give you a short tour of the campus."

"I understand," said Eric, "that relations between town and gown have improved since the student riots a year ago."

"We can thank Pope Gregory the Ninth for that," replied Reginald. "For almost a decade, the students were griping about the high cost of food and board. They rightly complained about garbage in the streets and the low quality of wine in the taverns. On the other hand, the citizens of Paris resented the proud and scornful airs of the professors and students."

"What was the riot like?" asked Eric.

"It went pretty far," said Reginald, "with both sides using swords, clubs, boiling water, bows and arrows, and pails of slop thrown from the windows. Several students were killed. This so shocked the teachers that they appealed to the papal legate for help. At first nothing happened, so the students and professors left town. It was the equivalent of their going on strike."

"That must have been when the pope stepped in," said Eric.

"The pope did intervene at that point," said Reginald, "by issuing a charter to the university that gave it the right to manage its own affairs, to determine rents and to suspend classes whenever the town harassed them."

"As a businessman I can appreciate that," said Eric, "for in leaving the city, the students deprive the storekeepers of lots of revenue."

The two of them were now at the campus, which was a series of Gothic-like quadrangles. The atmosphere was full of lively and youthful expectancy.

"Tell me what an average day is like for the students," said Eric.

"They get up at five in the morning for Mass," said Reginald. "Classes begin about six and last until ten, when they have breakfast. Classes resume again until five, when they pause for supper. Then they review their notes until about nine, when they go for a walk, after which they go to bed."

"What is the teaching like?" asked Eric.

"It's changed a good deal since I was a student," said Reginald. "In my day, we studied the 'authorities' such as the church Fathers. Our teachers handed on the traditional information. We never presumed to question or contradict the material."

"Who brought about a change?" inquired Eric.

"The man mostly responsible," said Reginald, "was the celebrated teacher, Abelard. He wrote a book called *Yes and No* in which he presented one hundred fifty-eight questions about religion and gave conflicting answers from the Bible and the Fathers."

"I've read about Abelard," said Eric. "I believe he said, 'The first key to wisdom is frequent questioning. By doubting we come to inquiry, and by inquiry to the truth.'"

"That wasn't too popular an idea at first," said Reginald. "Eventually he got into trouble, but his ideas about learning lived on and developed into the method of disputation that is used now."

"So now the students learn by debating the text readings through the question and answer approach," said Eric. "This must produce wars of logic."

"The disputation is like a tournament," said Reginald. "The students take sides with their favorite debaters and cheer and stomp and whistle. All agree, however, that it is training these young people to think."

"My goodness, that's an odd-looking professor," said Eric.

"That's Roger Bacon," replied Reginald. "He's our scientist. His most recent invention is a pair of glasses for reading. At first people wouldn't use them because they thought it was a devil's trick. They didn't want something between themselves and reality."

"Who is that very old professor lecturing in the Great Hall?" asked Eric.

"You are looking at the eighty-four-year-old German Dominican, Albert the Great," said Reginald. "He came here from Cologne to defend the teachings of his former student—and my master—Professor Thomas Aquinas."

"Someone told me," said Eric, "that Aquinas is the most radical professor this university has ever known."

"He's a mild man for such a title," replied Reginald, "but it's very true. I know the Bishop of Paris and the Archbishop of Canterbury believe that

Thomas is a heretic. It's easy to see why when you hear him going against the eight-century-old tradition set by Saint Augustine. Augustine said that all necessary knowledge comes by revelation from God and that purity of heart is more important than clearness of mind. Still, in spite of the disagreement, Thomas owes a great deal to Augustine and acknowledges him a master."

"But that doesn't leave much room for the work of reason," said Eric. "If God gave us a mind, doesn't he expect us to use it? I know it's important to be a virtuous man, but I tend to beware of the unthinking man."

"Just what Thomas would say," replied Reginald. "Thomas took the logic of Aristotle and applied it to morality, dogma, politics and psychology. People fail yet to see that Thomas is not denying that important truths are in revelation, but he asks us to have an equally healthy respect for human intelligence and its workings. Furthermore, he is not opposed to the life of virtue. I think he is the holiest man in Christendom."

Reginald led Eric into a broad-ceilinged room where Thomas Aquinas was conducting a lively exchange between himself and his students.

"Master Aquinas, what is the cause of love?"

"There are many causes, my friend, but I believe they can be reduced to these three— knowledge, goodness and likeness. A blind man cannot enjoy the beauty of spring flowers for he can't see them. A deaf person fails to appreciate the melodies of great music for he can't hear them. It is the same with love. You must know a person in order to really love.

Golgotha

Francis was known to practice a common devotional exercise of the Middle Ages: meditating on a skull. The purpose was to bring people concretely and vividly to the realization of mortality as well as to remind them of the death of Christ at Golgotha, "Place of the Skull." In correspondence with others Francis was even known to embellish letters with drawings of skulls.

"Goodness, too, is important. This is another way of talking about the magnetic attraction lovers have for each other. The lover is drawn to the beloved by the powerful goodness and beauty that is sensed.

"Lastly, likeness produces love. Lovers must have something in common. Birds of a feather flock together. Knights and stonecutters join different guilds since they have different interests. Lovers find each other through a common interest."

"What, then, is the result of such love?"

"As every true lover knows, ecstasy is the greatest effect. Those who really love can know the greatest happiness that is possible here on earth."

"Why do lovers talk so much?"

"That is because they want to live in each other's minds. Hence, hand in hand they walk under the chestnut trees, pouring out the secrets of their hearts to each other."

"Aren't lovers too possessive?"

"Those really in love naturally want to possess each other's hearts. God says in the Bible, 'My son, give me your whole heart.' That is why the girl may say to her boy, 'Tell me how much you love me! Tell me again a thousand times!'"

"Does this explain why they want to be with each other so much?"

"Of course. Love demands presence. Even when they are parted for one reason or another, the lovers remain bound to each other in affection and thought."

Eric and Reginald withdrew at this point and went toward The Lion and the Arrow for lunch.

"So that is your master," said Eric. "He speaks with such warmth, intelligence and gentleness that I wonder why anyone would oppose him."

"It's like everything else in life," said Reginald. "So much prejudice and misunderstanding is based, even as Thomas said, on not knowing the person. Those who really know Thomas as I do can't fail to love him."

With that they ordered strawberries and wine to eat and drink in honor of the great Christian University of Paris and its most honored professor, Thomas Aquinas.

Faith and Reason

On August 4, 1879, Pope Leo XIII issued the encyclical Aeterni Patris, *which sought to "restore scholastic philosophy in general and that of Saint Thomas Aquinas in particular." Using Saint Thomas Aquinas as its guide, the encyclical said: "Those therefore are the best philosophers who combine the pursuit of philosophy with dutiful obedience to the Catholic faith, for the splendor of the divine truths irradiating the soul is a help to the intelligence; it does not deprive it of the least degree of its dignity, but even brings it an increase of nobility, acuteness and strength."*

Thomas' harmony of faith and reason as presented in his Summa Theologica *was now a model for seminaries throughout the church. Thus a man who at one time had been accused of heresy now became the model theologian-philosopher for the church to imitate.*

The Catholic church sponsored the growth of medieval universities such as those at Paris, Oxford, Cambridge and Padua. From the very beginning, as in the case of Thomas Aquinas, academic freedom produced tensions. Scholars still have not resolved how much dissent can be allowed in a Catholic institution of higher learning.

. . . .

LOOKING BACK

. . . .

Friars

Saint Francis of Assisi

1181 Giovanni Francesco Bernardone was born at Assisi. His father was a wealthy textile merchant and his mother was a member of a distinguished French family. He was called Francis ("the Frenchman") because of his love of French clothing and lifestyle. Francis' youth was marked by a general spirit of worldliness; his wealth and love of life made him a leader among the youth of Assisi.

1202—1203 Francis participated in the inter-city feud between Assisi and Perugia and was imprisoned for a time. He became gravely ill and subjected himself for the first time to serious self-analysis.

1205—1206 Francis renounced his worldly possessions to embrace a life of poverty. Although a layman, he began to preach to the townspeople; after this, his first followers joined him. Francis composed his first rule, which made the gospel his way of life.

1209 When Francis and his followers numbered twelve, they went to Rome and obtained the approval of Pope Innocent III for the rule.

1212 Francis reactivated the missionary activity of the church and undertook a missionary journey to Syria.

1221 The rule of Francis' order, which had developed without much direction, was revised and promulgated. Francis devoted himself to the spiritual growth of his order. He preached throughout the countryside, but repeatedly interrupted his activity to retreat to a solitary hermitage.

1224 Francis received the stigmata on September 14.

1226 Francis died at Assisi.

The early rule of Saint Francis, which has not survived, set as its aim "to follow the teachings of Our Lord Jesus Christ and to walk in his footsteps." Probably no one in history set himself so seriously as Francis did to imitate the life of Christ and to carry out so literally Christ's work in Christ's own way. This is the key to the character and spirit of Francis. He was a lover of nature, a social worker, an itinerant preacher, a lover of poverty. Perhaps Francis is most widely recognized, however, for the deep sense of brotherhood he felt with all of God's creatures.

The Medieval University

The medieval university was a special creation of the Christians of the Middle Ages. Ancient Greece had a respect for education and founded academies for learning, but these were never as ambitious as the university turned out to be. The word *university* originally applied to any official grouping of people in medieval times. Eventually, it was applied directly to the educational enterprise itself.

Items stressed in the episode:

1) Student unrest was common. Records of battles between "town and gown" are a recurrent theme throughout history.

2) A papal charter was the medieval method of gaining academic freedom for the university. Generally, it was the city fathers who wanted to coerce and suppress freedom at the university. It was the church who threw a protective mantle over the campus.

3) Educational methods changed. In the early stage the main emphasis was on quoting authorities to explain a point. Hence, one would teach the meaning of the Incarnation by showing how great church authorities talked about it, quoting from Augustine, Ambrose, Chrysostom, Origen and similar people. To a great extent, the feeling was that these authorities had pretty much said all there was to say on the topic. Hence, it was the job of the student to master the thought of the authorities, organize it in his own mind, and present it in turn to the rest of the class.

But with the rise of the scholastics, especially Abelard, Bonaventure, Thomas Aquinas and Duns Scotus, the method changed from lecture and authority-quoting to disputation. This was somewhat like a debate, calling for maximum student involvement and the rigorous use of logic and careful research. The authorities were still quoted, not slavishly, but in a critical sense to make sure they were understood in a contemporary light. Other elements were also brought into play, such as the philosophy of Aristotle, the scientific style of Albert the Great and the special cultural elements of medieval times.

In terms of modern educational theory, it was a shift in emphasis from the lecture system to participative learning. This doesn't mean that lectures were ruled out, but they were no longer the sole basis for learning.

4) Aquinas was a radical, and was believed to be a heretic. This is all the more ironic when we observe that he is a favorite theologian among today's conservatives.

5) Aquinas taught that reason was friendly to revelation and that common sense was as important as virtue.

The parallels between thirteenth- and twenty-first–century universities are evident: Young people in universities have been perennially rebellious. Universities enjoy their academic freedom today as much as they did in medieval times. We are still moving from "authorities" to "disputation."

CONNECTING TO OUR TIMES

. . . .

Reverence the Environment, Serve and Love the Poor

Saint Francis of Assisi celebrated nature, ministered to the poor and probed the depths of the prayer of simplicity. For those who were migrating to the new medieval cities, he reminded them to stay in touch with the beauty of creation. For rich merchants who built fine homes behind city walls, he urged them to reach out and help the naked and the starving marooned outside those fortresses. For all busy Christians he modeled the need for meditative prayer and inspired them with poetry such as "The Canticle of Brother Sun."

FOR REFLECTION AND DISCUSSION

. . . .

1. A brilliant tenured professor at a midwestern Catholic college is teaching that the opinions of theologians are to be considered equal in weight to the teachings of the pope and bishops. A group of rich donors have warned the president to stop the professor: Silence him or remove him somehow. If not, they will withdraw pledges of several million dollars to the capital fund campaign. Should the professor be allowed his freedom of expression? Should the board try to silence or fire him? Is the intervention of rich donors a form of blackmail?

2. The editors of a student newspaper at a northeastern Catholic college have taken an extreme right-wing position on political and moral issues. They have angered a number of people not only with their positions, but also because they have made pointed personal attacks on certain faculty members and other students. Are they acting within the bounds of academic freedom and freedom of the press? If you disagreed with their approach, what would you do about it? What moral principles would you invoke in this case?

3. When approaching Francis, how can we get beyond the legendary and romantic, almost tame person and truly discover his radicalism? Where does Francis challenge us, the church and society today?

CHAPTER FOURTEEN

THE CRUSADES

> We are impressed and
> engaged to fight
> To chase those pagans
> in those holy fields
> Over whose acres
> walked those blessed
> feet
> Which fourteen
> hundred years ago
> were nailed
> For our
> advantage on the
> bitter cross.
>
> —Shakespeare, *Henry IV*

HOLY WAR: A SAD HISTORY
(1096–1270)

Holy wars are the most frightful of all wars. A holy war means that the people think God desires it; hence they bring all the ferocity of religious conviction to the fight. War is hell enough as it is, but when religious fervor is added, it is super-hell.

There had always been plenty of ordinary war between Christians. And the medieval church attempted to reduce the brutality of these "unholy" wars by enforcing the Truce of God and the Peace of God. The Truce of God allowed no fighting to take place from Wednesday evening to Monday morning—or on

4. Thinking that scholarship and learning would tempt one to substitute knowledge about God for knowing God, Francis discouraged his friars from such pursuits. Would you consider this a valuable warning or a display of anti-intellectualism?

5. Francis lived a life of absolute poverty and said that when his friars went into the world they were "to carry nothing for the journey, neither sack, nor scrip, nor bread; neither money, nor staff." Is this way of life possible or must compromise be made today? Where does Francis' love of poverty and simplicity fit into our consumer-oriented technological society?

6. It has been said that no one in history has imitated the life of Christ more closely than Francis. Do you agree? Why or why not?

holy days. Since there were so many holy days, combat would be at best an occasional sport. The Peace of God limited the extent of combat by forbidding attacks on merchants, farmers, nuns, pilgrims, priests, or on the animals and properties belonging to these people.

Knights and princes were urged to come forward and vow to keep these rules. They piously took the vows—and just as religiously broke them. The bishops raised armies to punish the princes for breaking their vows. Then the kings raised armies to stop the bishops.

The Council of Clermont in 1095 brought a stop to this "unholy feuding" and enlisted the efforts of all sides against a new enemy in a "holy" war. A plea for help had come from the Emperor Alexius at Constantinople. For almost a century, the East had been fighting off Asiatic invaders whom the Byzantines called *Sarakenos*, "Easterners." (The word *Saracen* came to mean any barbaric and fanatical fighters.) The latest invasion of the "Easterners-Sarakenos" was that of the Seljuk Turks, who occupied a good deal of Asia Minor and were threatening Constantinople itself.

"God Wills It"

Pope Urban II used the Council of Clermont as the setting for a speech that would bring about the first Crusade. The scene was decked out with the full forces of church pageantry—cardinals, bishops and noblemen with all the trappings of early medieval color and pomp. A vast crowd of people awaited the pope's talk. We have no accurate record of what the pope said that day, but whatever it was, he so excited the people that they cried out: *"Deus vult! Deus vult!"*—God wills it! And the holy wars began.

For the duration of the Crusades, Christians ignored Augustine's idea of a just war. Augustine had said that wars may be fought for the cause of justice, but now war was being fought for the cause of faith. Augustine also said that the state should manage wars; but now the church was sharing this responsibility. Ordinarily, the soldier is obedient to his prince, but now he marched in obedience to the cross.

The just war code insisted that we trust the good faith of the enemy and show special care for the civilian population. The Crusaders decided that these norms did not apply to the infidel. They found justification for their theory of holy war in the biblical account of Joshua's conquest of Canaan.

Orders of Knights

Knights Hospitalers (Knights of St. John): Founded in 1113 for the care of sick pilgrims in the Holy Land, they originally engaged in actual nursing. In 1118 they added defense of the "holy places" to their duties and thereafter became primarily a military order.

Order of Knights Templar: Founded in 1118 to protect pilgrims coming from Europe and to defend the Christian conquests in the East, these soldier-monks had few applicants until Bernard made them known and admired throughout Europe by writing a rule for them at the request of the Council of Troyes.

The immediate advantage of the Crusades was that they brought to an end the bickering among Christians and focused their hostility on a common enemy outside themselves. Further, it brought about the widespread sense of unity, fervor and idealism that would be captured by the word *Christendom*.

The Crusades began in 1096 with an unofficial phase known as the "People's Crusade." Fired up by the hypnotic, bearded, wild-eyed Peter the Hermit, nearly fifty thousand peasants surged out of Western Europe toward the East. It was a reckless and tragic venture.

Along the way these "crusaders" massacred communities of Jews and ravaged the rich farms of people they considered heathens in the Balkans. Those attacked fought back by slaying the peasants at night as they slept by their campfires and by poisoning the wells ahead of the crusaders with dead sheep.

Not many of the original fifty thousand were left by the time they arrived at Constantinople. The Emperor Alexius saw the ragged survivors as a potential threat. He shipped them over to the Turks, who promptly slaughtered them all.

The official "Crusade of the Princes," however, was a resounding success. The backbone of their expeditionary forces were the Normans, who still had the courage and cunning of their Viking forebears in their blood; and they were fresh from victories over England and Sicily.

Within two years the Crusaders captured Asia Minor and the important cities of Edessa, Antioch, Tripoli and—best of all—Jerusalem. Covered with blood, they sang in jubilation as they entered the Holy City and knelt in ecstasy before the tomb of Christ.

What was the result? The Crusaders set up four Christian states collectively known as Outremer —the land "beyond the seas." The four states centered around Edessa, Antioch, Tripoli and Jerusalem. Basically, Outremer was a string of fortresses that stretched along the Mediterranean coastline.

Outremer lasted for two hundred years and maintained the Christian presence in the Mideast. Italian ports such as Genoa kept the supplies coming. Two new religious orders, the Knights Templar and the Knights Hospitaler, defended the forts.

Seven more Crusades were to follow this first one, but none could quite match it. Romantic literature has dwelt on the Third Crusade (1189–1192), when Frederick Barbarossa, Philip Augustus and Richard the Lion-hearted set out to fight the great Saladin. It was a massive confrontation, but the Crusaders failed. Frederick drowned, Philip went home and Richard signed a treaty that reduced Christian holdings to a strip of coastland.

The two children's Crusades were the saddest. Twelve-year-old Stephen of Cloyes, claiming he had a vision from Christ to free the Holy Land, persuaded thirty thousand French children to follow him. They marched to Marseilles, expecting the Mediterranean to open for them as the Red Sea did for Moses. Instead, slave traders took them and sold them to the Muslims. Germany produced its own version with twenty thousand children who marched to Italy. It also ended in failure.

For the remainder of the Crusades, the knights' ever-increasing number, power and wealth were the mainstay of the holy war. Because these characteristics aroused so much political and ecclesiastical opposition, Pope Clement V ordered their dissolution at the Council of Vienna in 1311.

. . . .

The Rise of Islam

The Crusades were to free the Holy Land from the grip of the Muslims, the so-called infidels. Islam had its origins in the early seventh century with the Prophet Mohammed (570-632) and the revelation of the Quran, the sacred scripture of Islam, from the angel Gabriel. Mohammed saw it as his mission to restore monotheism to the peoples of Arabia. From about 610 forward, Mohammed proclaimed the message of Islam (Arabic for "submission to the will of God").

Finding little success in Mecca, Mohammed took refuge in Medina, founding the first Muslim city where religious and civil life were combined according to the principles of Islam. Shortly after this he and his followers set out on a military and political campaign through which they gained Mecca. By the time of Mohammed's death in 632, a major part of Arabia was in the control of Muslims. In steady succession the ancient centers of Eastern Christianity fell: Damascus (635), Jerusalem (638), Alexandria (642) and Carthage (695). Many people, having lived through so much intra-Christian hostility, saw the Muslims not as oppressors but as liberators and converted to this new faith. Muslim advance in Spain was halted only in 732, when Charles Martel defeated them at the battle of Tours. Constantinople was constantly under attack, yet withstood the pressure until its fall in 1453.

Thus, from the seventh century on Europe was effectively cut off from the East. The Mediterranean was a Muslim sea. For the next five hundred years Europe and Christianity would be threatened by the Muslims.

Among those who accompanied Christian armies on the Fifth Crusade to Egypt in 1219 was Francis of Assisi. During the siege of Damietta he crossed enemy lines to preach to the Muslim sultan, Malik-al Kamil. Despite his great admiration for the Christian holy man, the sultan did not convert, but did allow Francis safe passage back to the crusaders' camp.

. . . .

The Results

Culturally, the Crusades proved an enrichment for the West. Persian carpets, real mirrors, glassmaking techniques, silks, sugar and spices were among the numerous benefits of contact with the East.

In religious terms, the Crusades accelerated the worsening relations between the Eastern and Western church. The emperor Alexius and the Crusaders quarreled over control of the reconquered city of Antioch. The Crusaders made the awful error of expelling the Greek Patriarch in Antioch and putting a Latin one in his place.

The sack of Constantinople in 1204 by a Crusader army was the worst affront of all. The soldiers tore down the tapestries in St. Sophia cathedral, ripped apart the silver iconostasis (altar screen) and divided it as booty. They placed a prostitute on the patriarch's throne and toasted her with altar wine in stolen chalices. They installed a Latin patriarch and emperor. Cordial relations were virtually impossible after such a desecration.

Historically, the Crusades mark a bloody page in the story of a violent time. They remind us that holy war is a perversion of God's will and a disgrace to Christian moral behavior. The Crusades should teach us that holy wars have no place in Christianity; they are anti-Christian in theory, practice and outcome.

LOOKING BACK

. . . .

The Crusades

In our own time we have known the horrors of ideological war, as in the case of the Nazis or terrorists. Ideological war is a secular version of holy war. The Bible described holy war in the Book of Joshua, where the Israelites were instructed by God to wipe out the enemy completely, letting no man, woman, child, animal or piece of treasure survive the biblical equivalent of an atomic holocaust. Some of us may shudder at the prospect of holy war, but, as we have seen all too recently, it has an uncanny way of surviving.

The Crusades were holy wars in the unabashed raw. Popes, bishops, mystics and saints gave wholehearted support to the enterprise and fired up thousands of people to embark on war against the infidels.

The material in this section has been presented in historical narrative form rather than as a fictionalized account. It raises again the question of the church and war, and highlights the paradoxes of church behavior. The Abbey of Cluny had attempted to lower the temperature of wars between Christians by vigorously promoting and supporting the Truce of God and the Peace of God, which had been initiated by regional councils of bishops and nobles. Yet at Clermont, the church unleashed a war machine that was as cruel and heart-breaking as ever known.

It is difficult—perhaps impossible—to render an adequate judgment on the Crusades. There is much that we can lament and condemn, especially the exploitation of children, the massacres of the Jews and the brutalities toward both Eastern Christians and the Muslims. Centuries later, we wonder how religion could have gotten mixed up in all of this.

Yet, even in our own time, campaigns against the enemy sometimes assume a religious quality and thus become a kind of holy war. At the same time, every modern pope has strenuously spoken out against war and for peace.

Even though this account of the Crusades definitely deglamorizes expeditionary forces or crusading armies, it is not meant to take either a dove or a hawk position on war. Christ had a friendly relationship with army men: He cured a soldier's boy; a soldier was apparently the first one to call Jesus "Son of God" at the Crucifixion; the church uses a soldier's prayer, "Lord, I am not worthy," for the Communion service. The main purpose here is to urge the review of issues of war and peace in a thoughtful way.

The Peace Movement During the Crusades

Toward the end of the thirteenth century, a new attitude toward the Crusades appeared in war-weary Europe. Ramon Lull (1235–1315), Spanish preacher, prolific writer, mystic and practical politician, raised his voice throughout Europe and strongly urged that peaceful rather than warlike methods be used to achieve the goals of the Crusades. Educated preachers, he emphasized, would be more successful than armies in winning over Muslims. Although the constant, indefatigable efforts of Lull along these lines achieved little in his own day, he does represent a realization of the greater value of peaceful methods.

The Just War Theory in the Contemporary World

The theory of just war, beginning with Augustine and later developed by Catholic theologians such as Thomas Aquinas and Francis Suarez, required that certain conditions be met: The war must be declared only as a last resort, by a lawful authority, for a just cause, using just means and with reasonable expectation of success. The military action cannot produce a greater evil than it seeks to correct.

In applying an evolving just war theory to the contemporary world, persons sincerely trying to form their conscience must judge whether or not the end achieved by a particular war is proportionate to the devastation wrought by that war. On the basis of the judgment, they could justify either participation or abstention from war.

Some conclude that just war in the modern world is not possible, citing Pope John XXIII's statement in *Pacem in Terris*: "Therefore, in this age of ours which prides itself on its atomic power, it is irrational to believe that war is still an apt means of securing human rights."

CONNECTING TO OUR TIMES

. . . .

"Lord, Make Me a Channel of Your Peace"

Jesus said there will always be wars and rumors of war. But Jesus also urged us always to practice reconciliation and work for peace. Unhappily, the church of the Middle Ages became embroiled in holy wars with many tragic consequences. On the positive side, church leaders today advocate an unremitting search for peace. Human experience shows that it is harder to make peace and relatively easy to make war. Too many people enjoy a fight.

Negotiation is better. President Kennedy got it right when he said, "We must never negotiate out of fear, but we must never fear to negotiate." The passions of anger, revenge and pride have driven the world of the twentieth century into the two greatest wars in history. President Reagan said, "We seek peace through strength." He meant military power. The popes teach that we should quest for peace through justice for all and the development of inner moral strength.

The wars on the battlefields and in the skies begin at home. The quarrels that rack families are breeding grounds for the arguments that tear nations apart. Too many people get used to fighting as a way to solve problems. They practice the love of power and not the power of love.

Jesus lifted no hand against his enemies. He told Peter to put his sword back in the scabbard. Jesus taught us to love our enemies and proceeded to practice what he taught. He told Pilate he could enlist "legions of angels" to protect him from the force of the state, but he declined to do so. He taught and practiced that witnessing truth and love are better ways to resolve human problems.

War is always terrible, whether it is fought with spears or with missiles. Mothers lose sons and daughters. Wives lose husbands and husbands lose wives. The killing fields are not pleasant places for strolls. They only look that way when the heat of battle is gone and the grass has regrown.

Yes, there will be wars and rumors of wars, but we should not resign ourselves to this condition. We should make peace in our families and nations a constant goal. Love is better than hate. Reconciliation is better than murderous anger. Peace is better than revenge.

FOR REFLECTION AND DISCUSSION

1. Some historians argue that the Crusades were justified by medieval people on three grounds: The infidel Muslims should be driven out of Christian lands such as Spain; Christians, not Muslims, should be in charge of the holy places in Palestine; new land needed for a growing population was being acquired through conquest of lands held by the infidels.

2. How could Christians have drifted so far from Christ's teachings on peace and love, doing good to enemies, not living by the sword, loving one another?

3. Did the crusaders act as Pope Urban II and others instructed them to? Was the object to loot cities and try to gain personal power? Were the intentions of the crusaders good or evil?

4. In today's world would such an undertaking be possible? Are people more or less zealous than in the Middle Ages?

5. All recent popes have denounced any intention to wage nuclear war. The American bishops have echoed this teaching and called for arms reduction and a freeze on nuclear buildups. Is it right to have a nuclear deterrent so as to deal from strength in arms limitation talks? Is it right to possess nuclear arms so long as we have no intention to use them even if nuclear attack is launched against our country?

6. Is forcing conversion on people a reasonable way to salvation? Do you think it would be justifiable to baptize people who do not really understand Christianity? In the same sense, were the Crusades a "moral failure"?

7. Do we suffer from a cultural arrogance in this country? Because we feel our way of life is superior to others, do we have the right to force our way of life on others? Should we be respectful of the cultures of other countries?

8. Is war or any type of violence the answer to problems or does it cause problems of its own? Are nuclear weapons necessary? Should our tax money be used elsewhere? Are there any clear-cut answers?

CHAPTER FIFTEEN

THE GREAT SCHISM

> Being unable to bear
> these unprecedented
> injuries and these out-
> rages directed against
> the chief apostolic
> see…we sign against
> Michael and his sup-
> porters the anathema
> that our most reverend
> pope has pronounced
> against them if they do
> not return to their
> senses….
>
> —From the sentence of
> excommunication by
> Cardinal Humbert against
> Michael Caerularius

"LET THEM BE ANATHEMA"
(July 16, 1054)

On July 16, 1054, Michael Caerularius, Patriarch of Constantinople, stood before a bonfire with his assembled bishops. Into the fire he cast a parchment scroll. Solemnly he pronounced the excommunication of the papal legate who had deposited it in his cathedral the day before, along with "all who had helped in drawing it up, whether by their advice or even by their prayers." In that dramatic moment the final rupture between the Eastern and Western churches occurred.

The quarrel which precipitated the rupture was the result of six hundred years of developing strain. When Caerularius became patriarch, he reminded his clergy of the issues which had long divided the East and the West—clerical celibacy, the use of unleavened bread for Eucharist, the wording of the Creed—and forbade his priests to follow the Latin Rite on pain of excommunication. In 1053 he closed all the churches in Constantinople which persisted in following Rome's directives.

Pope Leo IX immediately responded to that action with a strongly worded letter demanding that all patriarchs recognize papal supremacy and branding any congregation which refused such acknowledgment as "an assembly of heretics, a conventicle of schismatics, a synagogue of Satan." His ire vented, the pope then sent a delegation under the leadership of Cardinal Humbert to discuss the differences between the two churches.

Humbert's approach was less than conciliatory. His legacy had not come, he insisted, "to listen and discuss, but to instruct the Greeks." The patriarch countered by challenging their competency to deal with the issues. In the midst of the stalemate Pope Leo died, and his successor would not be elected for a year. Three months after Leo's death, the frustrated and embittered Humbert decided to take matters into his own hands. The cardinal composed a bull excommunicating Caerularius and hurled it upon the altar of St. Sophia, the great sixth-century basilica in Constantinople. The scene was set for the patriarch's angry response—and for the division of Christendom.

LOOKING BACK

. . . .

The Great Schism

To some extent the division between the Eastern and Western churches goes back to the directions each took after the fall of the Roman Empire in 476. The bishops of the Western church filled the power vacuum (see chapter eight) and provided the stability and continuity needed during the chaos of the barbarian invasions. The bishops acquired a good deal of political and economic power as a result. This led to the papal theocracies of the Middle Ages wherein popes exercised vast temporal as well as spiritual power.

Filioque

Besides the political and cultural differences that divided the Latin and Greek churches, religious differences also added to the tensions which eventually broke in 1054. The most obvious concerned the Holy Spirit. Led by Photius, the patriarch of Constantinople, the Greeks severely criticized the Latins for tampering with the formula of faith as found in the Nicene Creed by adding filioque.

In the East, where the government remained relatively stable for many centuries, the church did not acquire political eminence as in the West. The Eastern church, however, did develop a sophisticated liturgy, theology and spirituality. The Eastern church's supremacy in these areas lasted for many centuries and fostered a sense of superiority in regard to the Western brothers and sisters. Not until the high Middle Ages, when universities like Paris and Oxford flourished, did Western theologians reach a competitive level. But by then the two churches had drifted alarmingly apart and the Crusades had eroded whatever common ground one might have hoped for.

The major split between Eastern and Western Christianity described in this chapter's episode took place just before the Crusades began. But strains had developed over the centuries ever since Constantine had moved the capital of the empire to Constantinople in 330. Rome had retained its place as mother church and primary seat of Christianity, but Eastern Christians found it increasingly difficult to submit to Roman rule in spiritual matters. Several times throughout these centuries the church in Constantinople had tried to make itself independent of Rome. As political instability afflicted Europe and infected even the papacy in the early eleventh century, relations between East and West deteriorated even more. When Michael Cerularius became Patriarch of Constantinople the stage was already set for a break.

The two sides disagreed about questions of liturgy, theology and church discipline; each felt the other held a foreign brand of Christianity.

The patriarch's persecution of Constantinople's Latin churches and the pope's angry response added fuel to the argument. The clash between the stubborn Cerularius and the hotheaded Humbert provided the final spark—and the name-calling in each writ of excommunication leaves no doubt that these two men were an incendiary combination.

Although the cardinal was later censured for his hasty action, Cerularius considered it sufficient excuse for the break from Rome his church had long wanted. At first Rome ignored the Eastern Schism, dismissing it as a personal quarrel between patriarch and papal legate; only years later did the pope acknowledge that a split had indeed taken place and appoint a bishop for the Latin churches in Constantinople.

Hopes of reconciliation between East and West plummeted in the thirteenth century when Crusaders plundered shrines and churches in Constantinople. The result of the Crusades was to confirm the separation in bitterness and hostility. Although attempts at reunion were made at the general councils of Lyons in 1274 and Florence in 1438, their success was short-lived. The Eastern church remained separate, adopting the name *Orthodox* ("holding the correct faith").

Zealous missionary efforts achieved reconciliation between a few groups and Rome. These groups, called Uniate Christians, were for the most part allowed to keep their traditional rites and customs. Over four hundred years, six such groups expressed their allegiance to Rome: the Chaldean, Syrian, Maronite, Coptic, Armenian

The old Creed read that the Holy Spirit proceeds "from the Father" to which the Latins added "and from the Son."

This addition brought with it a subtle theological nuance in the understanding of the role of the Holy Spirit —one that the Greeks were unwilling to accept. The Latins were so familiar with the phrase they went so far as to accuse the Greeks of having cut the expression out.

and Byzantine Rites. The vast majority of the East, however, remained within the Orthodox tradition.

The most dramatic step toward reconciliation since the schism occurred in our own century. In 1964 Pope Paul VI and Orthodox Patriarch Athenagoras met in the Holy Land and publicly embraced each other. In December of that year, they issued a solemn declaration expressing regret for the "offensive words...and reprehensible gestures" which marked the events of 1054 and removed the sentences of excommunication pronounced by Cerularius and Humbert as a first step in reopening the dialogue between East and West.

CONNECTING TO OUR TIMES

. . . .

Learning More About the Eastern Church

Pope John Paul II frequently said, "The church must breathe with two lungs, the East and the West." He was referring to the two main segments of the Catholic church, the Latin church of the West and the various communities of the Eastern church, such as that of the Byzantine Rite. In a special way he was thinking of the Orthodox churches, with whom he felt a special empathy. He hoped and prayed for reunion with them.

With the end of the Cold War it was hoped that significant progress might be made toward reunion with the Orthodox churches. Since the majority of their membership—except for Greek Orthodox—is in former Iron Curtain countries such as Russia, Ukraine, Romania and Bulgaria, their energies have been directed more to recovering after years of tyranny than to ecumenical endeavors.

The Russian Orthodox church, in particular, feels besieged and threatened both by fundamentalist Protestant missionaries and the rebuilding of Latin Rite Catholic life in that country. In Ukraine there is tension between the Orthodox and the Uniate Catholics (Eastern Rite Catholics in union with Rome). The Catholics want returned the thousands of churches taken from them by Stalin and given to the Orthodox. These problems will not be settled quickly or easily. Still, the faith-filled quest for unity must continue.

In the United States there are many Catholic Uniate as well as Orthodox parishes. We should vigorously pursue ecumenical dialogue with the

Orthodox. We should also become familiar with the liturgy and approach to doctrine of the Uniate churches. Their approach to worship stresses the divine and transcendent mystery of God. We have much to learn from them, for they can enrich our own approach to liturgy and catechesis. We must also pray to the Holy Spirit, who is living and active in Uniate, Latin Catholic and Orthodox churches, that a loving unity may be achieved.

FOR REFLECTION AND DISCUSSION

1. In John Paul II's encyclical on ecumenism, *That They May Be One,* Catholics are reminded that they can look to other Christian bodies as sources of truth about the mystery of Christ and the church. With this in mind, what can the Eastern and Protestant churches teach the Roman Catholic Church? What have you learned from other Christian traditions beside your own?

2. One of the major pushes for church union in the twentieth century began because of missionary experiences. In Africa and Asia efforts to gain converts were hampered because of competition and disputes between the various Christian groups. The scandal of church disunity became very apparent. What might be some of the advantages (or disadvantages) if Christians coordinated their missionary efforts?

3. The Decree on Ecumenism states that "in order to restore communion and unity or preserve them, one must 'impose no burden beyond what is indispensable' (Acts 15:28)." How can Christian union allow for diversity without division? In this process, can the various identities of each church be preserved or will one expression predominate?

CHAPTER SIXTEEN

. . . .

HERETICS

> There is one body and
> one Spirit…one Lord,
> one faith, one baptism,
> one God and Father
> of all…
> —Ephesians 4:4–6

. . . .

The church has always been active, not only in expressing religious truth but also in protecting against error in religious matters. The regulations below from the Synod of Toulouse show how tragically caught up the church has been, in certain times and places, in the fear of heresy. But the adaptation of the Vatican II statement on religious freedom that follows shows the balanced view the modern church takes with regard to persons' rights to believe as they see fit.

REGULATIONS OF THE SYNOD OF TOULOUSE
(1299)

Whoever allows a heretic to stay on his property either for money or any other cause, if he confesses or is convicted, loses his property forever and his body is handed over to the civil authority for punishment.

He is also subject to legal punishment whose property, without his knowledge but by negligence, has become the abode of heretics.

The house where a heretic is found must be torn down and the property must be confiscated.

The sheriff who lives in a suspicious place and is not diligent in searching for heretics loses his job—and is not permitted to be employed either there or in any other place.

If anyone who is tainted with heresy freely gives up the heresy, he is not allowed to live in the house where he formerly lived in case the house is under suspicion of heresy. He must move to a Catholic house which is free from suspicion. Besides he must wear two crosses on his coat, one on the right and the other on the left, and of a different color from his coat. Such persons cannot hold public office or be admitted to legal actions unless they are fully reinstalled after due penance by the pope or his legate.

Males and females who have attained the use of reason must confess their sins to a priest three times a year or, with their priest's permission, to another priest. They must perform the imposed penances humbly and according to their strength. They must receive the Eucharist three times a year. *Whoever does not do this is under suspicion of being a heretic.*

Laypeople are not permitted to possess the books of the Old and New Testament. But they can possess the Psalter, the breviary and the little office of the Blessed Virgin—but not in the vernacular.

Women who own castles and fortresses are not permitted to marry enemies of the faith and peace.

Pastors must explain these regulations to their parishioners *four* times a year. (Emphases added.)

VATICAN II'S GENERAL PRINCIPLE OF RELIGIOUS FREEDOM
(1965)

This Vatican Synod declares that the human person has a right to religious freedom. This freedom means that no one should be forced by any person or group to act in a manner contrary to his or her own beliefs. Nor, within due limits, is anyone to be stopped from acting in accordance with those beliefs.

The Synod further declares that the right to religious freedom has its foundation in the very dignity of the human person, as this dignity is known through the revealed word of God and by reason itself. This right of the human person to religious freedom is to be respected by the laws of all governments. It is to be a civil right of every citizen.

Ecumenism
Roman Catholic
participation in
interdenominational
services or events was
not allowed, except
with the Holy See's
permission, right up
until Vatican II. This
was especially
distressing in America,
a country where there
were multiple
Christian confessions.
Because of the
Vatican's stance against
interdenominational
cooperation, in 1947
Congressman John F.
Kennedy was forced to
cancel a scheduled
appearance at a
Philadelphia fundraiser
for a chapel to be built
in honor of four
chaplains—Catholic,
Protestant and
Jewish—killed during
World War II.

It is in accordance with the individual's dignity as a person—that is, a being who has reason and free will and, therefore, personal responsibility—always to seek out the truth, especially religious truth, follow it once it is known, and live all of life in accordance with it.

However, one cannot freely do so unless free from all types of pressure or force, whether physical or psychological, which impel a certain manner of acting. The right to religious freedom has its foundation in the nature of humanity itself. Consequently, each person, no matter who, has this right and can exercise it, provided that the just requirements of public order are observed.[1]

LOOKING BACK

. . . .

Heretics

There are differing arguments about the repression of heretics in an earlier time. The church argued for preserving the purity of the gospel and the faith of the people. The state argued that this approach sustained the public order. Critics today argue that this was a cruel repression of human freedom. They abhor the witch-hunting mentality that occurred as an offense against simple decency and a dishonor to the human person.

What are we to think? Certainly the church has the right to preserve the purity of the gospel and the faith of the people. Assuredly, the state has the right to insure the public order. Without a doubt, human freedom—not license—deserves to exist immune from harm. But how do you resolve conflicts that arise when gospel purity, human freedom and public order appear to clash?

The medieval world turned to such solutions as those found in the "Regulations of the Synod of Toulouse." Today's world addresses the issues with a position such as that of Vatican II's document on religious freedom.

Pluralistic democracies do not experience the tight repressiveness of the church in a medieval society. Yet we do see such behavior in totalitarian regimes of the left in China and Russia, and in the right-wing totalitarian governments of Latin America and Korea.

Medieval religion appears to have acquired the characteristics of an ideological state. We know how China and Guatemala handle dissent. They repress it because they apparently fear any permissiveness would lead to the dissolution of their societies. Those in power in the medieval period—church authorities and politicians alike—also feared deviant behavior. Hence their fierce repression of the Cathari and the Poor Men of Lyons in the south of France and their hot reaction to other pockets of resistance to orthodoxy that arose persistently despite all efforts to eradicate heresy.

We will see this dynamic again in the church's struggles with Protestantism and with the rise of secular liberalism.

Chronology of the Formal Treatment of Heretics

1139 Canon of the General Council of 1139 called on the civil power to repress the Albigensians.

1163 Decree of the Council of Tours demanded that heretics be tracked down and their property confiscated. In England, at the same time, it was decreed also to destroy their houses.

1179 A general council renewed the exhortation of Tours to Christian princes.

1184 The decree *Ad abolendam*, the outcome of a meeting between Frederick Barbarossa and Pope Lucius III at Verone, was passed.

1215 The Fourth Lateran Council adopted *Ad abolendam* and formed the law which Pope Gregory IX applied when he began the Inquisition in 1231. The Lateran Council set extremely severe regulations, but their enactment depended on the energy of local bishops. Pope Gregory found it impossible to police all the bishops, so he appointed inquisitors who had supreme power as papal representatives.

1231 Torture appeared in heresy trials, restored to use by Frederick II.

1233 Pope Gregory appointed the Dominicans as inquisitors in Languedoc,

France. They were unwilling to be identified with the project, however, and the pope ordered the Franciscans to help them.

1252 Pope Innocent IV prescribed the use of the rack for those suspected of heresy.

1478 Pope Sixtus IV reorganized the Inquisition (see chapter twenty-one) at the request of Ferdinand and Isabella of Spain. An important change, however, was that he allowed the king and the queen to choose the inquisitors.

1479 The Spanish Inquisition began and for years was motivated mainly by political rather than religious reasons.

Heresies of the Middle Ages

One of the great heresies of the Middle Ages was Albigensianism. Known in the beginning as Cathars, or "pure ones," this heretical sect spread through much of western Europe, gaining a foothold in northern Italy and southern France. They were especially strong in the town of Albi, France, from whence their name comes.

Like the earlier Manichees, the Cathars believed in two gods. The good god created an invisible spiritual realm, whereas the bad god, identified with the God of the Hebrew Scriptures, created the visible, material world. The body, the creation of the bad god, was evil. Following the example of Christ, the believer was to free the spirit from the body and attain salvation. Their antimatter dualism led them to reject central Christian doctrines including the Incarnation, the sacraments and the Resurrection.

Much of the Cathars' popularity and success was due to their austere and ascetic life, which contrasted sharply with the lives of the clergy. Thus, following the Cathars could be construed as a form of protest against the church's corruption. In response to the Cathars' continued presence and growth, Pope Innocent III launched a crusade against them in 1208. The establishment of the Inquisition followed and eventually rooted out the heresy.

. . . .

CONNECTING TO OUR TIMES

. . . .

Do You Demonize Those Who Disagree With You?

It is a common human tendency to "demonize" those who do not agree with us in belief, attitude and practice. In the Middle Ages this took a deadly form when church members branded dissenters from Catholic truth as heretics and used this as a chance to oppress and persecute them. In the Reformation of the sixteenth century and for many years thereafter, Catholics and Protestants considered each other heretics and practiced many forms of oppression on one another.

Today, thanks to the graces of the Holy Spirit, the ecumenical movement has considerably reduced and often eliminated this mutual demonizing of one another on religious matters. We do still disagree, frequently on substantial issues, but we do so in a charitable manner and engage in dialogues and mutual humanitarian endeavors which benefit society.

Within the Catholic church today, however, there are divisions between conservatives and liberals that sometimes become acrimonious. One side tends to invoke authority on doctrinal and moral issues while the other inclines to a political advocacy especially on social issues, but also on debates concerning married clergy, inclusive language and gender equity. A centrist group tries to hold the community together through persuasion and flexibility where possible.

Society itself is torn by political correctness and single-issue politics. The advice of Rudyard Kipling is pertinent, "Keep your head when all about you are losing theirs." Both in the church and society we will encounter these stresses. When we do, we should learn from history not to demonize those with whom we disagree, and certainly not seek to persecute them.

The New Testament church had many divisions of its own. Paul urged the medicine of kindness. "Let no evil talk come out of your mouths, but only what is useful for building up, as there is need, so that your words may give grace to those who hear....and be kind to one another, tenderhearted, forgiving one another, as God in Christ has forgiven you" (Ephesians 4:29, 32).

137

. . . .

1. Vatican II's Degree on Ecumenism refers to the division of Christianity as a rending which has "damaged the seamless robe of Christ" (#13). It affirms the richness of Eastern liturgy and spiritual traditions, and acknowledges the debt owed by the West for theological insights first formulated in the East.

2. Does the division of Christianity worry you at all? What do you think it does to the effective preaching of the gospel in today's world? What skills or insights were lost to each side in the schism?

3. The practice of celibacy differs between the churches of the East and West. In the Eastern churches bishops are required to be celibate and are usually drawn from the ranks of monks. Their priests may marry once, and must do so before ordination. In the Western church, celibacy is mandated for bishops and priests. Vatican II teaches: "There are many ways in which celibacy is in harmony with the priesthood. For the whole mission of the priest is dedicated to the service of the new humanity which Christ raises up through the Spirit" (Life of Priests, #16).

4. Uniate Christians maintain Eastern traditions in liturgy and discipline while acknowledging the primacy of the pope. How much room is there in the church for such diversity?

5. Holy wars were one dark moment in our church history; the torture and persecution of heretics is another blotch on our past. Inquisitors, or heretic hunters, were quite willing to torment their victims. They burnt their feet, snapped their muscles with tight ropes and choked them with force-fed water. Like an early form of the KGB, inquisitors created vigilante committees of informers who terrorized their neighbors with fear of being named a heretic. Heretics and their families were denied civil and human rights.

6. Heretics have often been called the "pioneers" of the faith in that they attempt to explain the truths of Christianity in new ways. Would you see them as having a positive benefit for the church?

7. Today we live in a world of plurality where individual rights and liberties are cherished. Unable to use the coercive methods of the past (which in the end were ineffective), how can the church preserve right belief or orthodoxy and yet respect the freedom of its members? How would you deal with those who deviate from Christian teachings?

8. In our world today, can the word heretic even be used? Is it an effective way of calling attention to those individuals, groups or practices which are at odds with traditional Christian teachings?

9. Given that heresies so often reappear in new forms, what role might religious education provide in combatting them?

10. Vatican II has taken a positive stand on religious freedom. John XXIII said that error has no rights, but people do. Is it ever all right to punish people for their religious belief? If someone disagrees with your beliefs, does that make the person a heretic? Exactly what is religious freedom and dignity?

11. Are there places in the world where people are being persecuted for religious beliefs? Discuss the following locations:
    - Rwanda
    - Sudan
    - Tibet
    - Bosnia
    - Palestine

CHAPTER SEVENTEEN

THE BLACK DEATH

> How many valiant
> men, how many fair
> ladies, breakfast with
> their kinfolk and the
> same night supped
> with their ancestors
> in the next world!
>
> —Giovanni Boccaccio

THE EZEKIEL REACTION: CHANGING CONCEPTS OF GOD
(c. 1390)

The characters:
- Conrad, a German merchant
- Lorenzo, an Italian cardinal
- Elizabeth, an English duchess

The scene: A pavilion at Lake Como, where wealthy survivors of the fifty-year Black Plague are on vacation. Their conversation touches on some of the facts and feelings of that terrible time (roughly 1347 to 1400).

Elizabeth: It looks as though we are getting some relief from the plague. I wish it were over for good, but I suspect it will return.

Lorenzo: I think your feelings are justified. At Rome the reports from our various embassies are far from optimistic.

Elizabeth: It's been a sorry time for us all. Tell me, how did the plague actually start?

Lorenzo: It came from Asia, where it had caused terrible trouble in China and Turkistan. During a battle in the Crimea the Asiatic enemy catapulted plague-infected corpses into the camp of our Genoese troops. They brought the plague back on the ships on their return.

Elizabeth: Couldn't anything have been done to stop it?

Lorenzo: The doctors tried everything but to no avail. The church urged fasting and prayer with no success. Some religious fanatics started penance processions in which the people whipped themselves bloody. And that certainly didn't help.

Conrad: What's even worse, my sister-in-law's family is Jewish and she tells me there were mass burnings of Jews. The Christians claimed the Jews caused the plague by poisoning wells.

Lorenzo: That shows what panic mixed with prejudice can do.

Conrad: The plague touched both the mighty and the lowly.

Elizabeth: How well I know. My home is Canterbury. The plague struck down two of our archbishops. And what was really sad—King Edward III's daughter Joan died on the way to her own wedding.

Lorenzo: And think of the great writer in our country, Petrarch, losing his beloved Laura, the inspiration of so many of his poems.

Conrad: A century ago Europe had nearly four million people. It's lucky to have two million today. I know of no war or plague that's ever struck us so badly.

Elizabeth: As a merchant, Conrad, you are probably in a position to know what it has done to our economy.

Conrad: It's had a terrible effect on food production, ruining the landowning classes. It's caused an excessive rise in wages. The expanding economy of such cities as Siena has come to a standstill. The citizens there have abandoned plans for enlarging their cathedral. Catalonia depended a great deal on a rising birth rate for its economic growth. So, of course, the plague has had a devastating effect on its economy.

Elizabeth: Cardinal Lorenzo, I believe the plague has had a profound impact on the spiritual life of our people.

Lorenzo: Of course it has. We are getting what I would call an "Ezekiel reaction."

Elizabeth: What's that?

Lorenzo: Do you recall that in the Old Testament Ezekiel was the prophet of the Jewish exile?

Conrad: You mean the time they were brought to Babylon and made slaves?

Lorenzo: That's right. Once upon a time all had been prosperity for them. God had seemed to be their friend. Now all is unutterable disaster. They are helpless. In a sense it's their Black Death.

Elizabeth: Then what is the Ezekiel reaction?

Lorenzo: Ezekiel composes for the people a picture of God that is awesome, almost frightening. He tells them their present misery is due to the fact that they have angered God. He is particularly hard on the priests: "Its priests have done violence to my teaching and have profaned my holy things; they have made no distinction between the holy and the common, neither have they taught the difference between the unclean and the clean, and they have disregarded my sabbaths, so that I am profaned among them" (Ezekiel 22:26).

Conrad: I see what you are getting at, Cardinal Lorenzo. There is a feeling that the Black Plague is really the result of the sins of people who have angered God.

Elizabeth: Is that what accounts for many of the scary sermons we've been hearing?

Lorenzo: I hope you haven't been hearing too many, Lady Elizabeth. But you're right. Some of our preachers are getting morbid, almost fanatical.

Elizabeth: Wouldn't you say this is an unhealthy approach to God?

Lorenzo: If it becomes exaggerated, it's a bad idea. No extreme is good. I believe this approach has value when it helps people toward moral responsibility. That's what Ezekiel had in mind for the people of his day.

Conrad: So he wasn't out so much to frighten people with an angry God as to draw them to holiness and spiritual backbone?

Lorenzo: Exactly. The Ezekiel reaction, when properly handled, begets a basic wisdom in thoughtless people.

Conrad: I guess it is only natural that with so much doom in the air these last fifty years, its mood would filter into religious thinking.

Elizabeth: All the more then must we work to balance this with the spirit of love and hope.

Lorenzo: You find the same in the gospel, Lady Elizabeth. Jesus gives his Last Judgment sermon the same week that he delivers his marvelous Last Supper discourse on love. If we had the balance and wisdom of our Master, we would never go overboard.

Conrad: I'm so glad we had a chance to talk about this. I was privately sharing Lady Elizabeth's concern.

Elizabeth: I'm grateful too. I hope we can get together again before we all leave.

Lorenzo: I'm sure we can. It's been a pleasure being with you both.

Jews and the Black Death

The Black Death has been called one of humanity's "epochal scourges." Jews of the time not only suffered the plague but also became scapegoats. Rumors circulated from town to town that Jews had poisoned wells by putting death-dealing drugs in them. Despite the efforts of Pope Clement VI (1342-1352) and other rulers to maintain order, for three years (1348-1350) Jewish communities throughout Europe were uprooted and destroyed. In some towns whole populations of Jews were burned; in others they were expelled and their property confiscated. It has been estimated that over two hundred Jewish communities, large and small, were destroyed.

. . . .

LOOKING BACK

. . . .

The Black Death

The Black Death is the name given to the great plague which raged during the reign of Pope Clement Vl between 1347 and 1350, the same period in which the Hundred Years' War between England and France was beginning. It struck every country in Europe, killing one-third to one-half of the population. No one has yet worked out a definitive analysis of its immediate effects.

Chronology of the Plague
In early 1347 the disease first appeared at Genoa, carried by a ship from the Genoese colony of Kaffa in the Crimea. It spread rapidly to Venice where a hundred thousand died. It then traveled down central Italy to Florence where another hundred thousand died. It reached Siena where about eighty thousand (four-fifths of the population) died. Sicily was struck very hard. In Marseilles fifty-seven thousand died in one month (two-thirds of the population) along with the bishop and nearly all of his clergy. Narbonne, Arles, Montpellier were all struck. Avignon lost over half of its people in seven months. Later in the year, northern France fell to the disease. In Paris eighty thousand died. In July the plague reached England and spread over it for eighteen months. No part of northern and western Europe escaped. It ravaged Spain in 1349. The plague crossed the Alps from Italy swept through Switzerland, struck the Rhine Valley and then Germany and the Low Countries. It continued by way of Denmark to Sweden and Norway.

The plague's traveling speed and the fact that so few who contracted it seemed to recover caused panic and despair everywhere. Wild outbreaks of lawlessness and debauchery took place.

At Avignon, Pope Clement VI organized medical and sanitation aid. He also intervened to protect the Jews (especially those from cities in the Rhineland); when they were accused of causing the plague Clement offered them sanctuary in his state.

Through the winter months of 1349–1350, this first onslaught of the plague wore itself out. But there were many recurrences from 1361 to 1400. In 1361 the plague struck England and France almost as severely as it had in 1348.

Results of the Plague

In many ways medieval life was never the same again. The European population did not climb back to its former density. The spirit of earlier centuries was totally lost. In religion, negative attitudes of fear and guilt became acute. The church suffered enormous losses in personnel; very few abbeys were ever filled again. Because the abbeys needed large staffs to operate effectively, the entire monastic system began to weaken. Steps should have been taken to institute stopgap measures. The existing houses should have been amalgamated but they were not. Much of Benedict XII's monastic reform was thus aborted.

CONNECTING TO OUR TIMES

. . . .

Why Worry About the End of the World?

Some people wonder how the world began. Others worry about how the world will end. The creation story in the Book of Genesis gives us a sense of the origin of the world and its creatures. The apostles pondered the end of time and asked Jesus when it would happen. Jesus told them that no one will know the day nor the hour except the Father. New Testament Christians believed the world would end in their lifetime. When it did not happen, they realized that the timing of the end is a mystery and that in the meantime, we should get on with Christian living.

In our own day there are Christian sects who claim they know an exact date when the end will come. Their followers gather on a mountain or in some remote space and fruitlessly await an end that does not happen. This does not seem to bother them. They simply believe they left some detail out of their

Dies Irae

This brooding, doom-laden hymn caught the mood of a world facing the Black Death and what seemed to be the end of the world. It remained part of the funeral liturgy until after Vatican II.

> *Day of wrath! O day of mourning.*
> *See fulfilled the prophet's warning.*
> *Heaven and earth in ashes burning.*
> *Oh, what fear man's bosom rends*
> *When from heaven the Judge descends*
> *On whose sentence all depends!*
> *Death is struck, and nature quaking.*
> *All creation is awaking,*
> *To its Judge an answer making*
> *Lo, the book exactly worded*
> *Wherein all has been recorded.*
> *Thence shall judgment be awarded.*
> *When the Judge his seat attains*
> *And each hidden deed arraigns*
> *Nothing unavenged remains.*
> *Ah! that day of tears and mourning!*
> *From the dust of earth returning*
> *Man for judgment must prepare him.*
> *Spare, O God, in mercy spare him!*

calculations and proceed to search for a new date.

The year 2000, for example, was met with fear that it was the beginning of the end and popular novels treat the Apocalypse as if it were imminent. All of these dire predictions should be taken with a grain of salt. We should live every day as though it were our last, filling it with love and service and prayer, whether there is a worldwide crisis or not. It does little good to increase panic when there is enough already to alarm people. Fear tends to paralyze people and impair their judgment. "Today's trouble is enough for today" (Matthew 6:34). The precious minutes we have are more valuable than the imagined ones that have not come.

FOR REFLECTION AND DISCUSSION

. . . .

1. The Black Death reached Europe by means of an early form of bacterial warfare: Asian soldiers catapulted plague corpses into Italian camps. Contagion spread through infected fleas who rode with the rodents aboard naval vessels headed for Italy. From 1350 to 1400 the plague occurred again and again, killing close to a third of Europe's population. The impact on economy, culture and religion was devastating. Thousands of teachers, scholars and spiritual leaders suddenly died. What happens to a church when the continuity and stability of its intellectual and spiritual tradition is abruptly broken?

2. During the fourteenth century, as a result of the Black Death, Europe was a death-oriented society. This orientation found reflection in the art, literature and theology of the time. Could one say that we too live in a death-oriented society?

3. In the face of great suffering, what is the role of the church? What purpose do you see it serving? What would you look for it to provide?

4. To many people the Black Death seemed like the end of the world. It was like the opening of the "sixth seal" in the Book of Revelation: "[T]he stars of the sky fell to the earth as the fig tree drops its winter fruit when shaken by a gale.... Then the kings of the earth...the rich and the powerful, and everyone, slave and free, hid in the caves and among the rocks of the mountains...for the great day of their wrath has come, and who is able to stand?" (Revelation 6:13, 15, 17)

5. What is the genuine Christian attitude about the end of the world?

CHAPTER EIGHTEEN

SPIRITUALITY IN THE MIDDLE AGES

> No longer resist the
> will of God, for the
> starving sheep wait for
> you to return to the
> see of St. Peter. You
> are the Vicar of Jesus;
> you must resume your
> proper seat.... Come
> as a bold man without
> fear; but above all, for
> the love of life, do not
> come with a military
> escort, but come with
> the cross in your hand
> like a gentle lamb.
>
> —Catherine of Siena

"Open to me the gates of holiness" (Psalm 118:19)

Saint Joan of Arc's incredible contribution to the ending of the Hundred Years' War between France and England should never obscure the seemingly less dramatic truth about her mystical life, short though it was. At the age of thirteen she heard the voices of Saints Michael, Catherine and Margaret urging her to win freedom and peace for her people. She spent three years pondering in prayer and in her heart what was God's will for her. She belonged to a communion of mystical saints who made a difference for the medieval world.

While Saint Catherine of Siena's historic achievement was to end the Avignon papacy, her life as a mystic and spiritual director better characterizes her everyday life. When one withdraws from the limelight of papal conflict with kings and emperors, the vitality of medieval spirituality becomes clearer. Saint Catherine's spiritual journey occurred in the centuries known as "The Ages of Faith." The soaring naves of Gothic cathedrals that looked like hands folded in prayer dominated the landscape of Christian Europe.

The sounds of monks' choirs were ever near at hand. There was an environment of constant prayer, an undercurrent of contemplation of God that sustained the church's progress through this history. The culture was radiant with God. Epic theologians were as admired for their holiness as well as their intellectual insights. In this fertile spiritual environment it was not unusual to find examples of spiritual direction given by three of our greatest theologians.

Saint Anselm of Canterbury (1033–1109)

When he was a boy, Anselm was privileged to grow up in the mountain air of the Italian Alps. In his young manhood he was a seeker, hiking through France and sampling the ways of the world wondering what God wanted of him. Providence led him to the Abbey of Bec where he settled down, learned the wisdom of Saint Benedict and grew into an insightful theologian. He was the greatest theologian of his time and wrote books that have withstood the test of time.

He became the Abbot of Bec and eventually the Archbishop of Canterbury. There is a prayerful quality to his theological writings as may be seen with the quote below from the first sentences of his book *On the Existence of God*. At the dawn of the High Middle Ages, Saint Anselm of Canterbury wrote these words of advice about how to meditate that were crystal clear and were accessible to God's people at any level:

> Escape from your everyday business for a short while. Break off from your cares and troubles and be less concerned about your tasks and labors. Make a little time for God and rest a while in him. Enter into your mind's inner chamber. Shut out everything but God and whatever helps you to seek him. Speak now to God with your whole heart: I seek your face, your face, your face, Lord, I desire.[1]

The Hundred Years' War

The dominant political and military event in the fourteenth and fifteenth centuries was the Hundred Years' War (1337-1453), an event to which Joan of Arc is inseparably linked. This conflict between England and France was due in large measure to the rising sentiment of nationalism taking place throughout Europe. People were becoming more conscious of their own language and traditions with rivalries developing as a result.

There were many reasons for the war, a semicontinuous series of military campaigns: chiefly England's continued possession of lands in southwestern France and claims to other French provinces, and a dispute concerning the succession to the French throne complicated by English intrigue. Armed with a new weapon, the longbow, the English won impressive victories in 1346 but were unable to remain in France due to lack of funds. In 1380 Charles VII came to the French throne, but soon gave signs of madness and was replaced by a regent; civil war followed.

It appeared that the English would secure victory in France, but in 1422 Charles VI died and his son the Dauphin, besieged in Orleans, declared himself King Charles VII. The tide began to turn when Joan of Arc entered the scene. She rallied the French people to the Dauphin's cause and eventually broke the siege. She then accompanied the Dauphin to Reims Cathedral where he was crowned.

Joan wished to return home, but was pressed into service and eventually captured in battle. This led to her trial by the English for heresy and witchcraft, for which she was burned at the stake in 1431. At the time of her death, Charles VII had ended the civil war and by 1453 secured most of France, thereby concluding the Hundred Years' War.

. . . .

He encouraged people to ask God to teach them how to find him, where to look for him. He stressed the importance of desire for God which energizes the search for him. This desire is an impulse of the heart, an act of the will, a movement of love: "Let me seek you in desiring you and desire you in seeking you, find you in loving you and love you in finding you."

Saint Bonaventure (1221–1274)

A century later, another notable theologian, Saint Bonaventure, echoed Anselm's advice on praying. For those in the academic life he cautions them to let go of their mental preoccupations and emotional strivings. In meditation, they should quiet the mind and calm the emotions and turn themselves over to God alone. Bonaventure urges his listeners to silence their anxieties and passions as well as the fantasies of their imaginations. If people would only give full attention to Christ's throne of mercy by gazing at him on the cross, then they would be open to the presence and power of the Holy Spirit who would grant them the gift of prayer and the wisdom of God. He writes:

> If you ask how such things can occur, seek the answer in the longing of the will, not in the understanding; in the sighs of prayer, not in research; seek the bridegroom, not the teacher; God and not man; and look not to the light but rather to the raging fire that carries the soul to God with intense fervor and glowing love.[2]

By inviting his readers to gaze at Christ on the Cross, Saint Bonaventure focused the process of meditation on a relationship with the humanity of Christ which opens us to his divinity.

Saint Thomas Aquinas (1224–1274)

The theologians of the medieval period, like their forbears among the Fathers of the early church, were not interested in theology for its own sake. They were spiritual directors luring people to imitate Christ. They were good shepherds with a passion for the salvation of souls. They did more than feed the mind; they spoke to the heart. Saint Thomas Aquinas perfectly followed this path. His mighty masterpieces such as the *Summa Theologica* were designed to bring people to know and love God, to be transformed by Christ's saving graces into the likeness of Christ himself. He often quoted the axiom of the Fathers, "God became man that man could become God."

In his commentary on the Gospel of John, Aquinas persuasively inspired his readers to place themselves in Christ as the way, the truth and the life; in his human nature Jesus is the way and in his divine nature Christ is the goal.

> If you are looking for a goal, hold fast to Christ, because he himself is the truth, where we desire to be... If you are looking for a resting place hold fast to Christ for he himself is the life. Therefore, hold fast to Christ if you wish to be safe. You will not be able to go astray, because he is the way. He who remains with him does not wander in trackless places; he is on the right way.[3]

Witnesses to Prayer

In the Middle Ages, new religious orders sprang up to serve God's people in a number of ways. Franciscans practiced radical poverty so that they could identify with the poor whom they served with dedication. Dominicans and Augustinians pursued the new learning that centered on the philosopher Aristotle so that they could serve the growing hunger for higher education in the new universities.

But the ancient hunger for contemplative prayer, ministered to by Saint Benedict in the West, survived for the men and women who lived in solitude so that they could enter the deeper mystery of prayer and win graces for the People of God. Following are witnesses to prayer in the lives of Blessed Hildegard of Bingen and Blessed Julian of Norwich. To their witness we add the remarkable work of Thomas à Kempis whose *Imitation of Christ* survives five centuries later as

Catherine of Siena

Catherine of Siena belongs to an elite group: the doctors of the church. This is a title conferred by a pope or general council to designate someone as a source of sound teaching and doctrine for the whole church. The norms for being a doctor of the church, set by Pope Benedict XIV, include the following: orthodoxy, personal holiness, eminent learning and explicit commendation by the highest church authority. Teresa of Avila and Thérèse of Lisieux are the only other women to hold the title.

Bridget of Sweden

A contemporary of Catherine of Siena, overshadowed but not diminished by her, was Bridget of Sweden. Like Catherine, Bridget was unafraid to call for reform and even reproach a pope (Gregory XI) for his continued papal exile in Avignon: "In thy curia arrogant pride rules, insatiable cupidity and execrable luxury."

. . . .

a reliable and enduring guide for Christian spiritual development.

Hildegard of Bingen (1098–1197)

At the beginning of the High Middle Ages a spiritual star was born, a baby girl who would combine divine and human learning in a way that would spur spiritual growth for many people. At age eight, Blessed Hildegard of Bingen was sent to be tutored by the anchoress Jutta in the Rhine valley. A number of girls from other families joined her for the lessons and, like her, were attracted to the consecrated life. Hildegard's daily contact with this holy woman over the years inspired her to commit herself to a similar vocation.

During these formative years Hildegard experienced visions. She confided these visions to Jutta and a monk named Volmar who were instructed by her to keep these experiences confidential. Volmar became her secretary, writing down her reflections that in time became books. Eventually she had a vision that profoundly affected her life:

> And it came to pass when I was forty-two years and seven months old, that the heavens were opened and a blinding light of exceptional brilliance flowed through my entire brain. And so it kindled my whole heart and breast like a flame, not burning but warming…and suddenly I understood the meaning of the many expositions of the books.

This vision marked her founding of a monastery of Benedictine nuns at Bingen. For the next thirty-six years she wrote books on theology, the practice of virtues, texts for her liturgical musical compositions, and scientific and medical matters. Her young years listening to monastic chant and music for the Mass influenced her style as a composer. She composed musical plays for her abbey. Currently, there are a number of CDs of her compositions. Observers call her a renaissance woman because of her broad intellectual and artistic interests.

As her fame spread she was contacted by wide number of spiritual, academic and secular leaders for advice regarding prayer, spiritual development and even on medical matters. Many traveled to her abbey to meet her personally and benefit from her wisdom. Doctors who have studied the symptoms recorded about her numerous bouts of illness have concluded she suffered all her life with migraine headaches. A few judged that this affliction was the cause of her visions, discounting the spiritual origin of her revelations. However, she herself distinguished between divinely caused visions and phenomena due to her headaches.

She was never formally canonized a saint, but local popular devotion has treated her as Blessed Hildegard and throughout the centuries she has been honored as a holy woman whose intercession with God they treasure.

Julian of Norwich (1343–1413)

Saint Catherine of Siena wanted to be a Dominican nun, but she was never accepted into the order. She settled for becoming a member of the Dominican Third Order where, as a laywoman in the world, she could benefit from the spirituality of the order and pursue her own union with Christ. Her contemporary Dame Julian found another path.

Though the monasteries drew the most people seeking union with God in a life of community under a rule and the vows of poverty, chastity and obedience, a small number of men and women chose the life of solitude. Certain women followed a form of this life in which they lived alone in a room attached to a church usually in a town or village for safety's sake. They were called *anchoresses*. The bishop blessed the women who sought this way of life and outlined rules to protect their calling. Male hermits or *anchorites* chose remote areas in forests or deserts for their living arrangements.

Julian of Norwich occupied a cell that was attached to a small church about one mile from the Norwich cathedral. Today the dwelling is reconstructed after it was bombed in World War II. Her cell is a comfortable size. There is

Saint Bernard on the Love of God

Saint Bernard, Abbot of Clairvaux, (1090-1153) was another member of the medieval community of teachers of spiritual growth, whose powerful sermons on the love of God inspired the people of his own time and continues to touch hearts today.

. . . .

"Love looks for no cause outside itself, no effect beyond itself. Its profit lies in its practice. I love because I love. I love that I may love. Love is a great thing so long as it returns to its fountainhead [in God], flows back to its source, always drawing from there the water which constantly replenishes it.

a window that looks out at the altar and tabernacle from which she could attend Mass and receive Communion and go to confession. Another window faces the street where she would have received visitors who stopped by to receive spiritual direction. There is a door to the outside which would have been used by a servant who brought her supplies of food, water, medicine, clothes, books and writing materials. The servant would also clean out the cell. Another window higher up on the wall provided more light. Julian probably had a cat to keep her company.

At the age of thirty, in May 1373, she received a series of sixteen visions or "showings" concerning the Holy Trinity and the Passion of Christ. She never had any more such showings. She passed the rest of her life meditation on these divine gifts. She wrote a first account of her showings under the title, "A Showing of God's Love." Twenty years later she wrote a longer version of the original text. Her second account illustrated her spiritual development and presented moving descriptions of the love of God as the origin and goal of all our lives.

She is popularly remembered for her wisdom saying, "And all shall be well and all shall be well, and all manner of things shall be well." After forty years in her holy solitude she died. She is not one of the official saints of the church calendar, but she has been one of England's favorite holy women and is popularly known as Blessed Dame Julian of Norwich. Following is her meditation on the pierced side of Christ:

The Heart of Christ

With a joyful expression our Good Lord looked at his wounded side and contemplated it with joy; and with his sweet gaze he led the understanding of this creature through the same wound into his side, right inside it. And there he showed me a beautiful and enjoyable place, big enough to contain all humankind that shall be saved that they might rest there in peace and in love. And with this he brought to my mind his precious blood and the precious water which he allowed to flow out of love for us.

In this sweet contemplation he showed his blessed heart cloven in two; and with great delight he showed to my understanding, partially, the blessed Godhead (as far as he wanted at that moment) strengthening in this way the poor soul to understand that which was without beginning, and is, and ever shall be. And with this our Good Lord said to me, "See how much I love you."[4]

The Imitation of Christ

Thomas à Kempis (1380–1471)

The year that Catherine of Siena died is the year that Thomas à Kempis was born. He was to write one of the most popular and influential devotional classics in the last five centuries—*The Imitation of Christ*. The fourteenth century was a time of mystics and interior prayer. Thomas inherited that spirit from his teachers at the school run by the Brethren of the Common Life who were advocates of the *Devotio Moderna* (Modern Devotion), a movement for spiritual

"Of all the movements, sensations and feelings of the soul, love is the only one in which the creature can respond to the Creator and make some sort of similar return however unequal though it be. For when God loves, all he desires is to be loved in return; the sole purpose of his love is to be loved, in the knowledge that those who love him are made happy by their love of him."—Saint Bernard, Sermon on the Song of Songs, 83, 4, LH, Vol. 4, p. 1333.

reform in northern Europe. Founded by Gerhard de Groote, the brethren focused on the development of the interior life, seeking grow in virtues and prayer by meditating on the life of Christ, especially on his passion.

Upon completion of his studies Thomas à Kempis was advised to join the monastery of Mount Saint Agnes near Zwolle, a community of canons regular—priests living under the Rule of Saint Augustine. He remained there for the rest of his life, writing, preaching and offering spiritual direction. His *Imitation of Christ* contains four parts:

Book One: Counsels on the Spiritual Life. He dwells on the first phase of spiritual development by describing the Christian teaching about life, aspects of human nature and the essential need for God.

Book Two: On the Inner Life. The disciple has made some progress in self-conquest and is gradually enlightened by a deeper knowledge of God. He comes to know the road to identity with Christ is the path of the cross.

Book Three: Inward Consolation. Christ calls the disciple to seek him alone who is the way to real peace. One should not seek the consolations of God, but rather seek the God of consolations. This consolation will not free him from trials, temptations and severe challenges. He is encouraged to have deeper faith and perseverance.

Book Four: On the Blessed Sacrament. This book outlines the theology of the Eucharist, the blessings of the Sacrament and the virtues of faith and love that enable the disciple to benefit more completely from the celebration of the Eucharist. "In this most holy sacrament, faith and love precede all else, working in ways unknowable to man."

At this point it seems fruitful to conclude with a brief selection from the *Imitation of Christ* from book four, chapter four:

> *On the Many Blessings Granted to the Devout Communicant.*
> O Lord, my God, so direct your servant with the blessings of your goodness, that I may worthily and devoutly approach your glorious Sacrament. Stir up my heart to seek you and rouse me from sleep and sloth. Visit me with your salvation, that my spirit may taste your sweetness, which in this Sacrament lies richly concealed as in a fountain.
>
> Give me light to reverence this great mystery; give me strength to

believe with unshakeable faith. For this is your work, and it is not within the power of man; it is by your sacred institution, and not an invention of men. No one of himself is capable of grasping and understanding these things which are beyond even the high knowledge of the angels… Therefore, I implore your mercy, and beg you to give me that special grace that I may wholly melt and overflow with love for you.[5]

The special attention to Saint Joan of Arc and Saint Catherine of Siena, that follows these reflections on medieval witnesses to prayer and spiritual direction, offer you a context in which to appreciate the contributions of Joan and Catherine to the spiritual lives of God's people in their days. They remain dynamic sources for inspiration in our own times.

FOR REFLECTION AND DISCUSSION

1. Joan of Arc was a young woman called by God in visions to crown the French king and to lead the French Army. Why did the church become involved in all of this? Why was she burned at the stake? Why is she a saint today?

2. People who claim to have visions are scoffed at today. What made Joan of Arc different? Is this kind of message possible today?

3. Catherine of Siena was a mystic, a charity activist and a social reformer— a rare combination. Why do some people enjoy prayer but feel no need to get involved in social action? Why do others love social action but have no time for prayer? Why do some love social action but grow impatient with one-to-one acts of charity and mercy? Why do others again prefer one-to-one charity and have no inclination to social action? For many, Catherine of Siena is a woman of contradiction: a defender of the Crusades and an opposer of the Avignon papacy. How do you see her—as a woman of contradiction or a woman of her time?

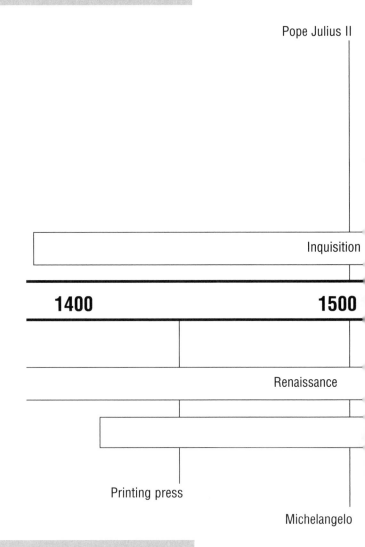

Pope Julius II

Inquisition

1400   **1500**

Renaissance

Printing press

Michelangelo

part three: REFORMATION

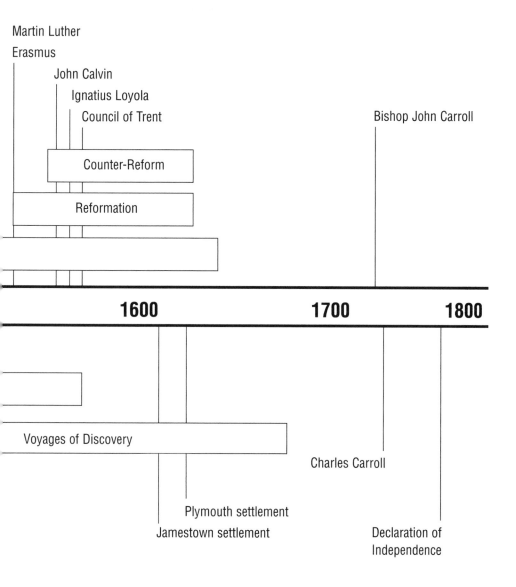

Martin Luther
Erasmus
John Calvin
Ignatius Loyola
Council of Trent
Bishop John Carroll

Counter-Reform

Reformation

1600   **1700**   **1800**

Voyages of Discovery

Charles Carroll

Plymouth settlement
Jamestown settlement

Declaration of
Independence

· ·

CHAPTER NINETEEN

REFORMERS: LUTHER AND ERASMUS

> If the pope rules while
> Christ is absent and
> does not dwell in his
> heart...what is the
> church under such a
> vicar but a mass of
> people without
> Christ?
>
> —Martin Luther

· ·

As the sixteenth century opened, the church could count some real blessings. The great problems of the late Middle Ages had passed. The attempt of late medieval church councils to replace the pope had failed. Spain, which had wavered between the church and Islam, cast its lot with Rome. The fierceness of the Inquisition, with its brutal treatment of suspected heretics, had let up.

Still, new problems arose for the church to solve.

The Black Death thinned the ranks of the clergy. It killed off so many teachers that educational systems broke down. It undermined morale in some places to the extent that clerics began to lead immoral lives.

The growing practice of selling church offices for enormous sums of money angered the faithful, since they paid the bill in the long run. In fact, this was an immediate cause of the Reformation. A man named Albert purchased the office of the Archbishop of Mainz with a loan from the banking house of Fuggers. The Holy See allowed Albert to institute a sale of indulgences so that he could pay off his loan. (Whatever was left would go to Rome to help build

St. Peter's Basilica.) One of the priests under the new Archbishop's authority was an Augustinian monk named Martin Luther.

Worst of all was the chaotic state of parish life. Many pastors were illiterate and untrained men. Since most of the money from parish collections went to support the princely ways of bishop and pope, a pastor then had to be given several parishes in order to have enough money to live on. But the pastor had too many people to work with. Hence the majority of his parishioners were neglected.

Reform was underway. Holland initiated education of the clergy. Spain brought order and discipline into the clerical ranks and attempted to explain in clear language what the people were to believe about faith and morals. The move to education and discipline was a healthy start. Regrettably, it was too little and too late.

The man who began the Reformation, Martin Luther, was born on November 10, 1483, in the village of Eisleben in Saxony, Germany. His father was a copper miner. Luther studied at the University of Erfurt, earning a master's degree.

Soon after his graduation, he was caught in a thunderstorm so frightful that he thought he was going to die. He vowed that, should he survive, he would become a monk. Several weeks later he fulfilled his vow by entering the Augustinian monastery at Erfurt. He was twenty-one.

The following is an interview with the man who set in motion the forces that gave birth to the Protestant churches. In the second half of this chapter we will meet Erasmus, Luther's contemporary, who approached reform from a very different perspective.

AN INTERVIEW WITH MARTIN LUTHER
(c. 1523)

Interviewer: Dr. Luther, by all accounts, the first real crisis between your conscience and the church was caused by the sale of indulgences in your diocese. Would you comment on this?

Dr. Luther: The Dominican friar, John Tetzel, was appointed to preach the special sale of indulgences. I can still hear the jingle he used: "As soon as the coin in the coffer rings, the soul from purgatory springs."

Interviewer: Was this what led you to post the ninety-five theses on the door of Wittenberg Castle church?

Dr. Luther: Yes. I was so angered by this abuse, along with so many others, that I felt someone had to speak up. As you well know, the best way to get a hearing is to post your views in a public place and call for a debate.

Interviewer: What were some of the questions you raised in the theses?

Dr. Luther: I wanted to correct a wrong impression that was being created by the sale of indulgences. I think when people sin they ought to do personal penance and thereby gain an indulgence, which is an elimination of punishment for sin. Buying off the punishment is hardly the same as a personal atonement. I strongly disagreed with the practice and said that it was a corruption of biblical teaching.

Interviewer: What did Tetzel think of that?

Dr. Luther: He was out for my skin. After he read my theses, he said, "Within three weeks, I shall have that heretic thrown into the fire."

Interviewer: Why didn't he?

Upon reading the "Twelve Articles," Luther was sensitized to the plight of the peasants and counseled the German princes to respond to the depressed conditions reported by them. The demands, however, fell on deaf ears and armed rebellion broke out under the leadership of Thomas Munzer. Luther attempted to resolve the conflict peacefully, but finally called on the princes to suppress the movement. Though he urged mercy, nearly a hundred thousand peasants were killed. Consequently, many peasants either returned to Catholicism or joined the rising Anabaptist tide.

Dr. Luther: Mainly because the pope was not too concerned. He spoke of it as a "monkish squabble."

Interviewer: But he changed his mind.

Dr. Luther: I can thank the invention of the printing press for that. I began turning out a series of pamphlets and became a best-selling author. The authorities couldn't ignore me.

Interviewer: Were you summoned to Rome?

Dr. Luther: Yes, the summons came. Thanks to my friend Prince Frederick, the pope allowed the hearing to take place on German soil. It took place at Augsburg and was conducted by the pope's representative, Cardinal Cajetan.

Interviewer: How did that hearing go?

Dr. Luther: Cajetan read me the papal teaching on indulgences, namely, that there is a spiritual treasury of merits gained by the saints. The pope claims the power to draw on that treasury and issue indulgences. I refused to accept that doctrine. I quoted from the Epistle to the Romans which says that people are saved by faith—hence, not by buying indulgences.

Interviewer: Did Cajetan see any merit in your argument?

Dr. Luther: Not at all. He demanded I accept the pope's position. I flatly refused. Negotiations broke down at that point.

Interviewer: Wasn't it soon after that that you had your debate with the theologian Johann Eck at the University of Leipzig?

Dr. Luther: Yes, and you should have seen the audience that day! Dr. Eck is quite a speaker and a powerful defender of the traditional faith. He didn't bother with the indulgence questions. Rather he dwelt on papal authority, saying that from the beginning it has been taught that the authority of the pope comes from God.

Interviewer: And you replied with the position of Jan Hus, a Bohemian scholar who was burned at the stake a century ago?

Dr. Luther: Right. I replied that the papacy as we know it is probably only four hundred years old. I denied that God founded the papacy and stated that it was a human creation. If I wanted authority I would look to the Bible, not to the pope.

Interviewer: That must have stunned the assembly.

Dr. Luther: Understandably enough. By appealing to the authority of the Bible and denying authority to the pope, I was undermining him.

Interviewer: What was the pope's reaction?

Dr. Luther: He wrote a document against my position. It began with these words, "Arise, O Lord, and judge your cause. A wild boar has invaded your vineyard." I was supposed to reply in sixty days, but I didn't even get the document until three months after he sent it. It was just as well, because I was deeply involved in writing at the time.

Interviewer: When did your final break with Rome occur?

Dr. Luther: At the Diet of Worms in 1521. I went there expecting a trial in the ordinary sense of the word. Emperor Charles was in charge. Prince Frederick promoted my cause among the bishops. The Dutch scholar Erasmus sought support for me among the professors of the university. The pope sent two legates as observers.

Interviewer: What was the mood of the city?

Dr. Luther: You should have seen it! Shop windows were filled with my books. Wall posters and signs flowered everywhere on my behalf. On all sides were shouts of "Luther!" and "Down with Rome!"

Interviewer: You mentioned it didn't turn out to be a trial.

Dr. Luther: That's right. I was shown a stack of twenty books, placed as prime exhibits. They asked me to recant the heresies contained therein. That was the critical moment for me. I said, "Unless I can be proved wrong from the Bible or from reason, I neither can nor will recant anything. Here I stand. I can do no other. God help me. Amen."

Martin Luther was excommunicated a month later. His stand paved the way for the breaking up of the unity of Christendom. He lived to see his behavior result in the appearance of other Protestant churches, such as the Presbyterian tradition begun by John Knox.

The imaginary interview in this episode hinges on several pieces of historical data about Luther, though they are not all explicitly stated in the episode:

1. *His trip to Rome as a young priest*
2. *The ninety-five theses*
3. *Three confrontations:*
   a. The hearing at Augsburg
   b. The debate with Eck at Leipzig
   c. The final break at the Diet of Worms
4. *Two of his major documents:*
   a. Address to the Christian Nobility of the German Nation
   b. Babylonian Captivity of the Church

. . . .

LOOKING BACK

. . . .

Luther

The historical and critical literature about Luther is large enough to fill a library. During the time when Catholics and Lutherans were actively hostile to each other, a good deal of the literature was embarrassingly prejudiced from both sides. In these ecumenical days, both groups have become less shrill and more cordial, and the literature more objective.

Luther pointed out a need for reform in the church. Tragically, when reform did take place it resulted in a revolt, splitting the unity of the church. We are now past the time for laying blame except to acknowledge humbly that there was fault on both sides. Beyond this we need to heal the divisions we have inherited in a humane and intelligent fashion. Above all, we must pray that the one God will abundantly pour forth the Spirit of unity upon us.

The Lutheran experience led the Catholic church to undertake a radical and fruitful reform of its discipline and a clarification of its doctrine, especially the teaching on the sacraments and the role of good works in religion.

This episode teaches many lessons: A living church must always be ready for reform and renewal. Christian doctrine always needs a fresh expression for its timeless message. Divided churches must heed Christ's insistent call "that they may all be one."

Timeline

1501   Luther entered the University of Erfurt as a lay student.

1505   Caught in a thunderstorm, Luther promised he would become a monk if he were spared. He was, and he entered the Augustinian monastery at Erfurt, thus disappointing his father, who wanted him to become a lawyer.

1507   He was ordained a priest.

1508—1517 Three events conspired to turn Luther into a radical reformer:

    1) *The fit in the choir.* Luther had a convulsion caused by the realization of his own sinfulness and the purity of God.

    2) *The revelation in the tower.* While meditating on Romans 1:17, he was overwhelmed by the teaching of Paul that we are justified by faith. Luther thought of himself as a sinner, but he felt the mercy and grace of God was greater. No human deed could move him toward God, but the grace-filled call of God could make it possible.

    3) *Tetzel's indulgence preaching.* Given Luther's conversion and new insight, it's easy to see how the Tetzel experience set him on the path of radical reform.

1517   Luther nailed his ninety-five theses to the door of Wittenburg Castle church.

1517—1521 Luther's productive mind plus the newly invented printing press made his teaching exceptionally available to the people of the time. He translated the Bible into German, wrote a catechism, composed hymns, created liturgies and issued a long series of spirited theological tracts. Various judicial hearings made attempts to reconcile Luther to the church; all failed. As the interview indicates, the Diet of Worms issued the final blow and Luther left the church.

1524   Luther broke with his former friend and defender, Erasmus.

1546   Luther died after a nine-year illness.

The Humanists

Luther was not the only one interested in reform in the sixteenth century. Popular preachers had long sought reform by calling the people to prayer, fasting and self-discipline. If they could improve the spiritual life of the common people, they believed, Christendom could be saved.

Others, such as Paris professor Jean Gerson and curial Cardinal Nicholas of Cusa, maintained that reform must take place in church organization. This group argued for regular ecumenical councils to improve church organization. They argued that the organization often speaks louder than sermons. Therefore, no matter how eloquent the preacher, the people were not likely to change unless the organization obviously witnessed the gospel.

The third reform-minded group was the humanists, including Thomas More, John Fisher and John Colet. They were called humanists because they devoted their energies to things that would develop the humanity of people. Hence they showed keen interest in education, poetry, art and ideals that would persuade people toward self-improvement.

The humanists put great faith in education and felt that good schooling would be the best instrument of church reform. They were grieved by the ignorance of the majority of people. Even with education, however, they saw little point in drawing the people into quarrels and arguments over religious doctrines, which tended to tear people apart and ruin the unity of the church.

Erasmus of Rotterdam was a member of this third group and the greatest humanist of them all.

Born in 1466, he grew to be the most brilliant man in Europe. Popes and kings, reformers and scholars turned to him for advice.

The interviewer who spoke with Luther now interviews Erasmus to get a broader view.

AN INTERVIEW WITH ERASMUS
(c. 1536)

Interviewer: What do you think of Martin Luther?

Erasmus: I believe he is a good man who saw evils and spoke out against them. Saint Augustine and Saint Bernard also wrote against such evils. I believe a good deal of what he says and I have defended his right to speak out.

Interviewer: If you agree with Luther, why have you gradually withdrawn your support from him?

Erasmus: I knew reform was needed and thought Luther would be just the man to spur it on. But then he became more and more headstrong, abusive and sometimes crude in his criticisms. He called the pope the Antichrist, the bishops seducers and Rome an abomination before God. That was a bit much.

Interviewer: You have a reputation for being advanced in your own ideas. How do you compare your own position with Luther's?

Erasmus: When I read his pamphlet on the Holy Eucharist, I knew the church would never accept his ideas. I didn't disagree with the ideas themselves, but I did disagree with their consequences. I knew that he would be excommunicated and that much of Germany would follow him. Germany had been itching for a long time to get out from under Rome's thumb.

Erasmus and Luther

It wasn't until 1524 that Erasmus and Luther, both of whom attacked church corruption, parted ways over the issue of freedom of the will. Though grateful to his one-time defender, in the end Luther would see Erasmus as a faint-hearted reformer unwilling to take his ideas about church reform to their final conclusion. As a result Luther said that Erasmus "would die ultimately in the wilderness without entering the promised land."

. . . .

Erasmus's "Credo"

Erasmus wrote no concise summary of his beliefs. The "Credo" in this interview pulls the consistent threads from a lifetime of writings.

. . . .

Interviewer: What is your reaction to this realization?

Erasmus: I fear it will cause much ruin. The reformers are growing rigid. They accused Rome of intolerance; now they are just as intolerant. They denounced Rome for having a party line; now they have a party line of their own.

Interviewer: Then you are not sympathetic to the revolution that is underway?

Erasmus: Not at all. I admit I have the head of a rebel, but not the behavior of one. I think the chaos of revolution is worse than the cruelty of tyrants.

Interviewer: Have you suffered for your moderate position?

Erasmus: Well, I've been exiled from my native Holland. But more painful to me was the death of my dear friend, Thomas More, who was beheaded in Protestant England. And comrades of mine have been burned at the stake in Catholic Paris. I hate to say it, but I think I am living in the worst century since Christ.

Interviewer: Would you be willing to give us a statement of your beliefs?

Erasmus: I would be pleased to do so. This is my creed:

I believe that we should pay more attention to our interior lives than to devotions and ceremonies. How foolish it is for people to revere the bone of the apostle Paul encased in glass and not to feel the glow of his spirit enshrined in his Epistles. How is it that the slipper of Thomas Becket, Archbishop of Canterbury, performs miracles now—which it could not do when he was alive?

I believe we should avoid quarrels about religious doctrine. Better to use our energies in piety and love.

I believe that nationalism is wrong: I can't understand why Frenchmen, Englishmen and Spaniards suddenly consider themselves natural enemies, when they have been born as brothers in Christ.

I believe in the reforming power of education. The enlightenment that comes through learning can do much to reduce the prejudices, superstitions and magic mentality that are currently the result of ignorance. I look for the day when every farm boy can whistle the Psalms as he furrows the soil.

I believe that the chaos of revolution is worse than the yoke of tyrants.

I believe that reason is to be preferred to angry deeds.

LOOKING BACK

. . . .

Erasmus

Erasmus (1466–1536) was the son of a priest. He was raised and educated at an Augustinian monastery and showed intellectual promise from the start. His guardians planned that he should be a monk, but Erasmus had no taste for the life, though he appreciated the education he received. He accepted ordination to the priesthood, but soon left the monastery to work for the bishop of Paris.

He continued his education both at Paris and later at Turin, where he took a doctorate in theology. His horizons were further widened by visits with the major members of the European intellectual community, including Thomas More in England. His intellectual tastes moved him away from the tradition of the medieval scholastics back to primary theological sources such as the Bible and the writings of the Fathers of the church. His careful translation of the New Testament into a new Greek edition became the basis of subsequent vernacular translations.

Erasmus lived during a time of great papal corruption. For example, the Medici Pope Leo X, after ascending the papal throne in 1513, said: "Now that we have attained the papacy, let us enjoy it!"

In his book, *Dagger of the Christian Soldier*, Erasmus emerged as a liberal academic calling for reform in the church and society. His writing technique was satire—not biting or sarcastic, but a gentle prodding of the high and mighty. He questioned the militarism of Pope Julius II and spoke for peace. He mastered the art of being a critic of the great while, at the same time, serving as their counselor.

He was a gentleman in Newman's sense of the word—that is, one who will never deliberately harm another. He could not bring himself to enter or approve violent controversy either at the level of conversation or the more brutal level of war. He placed great faith in the power of reason and education to solve problems. In short, he was the prince and father of humanists, putting great trust in the power of learning to liberate people from strife and pettiness.

In his relationship with Luther, he was at first sympathetic, but later withdrew his support. He liked Luther's biblical and patristic theology, but he could not support Luther's political ties and revolt against the church. It was one thing to explore new ways to preach the gospel and improve Christian behavior, but it was quite another to destroy the unity of Christendom.

He lived to see Luther's strategy prevail and to hear Rome cite humanism as one of the elements which aided the rise of heresy and the split in the church. In spite of his challenging ideas, Erasmus never lived under any threat of excommunication or of trial for heresy. In fact, in his old age he was offered a cardinal's hat. He graciously declined.

He saw no contradiction between humanism and faith. The tumult of the times obscured his quiet wisdom, but today we look at him again and are more prepared to see the direction in which he would have led the church.

CONNECTING TO OUR TIMES

. . . .

The Holy Spirit Is the Soul of Ecumenism

"Grow or die" is a principle of business. Conversion and renewal are watchwords of the religious and moral life. The Catholic church of the sixteenth century needed to grow out of its medieval cocoon and embrace reform and renewal. Because it was slow to do this, the conditions for the Protestant Reformation occurred. In our own day the church did not wait for a similar crisis to arise, but embarked on a process of self-renewal at the Second Vatican Council.

One of the productive outcomes of the Council was the ecumenical movement. Four hundred years ago we and the Protestants locked horns with each other. We practiced "no prisoners theology," fighting each other as though we were secular states at war. By the grace of God and the movement of the Holy Spirit we have been liberated from that contentious attitude and today strive to achieve spiritual unity—and possibly one day an institutional union.

For many years now there have been dialogues between the Catholic church and such major denominations as the Anglicans, Lutherans, Methodists and Presbyterians. At the theological level, many misunderstandings have been cleared away. At the pastoral level, covenants have often been made between Catholic and Protestant parishes. At the human level, people of all Christian faiths have formed a common bond in humanitarian endeavors and projects for the good of society in general.

It is clearer now that the goal of unity of Christian churches will be a long-range project. It is more evident that all Christian communions must be humbler and more open to the divine power of the Holy Spirit, for this worthy goal is in essence dependent upon the action of grace. We must continue to work for Christian unity at all levels, while being even more fervent in imploring the Spirit—the principle of unity—to bring us together in the bond of love and the blessedness of peace.

FOR REFLECTION AND DISCUSSION

1. If Luther were alive today what would he protest against?
2. Looking back, do you think that the Councils of Trent and Vatican II satisfied all of Luther's demands? Do any of Luther's concerns yet need to be addressed by the Catholic church?
3. Luther was a man of the *sola:* Scripture alone, faith alone, grace alone. How are these statements balanced by the Catholic church?
4. Luther gave the Christian world a profound insight into the glory of God's love, manifested in the saving grace of Christ. He illumined the essential need for a living faith. It was the issue of selling indulgences—without proper emphasis on the interior need for penance and prayer—that sparked the Reformation. Extremist statements were made by both sides. Luther said, "Christians should be taught that if the pope knew the demands of the indulgence preachers, he would rather the Basilica of St. Peter's be burned to ashes than built up with the skin, flesh and bones of his sheep" (Thesis #50, nailed to door of Castle at Wittenberg, October 31, 1517). Pope Leo X's private theologian Prierias wrote the document summoning Luther to Rome on charges of heresy. He was also unrestrained, as these words show: "Luther is a leper and loathsome fellow...a dog and the son of a bitch, born to bite and snap at the sky with his doggish mouth, having a brain of brass and a nose of iron" (see *Martin Luther,* by J. Todd).

5. Why can religious issues stir up such passion in people? Why do people lose all civility when quarreling about religion? Was there some wisdom in the old saying not to talk about religion or politics at a party?

6. When people debate religious differences instead of dialoguing, what is the inevitable result?

7. What rules for dialogue about religious differences would you lay down today?

8. Erasmus was a Christian humanist. He believed there was no fundamental contradiction between a scholarly life—research and learning—and living the Christian faith. Is this always true? Should scientific researchers have refused to invent the atomic bomb? Ought they avoid any further research on genetic engineering? Does the fact that so many of today's artists, poets, historians and writers are professedly nonreligious prove that Erasmus was naive about the presumed compatibility of humanism and religion? What examples demonstrate that Erasmus was right?

9. Erasmus believed it was better to study the Bible in a scholarly way than to concentrate on theology, which he felt caused too many quarrels. Catholics, however, have tended to concentrate on tradition and theology, while Protestants have tended to concentrate on the Bible. Which is the better way? What is the value of studying both Bible and theology?

10. It has been said that Erasmus was "a moderate man in the most immoderate times." In light of his own response to the corruption of the church during his day, how can we be critical of some of the church's practices while, at the same time, remaining faithful to it? In this process of questioning and change what situations need to exist to ensure that tolerance and moderation triumph over extremism?

11. It has long been said that Erasmus, given his travels, studies and intellect, read the signs of the times and foresaw the need for church reform. Reading the signs of the times in our own day, what, if any, church reforms would you suggest? Do you think they could be implemented without causing division?

· ·

CHAPTER TWENTY

THE RISE OF PROTESTANTISM

> Those who teach the
> word of God, yet not to
> the honor of God, but
> for themselves...and
> for protection of their
> fabricated high station,
> are harmful wolves,
> coming in sheep's
> clothing.
>
> —Hueldrich Zwingli,
> originator of the popular
> saying

· ·

Although the sixteenth-century protest against the church began with Luther in Germany, it soon spread to other countries. In Switzerland two distinct types of Protestantism developed: Anabaptism and Calvinism. The first was founded in Zurich by a Swiss priest named Hueldrich Zwingli. The second was begun in Geneva by the French lawyer John Calvin. These two leaders disagreed strongly with one another.

In Scotland John Knox led the revolt. Since he had lived for a time in Geneva and had been greatly impressed with Calvinism, Knox included many of its basic beliefs in the development of Presbyterianism.

For the most part the Protestant revolt was led by such differing personalities and views that all attempts at agreement failed. The movement on the whole brought about a splintering of the Christian church.

The following playlet will give some insight into the ideas of these Protestant leaders.

Henry VIII

While the Reformation was raging in continental Europe, the papacy had one of its ablest defenders in Henry VIII, King of England. In 1521 he wrote a book against Luther for which Pope Leo X conferred on him the title "Defender of the Faith." Henry, however, was soon to join the ranks of the Reformers.

Unable to produce a male heir with his wife, Catherine of Aragon, Henry sought an annulment from Rome. Since she was the aunt of Charles V, the Holy Roman Emperor, Pope Clement VII stalled, not wanting to alienate a needed ally. At this point Henry consulted the major universities, which declared that his marriage with Catherine was invalid.

BLUE LAWS AND CLEAN STREETS
(c. 1545)

The characters:

- Margaret, cousin of John Knox
- Karl, an original disciple of Zwingli
- Kristin, secretary to Calvin
- Frederick, a Lutheran clergyman

The scene: A hotel dining room in Geneva where four people have met at lunch to discuss developments in the Reformation.

Frederick: I'm amazed at how quickly Switzerland picked up the fire of the Reformation. Luther, however, sometimes regrets the direction it has taken here. He blames your hero Zwingli for that.

Karl: I was with Zwingli when he had his summit meeting with Luther. Zwingli argued that the church should be stripped of all pageantry. That was why he took the crucifixes, chalices, vestments, censers and even the organs out of the churches. He loved music and used to play the flute in class to quiet rowdy boys. But in church he wanted no interference between humanity and God.

Kristin: At least he had the good sense not to encourage his followers to smash the stained glass.

Frederick: Luther would say amen to that, but he was unhappy about Zwingli's other teachings.

Kristin: Didn't they have quite an argument over how to tell whether God liked you?

Karl: Yes, and you have to admit it's an important issue. I mean, after all, if you believe that some people are destined to go to heaven and others to hell and it all depends upon whether or not God likes you, then it's rather important to know if you can tell where you stand with God. Luther said no, you can't tell; only God knows whom God likes. But Zwingli said you could tell—those who publicly profess their faith and join in the Lord's Supper are God's friends.

Frederick: From what I gather they were not able to come to an agreement.

Karl: They came to the end of the meeting in total disagreement. Zwingli offered to shake hands with Luther, but Luther refused.

Frederick: That's too bad. That must be the reason for the statement I heard Luther make later when he said of Zwingli, "I will not let the devil teach me anything in my church."

Margaret: As a Scot, something that has interested me about the Swiss church is its apparently democratic style.

Karl: The smallness and mountain seclusion of Switzerland gave us a kind of democratic opening. Each of our thirteen cantons, or states, has a law-making body for both domestic and foreign affairs. In one canton every man is in the legislature. Even in the Catholic days, the legislature supervised discipline and taxation in churches and cloisters.

Kristin: We Swiss have always been a freedom-loving people. We like to determine things for ourselves. Our new church in Geneva reflects this spirit. We want to participate in the running of the church.

Margaret: You know my cousin, John Knox, owes a great deal to your John Calvin. Tell me a little about him.

Events culminated in 1534 in the Act of Supremacy, when Parliament declared Henry head of the church of England. It also forbade the payment of taxes and other contributions to Rome, ruled that Henry's marriage to Catherine was not true, and that their child Mary was not an heir to the throne. Thus the reformation in England was based not on doctrinal issues but political ones. Henry sought to restore the rights of the crown against undue papal intervention. This would lead to the beheading of Thomas More who, as chancellor of England, refused to recognize Henry as head of the church.

Transsubstantiation

One of the most divisive issues of the Reformation (and one that disallowed any union among the Reformers) was the understanding of the Eucharist. Luther believed in Christ's real presence in the Eucharist. He spoke of the bread and wine "coexisting" with the Body and Blood of Christ, which he termed transubstantiation. Furthermore, Luther said that the Mass was not a sacrifice because he could find no verification for it in Scripture. He saw the Mass as a "work" which went against his notion of "faith alone."

In 1530 the Marburg Colloquy was called by a German prince to reach doctrinal agreement and to present a united front

Kristin: Originally, Calvin was a French Catholic student of theology. It was when he studied law under the humanists at Orleans that he became a Protestant.

Karl: His law training served him well when he came to write *Institutes of the Christian Religion.*

Kristin: That has become a standard textbook for the Reform. In it Calvin spoke movingly of the majesty of God. Like Zwingli, he held there were visible proofs that God liked you: Belief in the true faith, leading a good life, going to the Lord's Supper regularly.

Margaret: Does this have something to do with the "holy commonwealth" here at Geneva that I've heard so much about?

Kristin: Yes, Calvin has transformed Geneva into a holy commonwealth. All its members attempt to live up to the three ideals of faith, behavior and worship.

Margaret: I've noticed the people are quite loyal to these ideals. I've also been astonished by their energy. They must be the hardest working people on earth. Does this have something to do with their religion?

Kristin: In some ways, yes. The people do seem to derive great strength and a sense of purpose from their faith. They see their prosperity as a blessing of God and a sign that God loves them.

Frederick: As an observer, may I mention something I don't like about your holy commonwealth?

Kristin: What is that?

Frederick: Like Margaret, I do admire the religious zeal and the devotion to hard work among your people. But as a German and a lover of the excitement of taverns, I dislike Calvin's "blue laws." They take all the fun out of tavern life.

Karl: Which ones do you mean?

Frederick: Well, if anybody so much as says "By the body's blood" or "zounds," he'll be punished. And you know how beer loosens the tongue. It's likely that a few off-color words will slip out after a few beers.

Kristin: I imagine you don't like the ban on gambling, dancing and indecent songs.

Frederick: How could I? It makes the place like a graveyard. I'm of peasant stock like Luther and we never saw anything particularly wrong in these matters. You're too solemn here. Imagine stopping at an inn and not being able to stay up after nine o'clock at night. Why, it's like a monastery!

Kristin: In many ways it is. All the Catholics, dissenters and heretics have left town. We have nothing but Calvinists here. By the way, we do allow informers to stay up after nine.

Frederick: Then you're like a police state.

Kristin: A holy one, indeed.

Margaret: It certainly is the cleanest town I've ever seen.

LOOKING BACK

. . . .

More Reformers

Hueldrich Zwingli (1484–1531)

Hueldrich Zwingli received a humanist education before being ordained a Roman Catholic priest. He was respected and esteemed in his ministry in Zurich, Switzerland. As his own thoughts veered away from orthodoxy, he continued to teach and preach traditional doctrine. It was not until 1516 that Zwingli openly manifested his beliefs. In

against Rome. There, in the presence of Luther, Zwingli stated that the Eucharist was a symbolic sign of Christ's presence, not a real one. He preferred to emphasize the importance of faith in the recipient.

Between Luther and Zwingli was Calvin. He stressed the spiritual nature of the communion with Christ in the Eucharist. Calvin said that in the Eucharist grace flows from Christ, who "is in heaven and not here."

Confronting the Reformers, the Council of Trent declared that in the Eucharist the bread and wine are substantially changed into the Body and Blood of Christ. This was termed
transubstantiation.

. . . .

The Puritans

Similar to European Calvinists were the English, and later American, Puritans. Intent on abolishing any remnant of Catholicism, the Puritans even banned Christmas. In the words of the famous American Puritan, Cotton Mather: "Can you in your conscience think, that our Holy Saviour is honored by mad Mirth, by long Eating, by hard Drinking, by lewd Gaming, by rude Revelling; by a Mass fit for none but a Saturn or a Bacchus or the Night of a Mahometan Ramadan?"

. . . .

many instances these resembled Luther's, since Zwingli also acknowledged the supreme authority of Scripture.

He felt only laws that agreed with Scripture were binding. Marriage was therefore lawful to all, clergy and laity alike.

He differed from Luther irreconcilably in his belief that human flesh, rather than humanity in general, was corrupt. Zwingli's view of the sacraments was negative. He considered the Mass a sacrilege, denied the real presence and forbade the use of art and music to uplift the spirit in acts of worship. Zwingli's major effort was to rethink all Christian doctrine in essentially biblical terms.

Soon Switzerland became a state divided over religious belief and, in 1531, Zwingli was killed in battle during a religious war.

John Calvin (1509–1564)

Calvin, born in 1509 to a bourgeois family and destined by his father for a career in the church, left home at fourteen for theological studies in Paris. At the college of Montaigu, he excelled in his studies. His ability won recognition from students and teachers alike, and by nineteen he had his master's degree in theology. His father then ordered him to transfer his studies toward a law career. In obedience, he journeyed to the University of Orleans, where he eventually took his doctorate in law.

In Paris, Calvin became aware of the tension between humanism and scholasticism. The connection between Lutheranism and humanism tended to make Catholic states wary of the "new learning." Calvin soon became friendly with a group that was translating Scripture into the vernacular in secret because of the church's ban on such projects. His connection with the group was evident and he became recognized generally as a gifted young Christian humanist, but his ties to the church were still strong. Transferring support from the authority structure of the church to a position of public protest against that authority was a gradual and painful move for Calvin. In 1534, when he was twenty-five, Calvin made the final step by renouncing his benefices and his ties with his local diocese and speaking openly on the side of the Protestants. Two years later he published the summary of his already matured thoughts, *Institutes of the Christian Religion*.

On one of his journeys, Calvin was detoured to the city of Geneva. There the leader of the evangelical reform movement appealed to him to stay and use his God-given talents to organize and solidify the advances already begun. It was not Calvin's wish, but he considered the request a divine call and decided to undertake it.

In Geneva, Calvin suffered from indigestion, sleeplessness, headaches and loneliness. His cold, reserved personality coupled with characteristic severity toward himself and others kept him alienated and aloof from the people. Yet he excelled as teacher, writer and organizer and was able to make Geneva the center of Protestantism. It became a theocracy, with the church in the driver's seat in state affairs. Leadership within the religious community fell to those who were "moved by the Spirit," thus threatening a professional ministry. This principle became the basis of all Protestant theocracies.

John Calvin
Testifying to the character and influence of John Calvin, Pius IV, the pope at the time of Calvin's death, is reputed to have said: "The strength of that heretic consisted in this, that money never had the slightest charm for him. If I had such servants my dominion would extend from sea to sea."

Calvin insisted upon his spiritual authority to teach, preach and censor. Often the people or the city council resisted him. Two years after he arrived in Geneva, with characteristic brashness, Calvin excommunicated the entire city on Easter, 1538. The next day he was banished from the city. For three years, Geneva lived in political and religious chaos.

Finally, in 1541, Calvin was officially invited back. He came determined to carry out the full reform which he envisioned. The "Ecclesiastical Ordinances" which he adopted were greatly influential in Europe and the British Isles. For twenty-two years, until his death in 1564, Calvin inculcated his theories and church policy into Geneva. It became a classical type for many attempts at reform.

John Calvin's brand of reform—with its emphasis on thrift, business, cleanliness and its Old Testament style of observing the Sabbath day—came to American shores with the Puritans. Zwingli had already introduced the idea of a church building shorn of all decoration in statuary and stained glass.

Probably the Swiss style of democratic government eventually led to the adopting of the "people's church" or congregational mode as it appeared in our country. Rome centered authority in the pope, Germany in bishops and Geneva in the leaders (presbyters).

Calvin's stern views about God carried over into the Puritan religion of early American Protestantism. It was a mood that affected all the churches with a "fire-and-brimstone" attitude toward sin.

Many have noted the link between this form of Protestantism and the rise of capitalism. The richer and cleaner people were, the more it seemed God had blessed them. Since no money could be spent on personal adornment or "foolish pleasure," everything was put back into the business. It was inevitable that the Calvinists and their posterity should become prosperous people.

Like Luther, Calvin did not believe that he was starting a new religion. He was reforming Christianity by returning it to a pristine state of existence. His theological theories were, like Luther's, based on the basic human inability to reach God. He believed that, for some mysterious reason, God redeems us even though we are unworthy or incapable of earning merit on our own. The Holy Spirit confers the grace of redemption, and the righteousness bestowed is manifested in personal life. The mystery of divine choice selects some and passes over others.

John Knox (1514–1572)

Knox was born in Scotland about 1514 and did not go beyond a bachelor's degree before ordination. He had a thoughtful, argumentative cast and initially became the tutor of nobles' sons. While thus engaged he came into contact with the reformed faith and was converted to it sometime before 1545. Soon his abilities were recognized and he became the spokesman and protagonist for Scottish Protestantism. During the period of religious persecutions and war which followed, he became a fugitive and, for a period of nineteen months, even lived as a galley slave. Freed through the intervention of the English government, Knox was made a licensed preacher in England. There he left a lasting effect on the church of England by helping to shape its *Articles* and its *Book of Common Prayer* and by encouraging the country to accept Puritanism.

When Mary Tudor came to the throne in 1553, Knox went into his second period of exile, spending his happiest years in Geneva until his return to Scotland in 1559. He then participated in the armed advance of the "true religion" and became its dominant spirit. A combination of circumstances brought victory to this group and Knox became the principal figure in drawing up the constitution, liturgy and doctrines of the Reformed church. The question of financing the church then became a stumbling block and a divisive factor between Knox and the nobles.

At this juncture Mary Queen of Scots arrived in Scotland and a grim war over religion ensued. The Reformed church was in real danger until Mary's abdication in 1567. When peace finally seemed to be in view, news of her execution threw Scotland into turmoil. Succeeding events literally taxed the life out of Knox, and he died in Edinburgh in 1572. Although a controversial figure, he had a strong effect on both the church of England and the church of Scotland.

CONNECTING TO OUR TIMES

. . . .

Celebrate a Positive Work Ethic

One of the enduring themes of the Protestant Reformation that endures to this day is the "Protestant work ethic." We trace this mostly to Calvin and Zwingli. The idea grew out of their teaching of predestination. God has predestined those who are to be saved. But how is one to know? Is it enough to be a good person, or should there be a sign—such as prosperity? If this is a reasonable indicator, then should not one work hard, be thrifty and save so that one has in hand the symbol of predestination?

Now this is an oversimplification. Doubtless Calvin and Zwingli would have thrown up their hands in despair at such a cheapening of their spiritual insights. They struggled with the doctrine of predestination and should be commended for trying to understand how it applies in a world of freedom. But by the time their theology reached a popular level, it often resulted in the Protestant work ethic and its tenuous connection of economic prosperity and divine salvation. In its most absurd form it would mean that only the rich and energetic are saved, while the poor and listless are doomed.

Regardless of how the idea of a work ethic originated, there is no question it has been a constant attitude in American life. Today it has been diluted and secularized in workaholism, greed and fast-track pursuit of money. This is prosperity divorced from faith. At the same time, we should heed its sensible teaching that hard work, thrift and perseverance are better for us than welfare dependency, living on the "edge of the plastic credit card," too much reliance on luck and a tendency to give up when the going gets tough.

Whatever its theological shortcomings, the Protestant work ethic made practical sense—and still does. It generated a tremendous middle class in our culture, a social group that provided stability and continuity for society. Of course, it is arrogant when it patronizes the poor and helpless and fails to reach out a helping hand. But, granting its deficiencies, the work ethic still has a significant role to play for us.

FOR REFLECTION AND DISCUSSION

1. Discuss your reactions to the following:
    • Work makes one holy and closer to God.
    • Religion means no fun anymore.
    • If you have fun, you can't be close to God.
    • God will reward you with money and good fortune if you work hard.
    • Faith is the only thing necessary for salvation.
    • Should churches ban drinking, smoking and gambling?
    • With freedom comes responsibility.
    • Are the rich obligated to care for those less fortunate?
    • Protestantism fits in best in the middle class.
    • What was the difference between the Pilgrims and the Puritans?
    • What is a "work ethic"?
    • Shops should not open on Sunday, because it is the Lord's Day.
    • Is the emphasis today more on money or the family?
    • God rested on the seventh day; shouldn't we?

2. Record your answers to the following opinion poll and then discuss with others:
    • Reformation Protestants stressed salvation by faith. Yet they became best known for the Protestant "work ethic."
       Yes___ No___ Not sure___

    • Of the two great reformers, Calvin had more influence on American Protestantism than Luther.
       Yes___ No___ Not sure___

    • It is easier to become rich when you do not waste your money on "wine, women and song."
       Yes___ No___ Not sure___

- The rise of capitalism coincided with the rise of the Protestant work ethic. Protestantism caused capitalism.

  Yes___ No___ Not sure___

- Historically, Catholic monasteries demonstrated the adage, "Diligence begets abundance." Is this a "Catholic work ethic"?

  Yes___ No___ Not sure___

- Prohibition of alcohol in America was an outgrowth of Protestant blue laws.

  Yes___ No___ Not sure___

- Our world would be better off if we had no drinking, smoking, gambling or dancing.

  Yes___ No___ Not sure___

- If all poor people practiced the Protestant work ethic, they would become prosperous.

  Yes___ No___ Not sure___

- American Catholics have become prosperous because they practiced the Protestant work ethic.

  Yes___ No___ Not sure___

· ·

CHAPTER TWENTY-ONE

COUNTER-REFORM

> Teach us good Lord, to
> serve thee as thou
> deservest; to give and
> not to count the cost;
> to fight and not to
> heed the wounds; to
> toil and not to ask for
> rest; to labour and not
> to ask for any reward
> save knowing that we
> do thy will. Through
> Jesus Christ our Lord.
>
> —Ignatius of Loyola

· ·

After Luther and Calvin, it seemed as though Protestantism would claim the whole of Europe. But the church of Rome responded vigorously in a stunning comeback known as the Counter-Reformation. One center of this movement was in Spain.

In the Middle Ages Spain had been a fairly tolerant country. Catholics, Jews and Muslims lived side by side. By the mid-fifteenth century the scene changed. The Spanish monarchy moved to eliminate all non-Catholics from Spain. Ferdinand and Isabella requested the church reestablish the Inquisition—an organization set up to find and punish heretics. In effect, this meant torture, prison and exile for Jews, Muslims and any Catholic who

The Fourth Vow

Like other religious orders of the day, the Jesuits took vows of chastity, poverty and obedience. What set them apart, however, and at times led to suspicion, was their fourth vow: "special obedience to the sovereign pontiff regarding the missions." Ignatius referred to it as "our beginning and the principal foundation of the Society." In contrast to the vow of stability made by monks, this is one of mobility, a commitment to travel anywhere in the world for the help of souls. Jesuits rely on the pope's vision of the church's role in the world to show where they are most needed.

. . . .

differed with the church's teachings. The Inquisition was a time of cruelty and intolerance.

Eventually, a positive movement developed in Spain. The man most responsible for the movement to bring about church reform in Spain was Cardinal Jimenez. As archbishop of Toledo, Jimenez, a man spiritually as tough as an oak tree, set out to discipline all of Catholic Spain. He purified the monasteries of corruption, eliminated moral laxity in the clergy and thus gave the church a foundation of steel.

Jimenez lived what he preached. Underneath his cardinal's robes he wore a hair shirt. In his palace he lived with the simplicity of a monk. He had a strong belief in the power of education and founded the University of Alcala, which very soon became an outstanding center of learning. He managed to reform the church in Spain and still keep it in union with Rome. The followers of Luther and Calvin made no headway there. Instead, Spain became prominent as one of the centers of the Counter-Reform.

Out of this world of reform and discipline came Ignatius of Loyola, the founder of the Jesuits.

IGNATIUS LOYOLA AND THE COMPANY OF JESUS (1491–1556)

Ignatius' early career did not suggest the future he was to live. He liked pleasure and the diversions of an army man's life. He enjoyed reading tales about knights and the art of courtly love. His ambition was to be an adventurous soldier. His hopes evaporated when a cannon ball blasted one leg, crippling him for life.

While the wound was healing, he passed his time reading the lives of the saints and the story of Christ. The idealism that once moved him toward the army now encouraged him to be a soldier for Christ. He spent a year in prayer, meditation and self-examination. The experience led him to write the *Spiritual Exercises*, a short book on how to develop self-control so that the will, the emotions and the body could be put at the service of the spirit.

Now he felt a strong need for education. He was in his mid-thirties, but was not embarrassed to go back to our equivalent of high school and learn Latin. He spent ten years at various universities in Spain and Paris.

It was at the end of this education period that Ignatius founded the order which would become known as the Jesuits. In 1534 in the small chapel of St. Denis in Paris, he gathered a group of men who promised to live a life of poverty and celibacy. They called themselves the "Company of Jesus."

They went to Rome to see Pope Paul III and to offer him their services. They said they were ready to do anything he asked of them; the pope could count on full obedience from the Company of Jesus. The pope accepted their offer, officially approved their order and made Ignatius the Father General. Ignatius and his successors have worked so closely with the popes that the general of the order has frequently been called "The Black Pope," a title derived from the black robe adopted as the official Jesuit garb.

In a short time the order expanded and met with enormous success. The Jesuits were particularly effective in two areas: the missions and education.

In the person of Francis Xavier, they dramatized the missionary enterprise. Francis, one of the original members of the Company of Jesus, went to Asia. There he preached simple sermons and exerted a personal, evangelical charm and faith that converted thousands in India, Japan and the East Indies.

But it was in education that the Jesuits emerged as international leaders. Ignatius founded many schools for the training of his seminarians. In time the Jesuits established and staffed many of the universities of Catholic Europe. The task required so many of their men that the majority of them were occupied in some form of education. Many feel that the secret of the Jesuits' success lay mainly in their firm discipline and stress on obedience. Ignatius had not forgotten his military days. He saw no harm in borrowing traits from military life and applying them to life in his order. But, equally important, he insisted that his men should have a good education. He did not want untrained men in the classroom. Hence, they received years of training before they themselves stood at the teacher's podium.

Ignatius shaped an army of men for the service of the church in the Counter-Reformation. He trained them to help people recover confidence in the church and remain loyal to it. Many other groups within the church helped spur the Counter-Reform, but few matched the energy and zeal of the Company of Jesus.

The reform of the Spanish church and the founding of the Jesuits were but two among many efforts to stem the tide of the Protestant advance. It was in the Council of Trent that these and other movements found fulfillment as the church pulled itself together and began a new life.

LOOKING BACK

. . . .

Counter-Reform

It was almost inevitable that the most powerful movement of the Counter-Reform should come from Spain. As the above commentary points out, Cardinal Jimenez had already brought to Spain a sense of order and reform that was so thorough that, had it been followed in Germany, Luther would have had no complaints.

The work of Ignatius fell into three areas. First, he provided the church with spiritual exercises that brought new and needed vitality to spiritual life. Second, he established an ideal of discipline and education that left a healthy imprint on the intellectual life of the church. Third, his fostering of the missions helped bring the Catholic message to the far-flung borders opened up by the exploration that followed the discoveries of Columbus and those who penetrated the Far East.

Today it is probably the intellectual competence of the Jesuits that is best known, since they still run so many educational institutions. Their missionary explorations have become part of the exciting literature of mission history. The method of prayer called the "Ignatian method," which was formulated by Ignatius, has long been an outline for meditations used in convents and monasteries throughout the Western church.

CONNECTING TO OUR TIMES

. . . .

Teresa of Avila

We rightly remember the Jesuits as the quintessential embodiment of the church's response to the Protestant Reformation. The Order of Saint Ignatius of Loyola inaugurated a worldwide system of schools and colleges and mission stations that should impress the multinational corporations of today. The Ignatian method of prayer remains a powerful and practical source of spirituality for the busy modern.

We should also remember Saint Teresa of Avila for her reform of the Carmelite Order, especially her order of cloistered Carmelite nuns whose great houses of prayer encircle the globe today. The Jesuits and other active orders have an intensely public presence in our church, hence we tend to notice them and admire the great work they do. But Teresa's cloisters are like our own souls—there, but not so evident amid the rush of modern life.

Just as our hearts beat silently thousands of times a day, sending our lifeblood to every corner of our bodies, so the women of these great cloisters are the heartbeat of the church, acting as channels of grace for every corner of the Mystical Body. These are not frail, frightened women running from the world. They are strong, purposeful women who have responded to God's call to a life of liturgical and contemplative prayer. They are missionaries of the Spirit. They know that just as no flesh lives without a soul, so the Mystical Body will not flourish without the life-breath of prayer.

Teresa of Avila
"Christ has no body on earth but yours, no hands but yours, no feet but yours. Yours are the eyes through which Christ's compassion for the world is to look out; yours are the feet with which He is to go about doing good; and yours are the hands with which He is to bless us now."

. . . .

Teresa's silent cloisters were born in the noisy turmoil of the Counter-Reformation. Four centuries have neither dimmed their vitality nor rendered their vocation irrelevant. Their cloisters dot our secular landscape like stars in the night and remind us all that there is a daylight of hope despite the pressures of contemporary madness. Thank God for their graces. Praise the Lord for their generous and joyful spiritual gifts to all of us.

FOR REFLECTION AND DISCUSSION

1. Traditionally the Jesuits have gone to some of the world's toughest mission fields. If you were the pope, where would you send them today? What do you think are some of the worldwide mission needs of the church today?

2. One of the great Jesuit missionaries was Matteo Ricci. He worked in China and spent his life adapting the gospel to Chinese traditions and culture. This brought with it the question of how far Christianity can go in accommodating to a new culture and still remain faithful to the teachings of Christ and the church. As the church continues to expand in Africa and Asia, how do you see this issue being settled? How much of Christianity lends itself to accommodation? What does not?

3. For many people the hallmark of the Jesuits is education, not only of their own members, but also through their establishment of institutions. Is education in the faith as strongly needed today as it was in Ignatius' time?

. . . .

CHAPTER TWENTY-TWO

THE RENAISSANCE

When painting the picture of hell and the souls of the damned in the Sistine Chapel, Michelangelo drew one of the souls so like a cardinal who was an enemy of his that protests were immediately voiced to Pope Clement VII to have it altered. To this Clement responded: "You know that I have power to deliver a soul out of purgatory, but not out of hell!"

. . . .

Amid all the fire and smoke of the Reform and Counter-Reform, the church played a key role in fostering the dazzling outburst of the art and architecture of the Renaissance. The humanists had recovered for Europe a taste for the wisdom and art forms of classical Greece and Rome. Mix this interest with an economic boom and you create an enormous demand for talented people.

The roll call of artistic giants in that period includes Raphael, memorable for his paintings of Mary; Michelangelo, creator of the dome of Saint Peter's, the ceiling of the Sistine Chapel and the statue of David, to mention but a few of his works; and Leonardo da Vinci, a genius who foresaw such inventions as the helicopter, the machine gun and the automobile. Leonardo's "Last Supper" is perhaps the best known representation of that event.

The merchant princes of Florence and the popes of Rome were the major patrons of these artistic geniuses. The works of art that resulted are now the delight of the tourist, the art expert and all people who love beauty.

The church did not insist that the artists restrict their work to the sacred. Popes and cardinals were equally willing to see the images of classical pagan myths produced alongside the traditional representations of the Bible, the saints and the history of the church.

Irving Stone's novel *The Agony and the Ecstasy* captures the mood of those dynamic days in presenting the life of Michelangelo Buonarroti. The section that follows describes the scene in which Pope Julius II commissioned Michelangelo to paint the ceiling of the Sistine Chapel. Michelangelo didn't want to do it, for he considered himself a sculptor rather than a painter. He finally gave in. He realized that his job was not merely to decorate a ceiling. He was to cover the ugliness of a building that had originally been designed as a fortress. His achievement became one of the masterpieces of the world.

"DECORATE THE SISTINE CHAPEL, MICHELANGELO!"
(c. 1508)

His eyes bulged when he saw the marbles dumped like a cord of firewood, discolored by rain and dust. Giuliano da Sangallo gripped his arm. "The Holy Father is waiting for you."

They passed through the smaller of the throne rooms of the papal palace, filled with a variety of supplicants hoping for an audience. Once in the large throne room, he advanced toward the throne, bowing to Cardinal Giovanni de Medici, nodding formally to Cardinal Riario. Pope Julius caught sight of him, suspended a conversation with his nephew Francesco, Prefect of Rome, and Paris de Grassis. Julius was dressed in a white linen cassock, his pleated knee-length tunic had tight sleeves, while the elbow-length scarlet velvet cape was trimmed in ermine, as was the scarlet velvet skullcap.

"Ah, Buonarroti, you have returned to us. You are pleased with the statue in Bologna, are you not?"

"It will bring honor on us."

"You see," cried Julius triumphantly, throwing out his arms energetically to include the entire room. "You had no confidence in yourself. When I made this splendid opportunity available to you, you cried out, 'It is not my trade!'" The pope's mimicking of Michelangelo's slightly hoarse voice brought appreciative laughter from the court. "Now you see how you have made it your trade, by creating a fine bronze."

"You are generous, Holy Father," murmured Michelangelo with a twinge of impatience, his mind occupied with the pile of stained marbles lying just a few hundred yards away.

"I intend to continue being generous," cried the pope heartily. "I am going to favor you above all the painting masters of Italy."

"'...painting' masters?"

"Yes. I have decided that you are the best artist to complete the work begun by your countrymen Botticelli, Ghirlandaio, Rosselli, whom I myself hired to paint the frieze in the Sistine Chapel. I am commissioning you to complete my uncle Sixtus' chapel by painting the ceiling."

There was a light patter of applause. Michelangelo was stunned. Nausea gripped him. He had asked Sangallo to make it clear to the pope that he would return to Rome only to begin carving on the sculptures for the tomb. He cried passionately:

"I am a sculptor, not a painter!"

Julius shook his head in despair.

There was an audible gasp from those around the throne. The Pope turned to his cardinals and courtiers.

"I had less trouble conquering Perugia and Bologna than I have in subduing you!"

"I am not a Papal State, Holy Father. Why should you waste your precious time subduing me?"

The room went silent. The pope glared at him, thrust out his bearded chin, demanded icily, "Where did you have your religious training, that you dare to question your pontiff's judgment?"

"As your prelate said in Bologna, Holiness, I am but an ignorant artist, without good manners."

"Then you can carve your masterpiece in a cell of Sant' Angelo."

All Julius had to do was wave a hand at a guard, and he could rot in a dungeon for years. Michelangelo gritted his teeth.

"That would bring you little honor. Marble is my profession. Let me carve the Moses, victors, captives. Many would come to see the statues, offering thanks to Your Holiness for making them possible."

"In short," snapped Julius, "I need your sculptures to assure my place in history."

"They could help, Holy Father."

"Do you hear that, gentlemen? I, Julius II, who recovered the long lost Papal States for the church and brought stability to Italy, who have cleaned out the scandals of the Borgias, published a constitution abolishing simony and elevated the decorum of the Sacred College, achieved a modern architecture for Rome.... I need Michelangelo Buonarroti to establish my historical position."

Sangallo had gone deathly pale. Cardinal Giovanni stared out a window as though he were not there. The pope loosened the collar of his cape against his own warmth, took a deep breath and started again.

"Buonarroti, my informants in Florence describe your panel for the Signoria as 'the school of the world'...."

"Holiness," interrupted Michelangelo, cursing himself for his envy of Leonardo that had led him into this trap, "it was an accident, something that could never be repeated. The Great Hall needed an accompanying fresco for the other half of the wall.... It was a diversion."

"*Bene*. Make such a diversion for the Sistine. Are we to understand that you will paint a wall for a Florentine hall, but not a ceiling for a papal chapel?"

The silence in the room was crushing. An armed courtier, standing by the pope's side, said, "Your Holiness, give me the word and we will hang this presumptuous Florentine from the Torre di Nona."

The pope glowered at Michelangelo, who stood before him defiant but speechless. Their eyes met, held in an exchange of immovability. Then a wisp of a smile drifted across the pontiff's face, was reflected in the tiny amber sparkle of Michelangelo's eyes, the barest twitching of his lips.

"This presumptuous Florentine, as you call him," said the pope, "was described ten years ago by Jacopo Galli as the best sculpture master in Italy. So he is. If I wanted him fed to the ravens I would have done so long ago."

He turned back to Michelangelo, said in the tone of an exasperated but fond father:

"Buonarroti, you will paint the Twelve Apostles on the ceiling of the Sistine, and decorate the vault with customary designs. For this we will pay you three thousand large gold ducats. We shall also be pleased to pay the expenses and wages of any five assistants you may choose. When the Sistine vault is completed, you have your pontiff's promise that you shall return to the carving of the marbles. My son, you are dismissed."

What further word could he say? He had been proclaimed supreme among his country's artists, made a promise that he would resume work on the tomb. Where could he flee? To Florence? To have Gonfaloniere Soderini cry out, "We cannot go to war with the Vatican because of you." To Spain, Portugal, Germany, England...? The pope's power reached everywhere. The pope demanded much, but a lesser pontiff might well have excommunicated him. And if he had refused to come back to Rome? He had tried that too, for a barren seven months in Florence. There was nothing to do but submit.

He kneeled, kissed the pope's ring.

"It shall be as the Holy Father desires."

Later, he stood by the front entrance of the Sistine Chapel, his mind awhirl with revulsion and self-incrimination. Sangallo was just behind him, his face haggard, looking as though he had been whipped.

"I did this to you. I persuaded the pope to build himself a triumphal tomb, and to call you here to sculpture it. All you have had is grief...."

Sangallo wept. Michelangelo shepherded him inside the protective doorway of the chapel, put an arm about the trembling shoulders.

"*Pazienza, caro*, patience. We will work our way out of this predicament."

"You are young, Michelangelo, you have time. I am old. Nor have you heard the crowning indignity. I volunteered to erect the scaffolding for you, since I renovated the chapel and know it well. But even this I was denied. Julius had already arranged with Bramante to build it.... All I want now is to return to my home in Florence, enjoy a little peace before I die."

"Do not speak of dying. Let us speak instead of how we can tackle this architectural monstrosity." He threw both arms up in a despairing gesture that embraced the Sistine. "Explain this...edifice...to me. Why was it built this way?"

The Renaissance in Italy

The birthplace of the Renaissance and humanism was Italy. It produced men and women devoted to developing their skills to the full. These humanists sought to be the pioneers of a new culture. One of the greatest was the Italian poet Petrarch, who emulated the Latin style of Cicero and brought about a revival of Platonism. Though a master of the Italian language, Petrarch felt his Latin writings were the more important. Due to his prestige and influence, they led to the growth of classical studies and increasing enthusiasm for the Latin language.

LOOKING BACK

. . . .

The Renaissance

Michelangelo belonged to a period of history known as the Renaissance. The Renaissance marked a new outburst in the fields of learning, the arts and architecture. Michelangelo lived in a time when men like Da Vinci, Raphael, Bramante and Donatello painted, sculpted, frescoed and built masterpieces that are works of genius. In the north of Europe, intellectual humanists like Erasmus, Thomas More, John Fisher and Colet revolutionized approaches to learning and education.

What were the principal characteristics of this Renaissance?

Three elements dominated the genius of those days: (1) a return to the classical cultural ideals of Greece and Rome; (2) a new interest in the human and the natural; (3) a belief that education was the best means of helping people be moral and pious.

Ancient literary classics and classical art existed all along. The monks copied the masterpieces of Greek and Latin learning. But at that time no one thought such "pagan" writing had much to say to the development of a Christian person. A major exception to this rule had been the rebirth of interest in Aristotle in the medieval period. Thomas Aquinas and the other medieval scholars adapted Aristotle's thinking to their explanations of Christian teachings. Aristotle's orderly synthesis suited the medieval thinker's structured world. His works were a philosophical form of a Gothic cathedral.

Renaissance humanists looked rather to Plato as their mentor and took his Socratic dialogues as a model for education. Rather than mount the orderly steps of an Aristotelian proposition to their peak, they wove their way according to the circular thinking of a Plato. Plato was more human, less confined to mental abstraction—round, poetic, idealistic. Thus the artists portrayed humans more realistically, though in their ideal and glorious form. Round domes on symmetrical churches, like the Duomo in Florence, gathered people as a human community in contrast to the medieval naves that drew one's eyes to the beyond.

Medieval artists had painted Mary as a stiff-looking woman, flat, holding her child forward on her knee like a stern little king. Renaissance artists painted a Madonna, a rolling cushion of a woman hugging her baby in the fold of maternal warmth.

Medieval artists had used pagan figures as ornaments on their canvases, set pieces like a Cicero or a Virgil or an Ovid robed in medieval clothes and standing like servants before the Christian Lord. They had no life or meaning of their own. How differently Michelangelo portrayed them! Bursting with anatomical energy, they stand out on their own, seemingly uttering their pagan wisdom alongside apostles and saints—and robed in classical folds, if indeed clothed at all.

The flat, perspectiveless figures of medieval paintings are always fully clothed, with the occasional exception of the infant Christ. The full-bodied, perspected figures of the Renaissance are often nude, with an occasional classical drapery—a conscious imitation of the Greek and Roman way of sculpting and painting.

Renaissance Popes
Giuliano della Rovere took the name Julius II as pope, indicating that his model would not be a Christian saint, but rather Julius Caesar. So feared in battle he gained the nickname "the Terrible," through his military and diplomatic exploits Julius was able to reorganize the Papal States, which had been opposed by France and Germany.

Perhaps the most corrupt of the Renaissance popes was Alexander VI. People of his day were heard to say: "Alexander is ready to sell the keys, the altars and even Christ himself. He is within his rights, since he bought them."

The Sistine Chapel
*In the early 1990s the
ceiling of the Sistine
Chapel was cleaned
and restored after
many years. Keep in
mind that for four
centuries the chapel
was lit by candles.
They produce quite a
bit of soot, which had
collected on the ceiling.
The restoration took
over three years; now
the colors on the
ceiling are vivid. One
can see the figures
much better. It was a
"renaissance" for
Michelangelo's famous
painting on the ceiling
of the Sistine Chapel.*

Michelangelo secretly dissected dead bodies (it was against the law) to learn how the muscles underneath the skin worked to produce their visual effect. Thus his David, Moses and the figures on the ceiling and walls of the Sistine Chapel pulsate with physical as well as spiritual vitality. No longer was the human figure hidden from view by neck-to-toe garments so that we might keep our mind on heavenly beings; now the glory of the human body was opened to view that we might celebrate the human form and rejoice in God's creation of natural order.

It was thus believed that the wisdom of the classical authors and the artistic models of the classical period, far from distracting us from God and good behavior, would in fact make us more moral and draw us closer to the Lord. The intellectual humanists promoted the study of Latin, Greek and Hebrew, not only that the classical authors might be studied, but also that the Bible be better understood and that the church Fathers be approached once again.

It was a heady time, intellectually and artistically. The humanists set in motion an educational ideal that ultimately led to the birth of the scientific mind and the value of mass education. But the dream that education would produce piety never materialized, but literacy did produce positive results. The concentration on the natural universe produced Newton, Descartes, Adam Smith and a host of inventors who made the industrial revolution and scientific advancement possible.

The revolution in art generated celebrations of landscapes, colorful impressionists and stately portraiture, and survived through the twentieth century's own revolutionary abstractions.

A homage to the classics, a love affair with the human, a dream of education-induced piety—these were the goals of the Renaissance geniuses. Their heritage remains to captivate us as well as to stimulate us to new achievements.

CONNECTING TO OUR TIMES

. . . .

Toward a Fresh Vision of Human Dignity

Renaissance artists and writers celebrated the human. They were humanists in the best sense of the word, viewing the person directly and boldly but always within a world of faith and God's presence. We style them "Christian humanists." They echoed the human idealism of Greece and Rome but within the context of a community of faith.

Once again in our own day there is a recovery of interest in the distinctly human. Our biblical scholars ponder the human side of the composition of the Bible. What were the human problems addressed by the biblical authors? What was the human history that shaped their insights and attitudes? Our theologians look at faith "from below" to meditate on the human side of the divine-human encounter. In religious education we explore human experience, its psychological stages and the social and cultural setting in which our students come to the table of word and sacrament. Our missionaries have become sensitive to enculturation, alert to the unique cultural patterns of the people they serve.

The doctrine of the Incarnation engages us today because we want to contemplate the humanity of Jesus as the door and window onto his divinity. We also do this because we wish to hold onto our human dignity in a culture that could easily treat us as a number, a thing, a category rather than a person. The threat to human dignity which the preoccupation with sexuality today poses must move us to consider more deeply that dignity and all that it entails.

The Renaissance began with much the same insight about the human and eventually framed it artistically in the works of Michelangelo, Palestrina and many others. We are only at the threshold of this perception about our human value. We can confidently anticipate that poets, playwrights, artists and sculptors will capture this for us in glorious new ways within the context of the faith.

FOR REFLECTION AND DISCUSSION

. . . .

1. Medieval culture and education emphasized the divine and the supernatural. The Renaissance period looked more at the human and the natural. Which approach do you prefer? What are some advantages and disadvantages of each approach? Are you more inspired by St. Peter's in Rome or Notre Dame Cathedral in Paris?

2. Renaissance humanists thought that education was an instrument of moral improvement and growth in piety. To some extent this did not happen. Why not? Today's public schools are not allowed to promote acts of piety or any express moral training. Is this a good idea?

3. One hears the term "secular humanism" quite a bit in today's society. Just what is secular humanism? We have discussed secular as being worldly and humanism as being concerned with the human aspect of life. Is this a bad term? Should we be concerned about things on a divine level? Is the human realm more important than the reign of God? Have worldly pleasures taken the place of spirituality? Is there room in today's world for both?

4. Discuss how one's human talents can be a source of spiritual development. Must singers sing only religious songs? Must painters paint only religious pictures? Must teachers teach only religion? How can we do what we are interested in and still lead a good life?

5. Did Renaissance artists paint only for the church or did they paint what they wanted to? Could this repeat itself today? Are we involved in a renaissance?

6. For some humanists the Renaissance, with its belief in the dignity of human persons, gradually took on secular overtones. They said that worship of God served only to distract humanity from developing its own powers and creativity. Do you think that belief in God promotes immaturity? How does an authentic Christian humanism promote maturity?

7. The Renaissance was a time when human reason was praised. Many suppressed the supernatural. Did the church of the Renaissance achieve a balance between these two? Does society today favor one over the other?

. . . .

CHAPTER TWENTY-THREE

THE COUNCIL OF TRENT

> This has been a time of
> such disaster, and the
> malice of heretics so
> obdurate, that there is
> nothing they have not
> infected with error at
> the instigation of the
> enemy of the human
> race, even in what was
> clearest in our profes-
> sion of faith or most
> certainly defined.
>
> —Council of Trent

. . . .

WINTER LIGHT AT TRENT: A DIARY ENTRY
(December 4, 1563)

Eight inches of snow greeted me this morning as I prepared to attend the closing session of the Council of Trent. This won't disappoint my nephews, who made the eighty-mile trip north to Innsbruck for a ski weekend; the winds were taking the storm in that direction. The weather may be chilly, but I feel a warm glow of satisfaction in knowing I have been part of one of the greatest achievements in the history of the church.

I have often wondered why it took so long to call a council in the first place. Why, I believe it was twenty-five years between Luther's break with the church at the Diet of Worms and the opening of the Council of Trent.

The Roman Catechism

One of the most important decisions the Council of Trent made was to commission the writing of a Catholic catechism. This was the first time that the church officially sought to present the truths of Catholicism in a comprehensive and systematic way. Completed in 1566 and popularly known as the Roman Catechism, it was intended to serve as a guide for clergy in instructing the faithful.

The Roman Catechism presented a positive and nonpolemical account of the teachings of the Catholic church. It did not dwell on condemning Protestant errors, but addressed them by stating exactly what Catholics believe and teach. Given the heated and antagonistic spirit of the times, the Roman

Apparently politics had a lot to do with it. One of the old cardinals told me that Pope Clement VII was more interested in settling the financial problems of his Medici relatives in Florence than in facing the Protestant question.

Francis I of France was hostile to any idea of a council, but Charles V of Spain was eager to see it come about. The German Catholics were interested, but they wanted a council that unreasonably limited the role of the pope in the proceedings.

Still, I know some work was done to reconcile Rome with the Protestants. I have reports on ecumenical meetings between Catholic and Protestant theologians. I mustn't forget the ecumenical conference at Ratisbon. Young John Calvin was there, as well as all the princes of Germany, the Emperor himself and a papal ambassador. What a shame it failed. The two sides were no longer able to communicate.

I was in Rome for the election of Pope Paul III. What excitement he generated when he told the cheering throngs that he would devote all his energies to calling a council. How disappointing to note that he first used his energies to find a comfortable royal position for his son, Pierluigi, and then to expend himself in making sure that his grandson married the daughter of Charles V of Spain.

When he did get around to calling a council, he met troubles on all sides. The cardinals said no. The French king said no and refused to let his bishops attend. I myself bore the personal invitation of the pope to the German Protestants. But matters were too far gone; they would have nothing to do with it.

Somehow, Pope Paul overcame all immediate obstacles and announced that the Council would open at Trent on November 22, 1542. Three papal legates arrived, but found no one there. By spring of the next year, about a dozen bishops had assembled, but in the meantime war had broken out between France and Spain, so the meeting was closed until the war ended.

Eventually, the Council did open. It was on December 13, 1545. Thirty-one bishops and forty-eight *periti* (theologians, canon lawyers and other religious experts) gathered that day. Reginald Pole, the English cardinal, gave the opening speech. He said it was clerical sin that had brought religion to such a sad state of affairs. He made a passionate plea for sincerity in the task that lay before us.

Our first problem was one of procedure. We settled on three different kinds of gatherings: Each new matter would be first debated by the experts, with the bishops listening in on the discussions. Then the bishops would take up the matter themselves in private session. Finally, when they had hammered out a satisfactory statement of the case, it would be presented for a vote at a public session. Their decree would be read out as a Council conclusion.

I'm rather glad that all the bishops didn't attend. It was much easier to get work done. We ranged in attendance from thirty-two to two hundred and twenty-eight bishops. The majority were from Italy, but there was no unity of opinion among them. Italy was divided into the Kingdom of Naples, the Papal States and the Venetian Republic. Charles V controlled Naples. The pope

Catechism *was a model of calm and confident proclamation. Its extensive use of Scripture enabled Catholics to see more clearly the biblical basis of their faith.*

With its authority resting on the fact that it was decreed by an ecumenical council and approved by the pope, the Roman Catechism *proved to be enormously influential. It went through 817 editions in four centuries (the first known English one was published in 1829). The renowned English theologian Cardinal John Newman spoke highly of it: "I rarely preach a sermon, but I go to this beautiful and complete catechism to get both my matter and my doctrine." As late as 1960 Pope John XXIII was still recommending it.*

A Reforming Council

In 1906, while secretary to Bishop Radini Tedeschi of Bergamo, the future Pope John XXIII came across the archives of Saint Charles Borromeo, the great Counter-Reformation saint who, some 350 years earlier, had been bishop of Bergamo. In these thirty-nine volumes Roncalli, whose scholarly vocation it would be to edit them, saw how Borromeo set about the reform of the diocese according to the decrees of the Council of Trent. Throughout his work as editor, Roncalli was heartened to discover that the Council of Trent was not an anti-Protestant council but a reforming one.

set the tone for the bishops from his domain. The Venetian Republic held its own maverick position.

The Dominican Order wielded a deep influence on our proceedings. Twenty-three of the bishops and twenty-eight of the theologians were from the Order of Saint Dominic. That is why the teachings of Saint Thomas Aquinas were so central to our deliberations.

We had two vast areas to cope with: namely, the question of discipline and the clarification of doctrine. Every reformer, both Catholic and Protestant, had cried out about the abuses in the church. Trent heard the complaints and did something about them.

Take the question of *benefice*. This was just another word for a source of income such as a diocese, an abbey or a parish. The problem arose when one person gained control of a large number of benefices and thus became mainly interested in the funds and not in the spiritual welfare of the people. Scandals arose when sales, trading and shady transactions concerning benefices made a mockery of religion and nursed the greed of the beneficiaries.

Another abuse was the custom of the absentee landlord. For example, the Bishop of Parma might also be the Abbot of Palermo. If he lived at Parma, he might never see Palermo even though he collected income for being abbot there. Milan hadn't seen its bishop for over a hundred years!

A peculiar variation of this, which happened in my uncle's family, was the custom of delaying the consecration of a bishop. My fourteen-year-old cousin was named Bishop of Pisa. From the moment of his appointment he began to receive income from the diocese. He put off ordination to the priesthood and consecration to the episcopacy until he was twenty-four. At that ripe age, he fell in love and decided to marry. He simply renoun-ced his right to the mitre of Pisa, but meanwhile had ten years of income in his savings account.

Needless to say, at Trent we legislated a stop to all this. From then on, we allowed only one benefice to one man. We abolished absentee landlords. We insisted that a man be consecrated within six months of his appointment as bishop.

We also decided to eliminate the practice of fund-raising through the sale of indulgences. Luther had raised strong objections to this years before, and we could only agree that it was a custom that caused much mischief and mis-understanding among the people.

Our second task was the doctrinal one. We attempted to clear up key issues rather than give full expositions of the doctrines discussed. We tried to put forward the traditional teaching of the church in such a way as to avoid con-fusion. A good part of our work was devoted to the doctrines of justification and the Eucharist.

Luther had taught that a person is justified by faith alone. What he meant was that the act of faith alone made a person a friend of God; good human deeds did not merit divine friendship. We said that both were needed: the act of faith and good human deeds. Thus God becomes our friend both through our faith and the human acts that please God. I realize that Luther knew the importance of good behavior in Christian life. But it's amazing to me that he couldn't see how it merited friendship with God, at least in some way.

As to the Eucharist, we preferred the term *transubstantiation* as the way of describing the mystery. The very substance or reality of the bread and wine change into the substance and reality of Jesus at the Mass. We further argued that Jesus is totally present under each species. There is, therefore, no neces-sity to receive him under the form of both bread and wine at Mass.

In speaking of the Mass as a sacrifice, we made clear that there was only one true sacrifice, that of Jesus at Calvary. The Mass simply makes that same sac-rifice present in our own time and place.

At our closing session the Bishop of Catania asked the fathers of the Council, "Are you agreed that the Council should be closed and that the pope should be asked by the legates in the name of the Council to ratify all the decrees and definitions accepted under the three popes: Paul III, Julius III and Pius IV?" All agreed. Cardinal Guise then said, "May we all confess the faith and observe the decrees of the most holy ecumenical Council of Trent!" The fathers replied, "We shall always confess that faith and observe those decrees."

The cardinal went on. "That is the faith of all of us. We are all united in it, we embrace it and subscribe to it. That is the faith of Peter and the apostles. That is the faith of our fathers. That is the right faith."

Then we sang the *Te Deum*. We had tears in our eyes. I saw many bishops who had fought and argued with each other these long years now embrace and kiss each other. I believe that we have produced a brilliant achievement with God's help and the endless goodwill of our participants. I leave the winter light at Trent with hope for the church we have tried to renew.

LOOKING BACK

. . . .

Council of Trent

This imaginary diary of a bishop at the last session of the Council of Trent stresses several items: (1) why it took nearly twenty-five years to get the Council going; (2) the disciplinary decisions of Trent; (3) the theological issues faced at this Council.

Political intrigue and selfish motives kept the Council from being a reality for nearly a quarter of a century. It's obvious that we should lament this. It is a pleasure, however, to report that the church had the wisdom and good grace eventually to face up to the problem and bring about a stunning reform of its internal life along with a theological statement that served as the backbone for religious faith and thought up to our own days.

The disciplinary measures dealt with the church's economic policies and the training of seminarians. Through abuses, churchmen were gathering benefits from places where they did not labor. Trent struck firmly against absentee landlords, the appointment of unsuitable men to the episcopate and the strange custom of "delayed consecration." While our diarist doesn't mention the reform of the seminaries, it should be noted here that the general principles Trent enunciated for seminary education and training have endured to our own time.

The doctrinal statements faced the Lutheran challenge of justification by faith alone, the matter of the real presence and the sacrifice of the Mass. Since the rhetoric of Luther seemed to exclude human free choice in justification, the church spoke strongly on this matter. Because the Protestant position seemed to dilute the doctrine of the real presence and the sacrificial character of the Mass, the Council of Trent took up the language of transubstantiation to explain the meaning of the real presence and emphasized the continuing re-presentation of the sacrifice of Christ in each Mass.

Today's ecumenical discussions are clearing up many of the misunderstandings that developed at the Reformation, but many divisions still remain. The gulf opened by four hundred years will not be healed in a day.

Enduring Impact

The work of the Council fathers at Trent (1545–1563) produced a powerful and enduring impact on the church. It helped shape the direction of liturgy, catechetics, theology, church law and authority for the next four centuries.

Liturgy. Trent established an Order for the Mass that precisely outlined the rubrics, texts and behavior to be expected at liturgy. In its dogmatic coverage of the Mass, Trent stressed the Mass as a true sacrifice that made present the sacrificial event of Jesus at Calvary. Trent also insisted on good preaching at Mass and urged people to receive Communion on Sundays. Saint Pius V, the post-Tridentine pope who worked hardest on liturgical reform, established the Congregation of Rites, a clerical commission to watch over liturgical behavior in the church.

Catechetics. The *Roman Catechism* was a product of the Fathers of Trent. It may surprise many, but it is a masterpiece of *kerygmatic* composition, that is, founded in biblical content and style. Its outline was creed, liturgy, law. Its theory was that religion begins with God. Hence the creed was a statement of God's work for humanity. Liturgy was the expression of this relationship with God experienced in the Mass and the sacraments. The law (the Commandments) was the outline of what people should do in the light of what God has done for them. Through the catechism Trent emphasized the need for all Catholics to have a good catechetical training.

Theology. Trent relied on the work of Thomas Aquinas for its theological expression. Most manuals of theology followed the same general outline: God, Trinity, Incarnation, Church, Sacraments, Morality, Last Things. The approach reflected the preference for clear statement of doctrine and the role of faith as firm agreement with church teaching and fidelity to tradition.

Church law. Trent touched the day-to-day life of Catholics with laws about Communion fast, the lenten fast, Friday abstinence from meat and extensive marriage laws. Since Vatican II Catholics have seen changes in these fast and abstinence laws. Marriage laws, especially those dealing with annulments, were recently updated and revised in the Code of Canon Law.

The magisterium. Because of the confusion generated by both the cultural chaos following the Black Death and the ecclesiastical chaos following the Reformation, it was important for Trent to make a strong case for the authority of the official teachers of the church, particularly the pope and bishops. Without the kind of unity this would bring, there was no real guarantee that the hard work of Trent would last. Hence, in the following centuries the term *magisterium* applied mainly, if not exclusively, to this group within the church.

It is popular among current church reformers to look down on Trent. This is unfair: Trent provided a framework for the church's operations that lasted four hundred years.

CONNECTING TO OUR TIMES

. . . .

From Protestant Challenge to Pastoral Concern

We have already made several substantial connections to the Second Vatican Council in this book. We must do so repeatedly because it stands as the turning point of the church's history in modern times. So once again we draw a link between Vatican II and an event of the past, this time, the Council of Trent. The angle that engages our attention here is the contrast between a Trent that strove to respond to doctrinal and disciplinary challenges and a Vatican II which was primarily pastoral in nature.

The Council of Trent was born in an age of ecclesiastical controversy and necessarily had to deal with the Protestant Reformation. Vatican II was called to update the church's pastoral responsibilities in the area of liturgy, Scripture, catechesis, priesthood and relations with other Christians and non-Christians, particularly the Jewish community.

Central to Vatican II's approach to pastoral mission was the understanding of the church. At Trent the bishops stressed the eternal, hierarchical nature of the church in the face of the Protestant emphasis on the church's "invisible side." At Vatican II the bishops dwelt much more on the church's spiritual nature as a mystery, as God's people, as the body of Christ, as a temple of the Spirit, while not ignoring its institutional reality. This was embodied in the document *Lumen Gentium* (Light of Nations).

But the bishops went beyond this internal reflection. They also explored the church's relation to the modern world. How can the church minister to a new world with its global awareness, the information explosion, the scientific mind and the enormous social problems presented by the developing nations? They wrote their conclusions in *Gaudium et Spes* (The Pastoral Constitution on the Church in the Modern World).

Ecumenical Councils intensely reflect a church in historical progress. Through the lens of Trent and Vatican II we encounter a church in action, living by the Spirit and ready to move forward.

FOR REFLECTION AND DISCUSSION

. . . .

1. For the everyday life of the church, Trent's reform of the Mass was a significant achievement. Trent abolished simony, the selling of Masses as well as the selling of ecclesiastical posts. Trent unified the texts of the Mass, eliminated the superstitions surrounding the Mass and put priests under strict notice to follow the rubrics perfectly and avoid any fanciful or eccentric additions. Historical understanding of the evolution of the Mass was still at a primitive stage. Common opinion at the time traced the Catholic way of saying Mass back to Saint Peter. Below you will find some value judgments flowing from Trent's treatment of the Mass. What is your reaction? Discuss.

   - The universal Latin Mass, the same all over the world, was good because it emphasized the clarity, stability and universality of Catholic teaching and identity.
        Good___ Bad___ Don't know___
   - This unchangeable Mass made people feel the church was unchangeable.
        Good___ Bad___ Don't know___
   - Trent felt it could not put the Mass in the vernacular because that would prove the Protestants right in saying the church has no claim to divine authority.
        Good___ Bad___ Don't know___

- The hostile spirit of the times prevented Catholics from admitting that Protestants could be right about anything.

    Good___ Bad___ Don't know___

- Trent's failure to give people a sense of participation in the Mass forced them to run after extra-liturgical devotions so they could have a sense of participation in the worship of the church.

    Good___ Bad___ Don't know___

2. The Council of Trent unified the church after the Reformation had landed some serious blows. The Mass is a central part of Catholic life and the Eucharist is the central part of the Mass. Some of the reformers made the Bible the most important part of worship. Trent said that the celebration of the Mass had to be universal, meaning that it must be the same no matter where you were. It made the church seem unchangeable.

3. Latin was the official language of the church. Have you ever attended a Latin Mass? Why would the church want to have the Mass said in a language that most people do not understand? What languages is the Mass said in today? Is it still the same? Does the language change what is going on there?

4. How much participation would you have in the Mass if it was only said in Latin? How much participation do you have in the vernacular (the language of the people)?

5. How has the ritual of the Mass changed since the Council of Trent?

6. Many of the laws introduced at the Council of Trent were changed or modified at Vatican II. It is interesting to note how laws and rules change but essential doctrines or beliefs never do. We believe the same things now as Christians did in the apostles' time.

7. Do you know the present day laws that pertain to fasting before Communion, lenten fast and abstinence, wearing hats in church, Saturday night liturgies?

8. Why are church councils good? Does the church need one of these every so often? Why do changes upset some people? Do we equate change with weakness?

CHAPTER TWENTY-FOUR

. . . .

THE AMERICAN SCENE

> Without morals a
> republic cannot subsist
> any length of time;
> they therefore who are
> decrying the Christian
> religion, whose moral-
> ity is so sublime and
> pure [and] which
> insures to the good
> eternal happiness, are
> undermining the solid
> foundation of morals,
> the best security for
> the duration of free
> governments.
> —Charles Carroll

. . . .

Catholics came early to what would eventually be the continental United States. Spanish Catholics arrived in St. Augustine, Florida, in 1565 and penetrated California as early as 1542. By 1772 there were mission stations in San Diego, San Carlos (Carmel), San Gabriel (near Los Angeles), San Antonio and San Luis Obispo. Spanish Catholic activity in the Southwest was equally impressive. They founded Santa Fe in 1609 and, in 1630, reported baptisms of five thousand Native Americans in New Mexico.

213

French Catholics settled in the Louisiana Territory in 1699 and controlled the area until 1766, when the Spanish took over. In 1755 the French exiles from Acadia (see Longfellow's "Evangeline" for a poetic take) added to the number of French Catholics in Louisiana. The Acadians are the ancestors of the Cajuns.

But the civilization that laid the foundations of the future United States was English and Protestant. England's continuing religious reformation in the sixteenth and seventeenth centuries affected the religious aspects of American colonization. First roots were struck in Jamestown, Virginia, in 1607. By that time England had definitely split with Rome. The Pilgrims came to Plymouth in 1620. They and their fellow Puritans founded the Massachusetts Bay Colony.

The Puritans represented the dissenting wing of England's reformation. Calvinist in their theology, they were resolutely opposed to Roman Catholicism and stoutly repudiated any Catholicizing influences in Protestantism; they would have nothing of the "papists." One reason they blocked any celebration of Christmas was because they identified such merrymaking as a papist creation—too Catholic.

Puritans firmly believed that Catholics had corrupted the gospel. They viewed Rome as "Babylon on the Tiber" and they believed the pope to be the Antichrist of the book of Revelation. Their recent historical experience gave them plenty of evidence that their religious judgments were unassailable. Catholic Queen Mary I ("Bloody Mary") had appeared to support the burning of three hundred Protestants between 1555 and 1558.

They read and reread John Foxe's *Book of Martyrs*, reminding them how Catholics had martyred Protestants. Vivid in their memory was the recent Gunpowder Plot of 1605, when Guy Fawkes and a group of Catholic subversives planned to blow up King James and the Houses of Parliament. On top of this, England's worst political enemies were France and Spain—both Catholic countries.

These English settlers barely had a foothold on the northeast coast of the United States. Not unreasonably, they feared the possibility of hostile action from Catholic New France to the north in Canada and Catholic New Spain to the south in Florida, Texas and Mexico. Protestant New England had skirmishes with the French and Indian alliance from Canada, and Protestant Georgia tangled with Catholic Floridians to the south. Religious and political poison soured the environment of the English colonies.

The Puritans set the pace for a strain of anti-Catholicism that became endemic to the American scene. In 1647 they enacted a statute against any priests who might appear. (Priests were automatically considered to be disturbers of the peace and enemies of the true religion.) If caught, a priest was to be put in jail for life. The statute further held that, "If he escapes and is afterward retaken, he shall be punished with death."

Actual persecution of Catholics in the colonies was, in reality, relatively mild, mainly because there were so few of them. Despite the restrictive laws and unwelcoming atmosphere, some Catholics did arrive and settle mainly in Maryland, Pennsylvania, Virginia, New York and New Jersey.

The most predominant Catholic settlement was in Maryland. Catholics tried to keep a low profile religiously in colonial days, while at the same time building up their prosperity. They belonged to the social and political elite of the Maryland colony. They were pragmatic, rather than ideological, Catholics. Maryland governors were to "instruct all Roman Catholics to be silent on all occasions concerning matters of religion, and treat Protestants with as much mildness and favor as justice will permit."

Catholic backing of the American Revolution won grudging acceptance from the Protestant majority, and anti-Catholic prejudice, articulated powerfully by the Puritan intellectuals and divines, abated slightly. But it penetrated Protestant consciousness and would flare up again and again in American history. Catholics would live with the

The New World

The New World was discovered in 1492 during the papacy of Innocent VIII. There was a scramble to see who would rule and who would settle the newly acquired lands. Pope Alexander VI sent the first missionaries and also set up the Papal Line of Demarcation in South America.

The Reformation came right on the heels of this discovery. The New World afforded a haven for many persons fleeing from religious persecution, both Catholic and Protestant. These groups who could not live in harmony in Europe eventually would do so America.

. . . .

tension of proving to Protestants that they could be good Americans—and proving to the pope they could be good Catholics.

The story of Charles Carroll, cosigner of the Declaration of Independence, and of his cousin Bishop John Carroll is the first—and one of the more pleasant —chapters in the stormy relationship of American Catholics to American Protestants.

The setting for the imaginary dialogue that follows is the park in front of Independence Hall in Philadelphia a few years after the victory over the English. A prominent Catholic woman, Mrs. FitzSimmons, is engaged in a discussion with John Carroll, America's recently elected first Catholic bishop.

"FOR GOD AND COUNTRY": A DIALOGUE
(c. 1791)

Mrs. FitzSimmons: I'm amazed that we have created a country that has separation of church and state. That certainly wasn't William Penn's intention. Over our fireplace is an engraving of his theory of government: "Government seems to me to be a part of religion itself, a thing sacred in its institution and purpose."

Bishop Carroll: All the first colonists felt the same way. The Mayflower Compact of 1620 reflects the sentiments of your William Penn. The Pilgrims and others came here to establish religious states purged of the problems back home. Separating the state from religion was farthest from their minds. The Pilgrims were blunt in their intentions: "Having undertaken for the glory of God and the advancement of the Christian faith a voyage to plant a colony in the northern parts of Virginia, we covenant and bind ourselves in a body politic to further the needs of the aforesaid."

Mrs. FitzSimmons: The colonists created a new style of church-state relations. They reduced the clergy's authority and would not let them be quasi-nobility. The laity managed the churches and introduced a democratic style.

Bishop Carroll: I think the best thing the colonists brought with them was the concept of freedom of religion. They practically invented the idea of freedom of conscience in religious matters.

Mrs. FitzSimmons: Except for Catholics and witches!

Bishop Carroll: Old prejudices die hard. The Salem witch trials of 1692 were a disgrace.

Mrs. FitzSimmons: I still resent the righteousness of the Puritans toward Catholics and other non-Puritans.

Bishop Carroll: Thank God for Roger Williams and Anne Hutchinson. They made Rhode Island the home of religious tolerance.

Mrs. FitzSimmons: Except for Catholics! It was a little pompous for them to say, "Let the saints of the Most High walk in this colony without molestation in the name of Jehovah." Just let a Catholic try it in those days.

Bishop Carroll: Still, the ideal of religious freedom was born there. I can appreciate their fear of Catholics. They still recalled too vividly the Catholic brutalization of Protestants in Europe.

Mrs. FitzSimmons: Anti-Catholicism lingers in our new republic. I am furious with New Hampshire for still forbidding Catholics to hold public office fifteen years after the Declaration of Independence.

Bishop Carroll: It will take time to convince Protestants we are coequal citizens. Massachusetts and Connecticut still make Protestantism the official state religion within their boundaries.

Mrs. FitzSimmons: I sometimes think it is only because of the wealth of Catholics that we have any freedom at all.

Bishop Carroll: Money brings power. We have comparatively few Catholics in the United States, but many of us are big landowners or engaged in rich shipping enterprises like the Moylans.

Mrs. FitzSimmons: Why did we back the Revolution?

Bishop Carroll: The English kings favored freedom for Protestants, but not for Catholics. Even in our "Catholic" colony, Maryland, there was difficulty for Catholics.

Mrs. FitzSimmons: And don't forget my Quaker state. We could not worship in public, have voting rights or hold public office. Mr. Penn was for it, but not the king.

Bishop Carroll: Our church was in a sorry state on July 4, 1776. We had only twenty-five priests in the thirteen colonies, mostly in Maryland and Pennsylvania. Virtually all of them were Jesuits, an order which had been suppressed in Europe. The priests could not look there for leadership.

Mrs. FitzSimmons: I felt we had no leadership. How could we when the Catholic bishop of London was in charge of us? How was he going to take much interest in a flock three thousand miles away?

Bishop Carroll: Chaos, that's what it was. No leadership. The church needed organization. All twenty-five priests favored revolution.

The Suppression of the Jesuits

The prevailing reputation of Jesuits was such that former President John Adams wrote a letter of warning to President Thomas Jefferson in 1816 stating: "If ever there was a body of men who merited eternal damnation on earth and in hell, it is this Society of Loyola's. Nevertheless, we are compelled by our system of religious toleration to offer them asylum." Asylum was granted in part because of the Society's suppression in 1773 due to political pressures in Europe. The Jesuits were not fully restored as a religious order until 1814.

. . . .

Mrs. FitzSimmons: So did most of their parishioners.

Bishop Carroll: That is why my cousin Charles and I joined Mr. Franklin on a diplomatic mission to Canada to enlist the support of French Catholics for our revolution.

Mrs. FitzSimmons: So we joined the Protestants in fostering armed revolt. It was the first time Protestants looked at us as partners. We all had a vested interest in preserving freedom of religion.

Bishop Carroll: Not to mention our common economic interests. Political freedom would lead us to religious freedom and economic independence.

Mrs. FitzSimmons: Oh, how we joined in that fight! Washington made Moylan an aide-de-camp. John Barry put his ships at the service of the navy and became a hero.

Bishop Carroll: My Maryland produced the Maryland Old Line Contingent from St. Mary's County. They are very proud down there about their role in the protection of New York and the defense of Boston.

Mrs. FitzSimmons: Yes, the Protestants have warmed up considerably toward us because of our clear patriotism. Imagine that bigot Jonathan Boucher preaching a sermon on toleration for Catholics.

Bishop Carroll: Our best supporter was President Washington. They all knew my cousin Charles Carroll was right when he said, "Our blood flowed as freely in proportion to our numbers to cement the fabric of independence as any of our fellow citizens."

Mrs. FitzSimmons: Our courage has paid off. We have a Bill of Rights that guarantees religious freedom for Catholics and everyone else. And now we have our own bishop in you, my dear John Carroll.

Bishop Carroll: I cannot help but think that our American Revolution is part of God's plan. In a recent sermon I said, "Since the American Revolution, I have always thought that Providence was reserving an even more extraordinary revolution in the order of grace."

Mrs. FitzSimmons: Church and state are now separated. But church and society are not. I believe that is how God's grace has touched us and I am convinced the old church of Europe will see it our way one day.

The Councils of Baltimore

The Councils of Baltimore were a series of provincial (meetings of the province of Baltimore) and plenary (including all archbishops and bishops) councils which met in Baltimore, Maryland, throughout the nineteenth century.

The First Provincial Council was convened in 1829 by Bishop John England of Charleston and discussed such issues as rising anti-Catholic prejudice, trusteeism and appropriate Catholic literature. Six more councils followed. In 1846, at the Sixth Provincial Council, Mary was chosen as the Patroness of the United States under the title of the Immaculate Conception.

The First Plenary Council was convened in May of 1852 and addressed the growth of the Catholic community, pastoral and parochial life, ritual, liturgy and church finances. It decreed that parochial schools be built wherever possible, that catechism instruction be given to children and that seminaries be created in every diocese or province. The Second Plenary Council was held in 1866, soon after the Civil War, and was primarily one of consolidation.

The Third Plenary Council convened in November 1884 under the direction of Archbishop James Gibbons. Its decrees shaped the direction of American Catholicism until the Second Vatican Council. Its chief concern was education, mandating both the establishment of elementary schools within two years and the founding of The Catholic University of America. The Council's most notable achievement was the drafting of a uniform catechism for the United States: the Baltimore Catechism.

. . . .

LOOKING BACK

. . . .

The American Scene

During the colonial period in America, the Catholic church was generally out-
lawed. There was mutual distrust and fear between Protestants and Catholics.
Protestants thought of the church as a political power rather than as a religious
community, while Catholics looked on the Protestant churches as Christianity
in various states of deterioration. As a result of these attitudes, the Protestant
majority withheld from Roman Catholics both active and passive participation
in colonial affairs. In 1776 Maryland and Pennsylvania were the first to pass a
declaration of religious freedom which offered Catholics the opportunity to
participate openly in the public life of the republic. After the Revolution,
when the Constitution was being written, the authors thought that a declaration of religious freedom was the only possible solution to allow for the variety of beliefs that existed in the republic.

The First Amendment to the Constitution put the church within the law
and legally enabled Catholics to participate in government.

In spite of discrimination, Catholics did contribute to the formation of the
American nation. Two outstanding Catholics noted for the part they played in
this early period are John and Charles Carroll.

The Carrolls

John and Charles Carroll were cousins born during the colonial period to a
wealthy, landowning family whose status raised them above the usual condemnation of "papists." Both boys attended a Jesuit school in Saint Omer, France.
Charles returned to Maryland to become one of its wealthiest citizens and,
after 1776, one of the most prominent public figures in the young republic.
John went on to the Jesuit novitiate.

After ordination John taught in Europe until 1773 when the Jesuits were
suppressed. At forty years of age, he returned to his mother's home in Rock
Creek, Maryland, and assumed the duties of a parish priest while watching
the mounting conflict between England and the colonies. Apparently there
was no question in his mind on which side his allegiance lay. When the
request came to accompany the committee to Canada, John accepted the

appointment although he had strong convictions about the inadvisability of clergy entering the political arena. Later, as first bishop of the United States, he converted this conviction into one of the guiding principles for the American clergy.

The public role of the Carrolls did a great deal to aid the social acceptance of Catholics. The well-known and staunch patriotism of Charles made the Carroll name respected throughout the colonies. Thus, the choice of a member of the Carroll family as the first Roman Catholic bishop of the United States did a great deal to bridge prejudice.

In 1790, John Carroll was consecrated the first bishop of Baltimore after having acted as vicar apostolic for a few years. For thirty years he did much to set the direction for the American church. He forged a creative role for the church in a new type of country rather than transmit a medieval institution to the infant republic. He requested of Rome the right for the American clergy to elect their hierarchy. (After he himself was elected, however, this privilege was withdrawn.) He also requested of Rome the right to use vernacular in the liturgy, but this was denied.

He set out to establish Catholicism in this young country and, to this end, he influenced the foundation of schools, the institution of new religious orders, the creation of dioceses and the repression of schisms. This work set the stage for a strong church community and built a foundation on which the church could grow.

John Carroll died in 1815, just prior to the arrival of waves of Catholic immigrants that would inundate and outnumber native-born Catholics. The newcomers brought with them new problems, but a secure foundation for the Catholic church in the United States had already been laid.

During the administration of John Carroll, the uniquely American policy of separation of church and state was inaugurated. To Europeans, this phrase seemed to mean that the new republic had made a conscious effort to eliminate religion as a force in public life. They interpreted it as a demeaning of religion. Yet this was not the American intention or meaning. The Declaration of Independence begins with a profession of faith in God, and the first article of the Bill of Rights prohibits the state from interfering with religion or its exercise. The American tradition, begun by the constituting body of the republic, put religion beyond the state, not the state beyond religion. It granted liberty to the church, not exile from public life.

CONNECTING TO OUR TIMES

. . . .

The Catholic Moment Has Come

The election of President John F. Kennedy marked a turning point in the acceptance of Catholics by the Protestant majority in the United States. Electing a Catholic president was the ultimate act of affirmation of the Catholic community. Now, affirmation is not the same as agreement. Nor does it imply that Catholicism will be immune from the bias and prejudice that was ordinary fare in American history from the days of the Puritans on. Catholic-bashing is still around.

But by and large Catholics can rest free and easy in American society as accepted partners in the great democratic experiment. In fact, Father Richard John Neuhaus, a convert from the Lutheran church, argues that the "Catholic Moment" has come. Until now, he explains, the American struggle to maintain and advance democratic values, virtues and ideals has been supported by the guidance of the Protestant churches. But with the weakening of the mainline churches, there is need of a fresh and strong religious community, such as Catholicism, to take up the traditional role of fostering the virtues of participation, respect for others, family strength, education, faith and patriotism.

Neuhaus believes the Catholic church is historically prepared, numerically significant (twenty-five percent of the population), spiritually vital and morally disciplined enough for this task. He intends no hint of "takeover" or any intent to subvert the freedom of religion in our country. He is simply saying that what a vital Protestantism offered to the success of our democracy, Catholicism is presently able to continue. He is not saying that Protestantism no longer has anything to offer, or that Judaism and other people of good will have no place in the public square. He observes that Catholicism has received a lot from America and should now shoulder responsibility equal to its gifts for the good of American society.

The tiny seed of Catholicism, born in colonial days, has now become an oak tree in the American garden along with the others. We have received much. We should now be givers more than takers.

FOR REFLECTION AND DISCUSSION

· ·

1. Protestants were a minority in Europe but became the majority in America. Catholics were generally not trusted by these Protestants, so Catholics did not participate in much of the secular society. Do you think that this religious discrimination is still alive today? Are Catholics welcome everywhere today? Can a Catholic successfully run for office anywhere in the U.S.?

2. A generation or two ago this country had many ethnic churches. If an immigrant came from Italy or Spain or Poland or Ireland, he or she would join a parish of other immigrants of like background. Why did the church have these ethnic parishes? Did these people feel more "at home" in these churches? What ethnic churches are found today? Who are today's immigrants?

3. The only Catholic to sign the Declaration of Independence was Charles Carroll, cousin of John Carroll, the first American bishop. Are many Catholics involved in public office today? Is it a conflict of interest to be Catholic and a political leader?

4. There has been only one Catholic President of the United States. Al Smith from New York was the first Catholic to run for president in 1928 but was defeated. Catholic John F. Kennedy won election in 1960. Why would people question the performance of a president because of his religion? Are there any religious groups that could not be elected? Why? What are your feelings on this?

5. Saint Elizabeth Ann Seton was instrumental in the beginning of parochial schools. Today there are Catholic schools from preschool to university. At all levels of education many non-Catholics attend these schools. Why? When might a non-Catholic feel out of place in a Catholic school? Many other denominations now have schools as well. Why does the country seem to be in need of religiously affiliated schools?

Rise of Liberalism

Pius IX

Vatican I

1800

Franco-Prussian War

part four: MODERN CHURCH

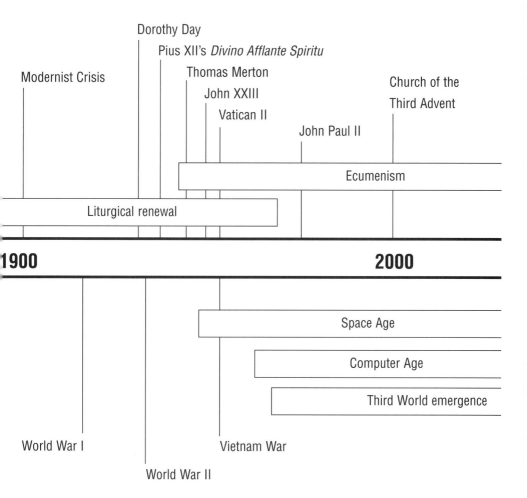

Dorothy Day

Pius XII's *Divino Afflante Spiritu*

Modernist Crisis

Thomas Merton

Church of the
Third Advent

John XXIII

Vatican II

John Paul II

Ecumenism

Liturgical renewal

1900

2000

Space Age

Computer Age

Third World emergence

World War I

Vietnam War

World War II

. . . .

CHAPTER TWENTY-FIVE

ON GUARD AGAINST LIBERALISM

> Our Predecessors have... constantly resisted the nefarious enterprises of wicked men, who have striven by their deceptive opinions and most pernicious writings to raze the foundations of the Catholic religion....
>
> —Pope Pius IX

. . . .

PIUS IX AND THE FIRST VATICAN COUNCIL
(1846–1878)

Pius IX was a charmer. A "people's pope," he loved strolling about Rome, chatting and joking with those he met. To him we owe the now common custom of large papal audiences. He wanted people from all over the world to come and see their Holy Father. He established the tradition of personal devotion to the pope.

Still, few popes have been more controversial; "Pio Nono" was hated as much as he was loved. Holding the longest tenure in the history of the papacy—thirty-two years—Pius had ample opportunity to dismay liberals and dash their hopes; he championed conservative causes right up to his death at eighty-six.

Things didn't start that way. Liberals cheered when they heard of his election. They misunderstood Pius from the beginning. At most an enlightened conservative, Pius was never a liberal. Admittedly, his first decisions had a liberal ring: He granted amnesty to political prisoners in the Papal States. He created some representative government in which the laity could have some jurisdiction over certain matters. He lifted censorship restrictions on political news (but not church news). He retained absolute veto power, however. He did not approve of freedom of religion and forbade Jews in the Papal States political equality with Catholics.

Political developments soon drew Pius back from even his tentative enlightened measures. The leaders of the Risorgimento, a movement to unify the Italian states into one nation, were determined to remove northern Italy from Austrian control. The pope's parliament declared war on Austria, but Pius vetoed their decision. He would not allow a war against a Catholic nation.

The people were not pleased with his decision. Mobs rioted in the streets of Rome and an assassin killed his prime minister. Armed demonstrators surrounded the papal palace and aimed a cannon at it.

Pius disguised himself as a parish priest and escaped to Gaeta, where he took up residence in a small hotel. Risorgimento leader Garibaldi entered Rome and declared a republic. This happened in 1848, two years after the election of Pius IX.

A coalition of European diplomats met to find a way to return the pope to Rome. They backed a French expeditionary force which successfully

The Papal States

In the eighth century, when the popes needed protection from some barbarian tribes, Pepin the Short, king of the Franks, donated much conquered land to the papacy. On this land, known for centuries as the Papal States, was maintained a papal army to protect the pope. Little by little over the centuries, this land was ceded back to Italy. All that remains today is the Vatican and certain churches and palaces in Rome.

Pope Pius IX was pope longer than any other pope—thirty-two years. The Middle Ages were over and people were looking for more power within the church. Pius IX kept the church hierarchy intact.

. . . .

Syllabus of Errors

The Syllabus of Errors characterized the papacy of Pius IX. Written in 1864, the Syllabus was appended to the encyclical Quantra Cura. It condemned eighty theses attributed to modern thinkers, including pantheism, religious freedom, rationalism, socialism's position on the right to private property, denial of the temporal power of the pope, subjection of the family to the state, freedom of the press and separation of church and state.

Many Catholics, as well as other committed Christians, were disappointed with the Syllabus, which simply listed errors to be condemned and contained no explanation of their context. Lacking

recaptured Rome and gave it back to the pope. Whatever tender feelings Pius may have had for liberals, they no longer existed. As far as he was concerned, liberalism was synonymous with persecution of the church.

Camillo Cavour and his Piedmont plan confirmed Pius's convictions. Cavour, leader of the liberals in the north Italian province of Piedmont, had abolished religious orders and stripped the church of its control of education. Cavour envisioned uniting all of Italy under the leadership of the kingdom of Savoy. His conquest of Italy would begin by the seizure of the Papal States, though he planned to let the pope keep Rome.

By 1860 Cavour had taken the Papal States. (The French still held Rome for the pope.) Cavour asked the pope to renounce his right to the Papal States. In return the Italian government would recognize his right to the Vatican and the papal palaces and galleries; take a hands-off policy regarding the appointment of bishops and pastors; pay their salaries and provide the pope with funds to maintain his operations. The church would have the freedom to teach and preach. (Cavour's proposal to Pius IX in 1860 was virtually the same as the one made by Mussolini to Pius XI in 1929—and accepted in the Lateran Treaty.)

One side of Pius IX agreed with the proposal: He did believe in the unification of Italy and was sympathetic to the goal of Risorgimento. But the other side of him prevailed in this dilemma: He could not bring himself to concede to a liberal ascendancy. It was too godless and too secular. Moreover, it seemed to him to be God's will that the Papal States remain in the hands of the pope. So he said no to Cavour.

A New Kind of Papacy

The twists of history benefited the pope more than he knew at the time. At the very moment his political power virtually vanished, his spiritual power exploded. From being the temporal monarch of a small Italian principality, he emerged as a worldwide spiritual leader. In theory the popes always had this role; in practice this was less true. Local aristocratic bishops held great power in the various monarchies and checked papal influence on local diocesan affairs.

The decline of papal political power marked the rise of papal spiritual eminence. A trend called ultramontanism (literally, "beyond the mountain") contributed to this development. The movement centered in France, that country "beyond the mountain," north of the Alps. Ultramontanists were Rome-centered, pope-oriented Catholics. What motivated them? Many were political conservatives who viewed the pope as a defense against revolutionary ideas.

The move toward centralization had begun with the Concordat of 1801 between Pope Pius VII and France, which called for all the French bishops to resign. From that moment on, the pope could appoint his own men. They owed him their job, not the French king or some local baron. At the same time Pius IX encouraged the parish clergy to turn to him for help against their bishops' arbitrariness.

Suddenly the politically shorn Pius was the magnet for a host of new forces. He championed the conservatives who hated political liberalism, tied the bishops to him by the favor of his appointment and allied himself with the parish

understanding of modern developments and their foundations, it only served to polarize liberal and conservative elements within the church.

In his conclusion to the Syllabus, *Pius IX refuted the notion that "the Roman Pontiff can, and ought to, reconcile himself and come to terms with progress, liberalism and modern civilization." Many would thus consider it the "charter" of conservative ultramontanism.*

. . . .

Modernism

Modernism describes an attempt by some early twentieth-century thinkers to bring Catholic teachings more into line with contemporary science, history, philosophy and Protestant biblical scholarship. Some of them altered Catholic doctrine to make it more acceptable to modern men and women. Pope Pius X condemned these errors in his decree, Lamentabili, *and in his encyclical,* Pascendi *(both on September 8, 1907). Modernism's most extreme form questioned the divinity of Jesus, saw the church in purely sociological terms, viewed Scripture as just literature and held that doctrine must change to suit the times.*

. . . .

clergy (and in turn their parishioners). His audiences endeared him to thousands of pilgrims who went home with the good news that they had actually seen—maybe even met and touched—the pope.

Pius IX made the papacy an international spiritual force in a way no pope had ever done before. He became a single ruling figure, a holy and international force around whom the world's Catholics could focus their allegiance. In the very death of the old order, the pope led a movement of faith. One might call it a "triumphalism for the millions."

This papal role is so familiar to us we forget it was not always this way. In fact we owe this role to Pius IX's thirty-two years of shaping the posture of the papacy in this manner.

Vatican I and Papal Infallibility

In 1867 the Papal States were gone. Pius still had Rome, thanks to the French. International papalism was on the rise. Pius decided to call the First Vatican Council. It would celebrate the eighteen-hundredth anniversary of the martyrdoms of Peter and Paul. Pius intended to rally the church against the liberal rationalism of the nineteenth century just as Trent stood against the Protestantism of the sixteenth century.

Seven hundred bishops gathered for the opening of the Council on the Feast of the Immaculate Conception, 1869. The bishops planned to study the nature of the church, the roles of bishops and pope. As things turned out, the issue of papal infallibility quickly engulfed the Council Fathers. About 80 percent of the bishops favored making papal infallibility a dogma. The opposing 20 percent came from dioceses in Austria, Hungary, France and the United States.

The liberal bishops argued that the trend of history was on the side of freedom and that this doctrine would make the church look too authoritarian. Conservatives countered that this new freedom constituted a grave danger to the church's existence. Liberals worried that papal infallibility would give too much power to the pope and not enough to the bishops. Conservatives replied that it would temper the excessive independence of bishops, such as had occurred in France.

Despite the polarization, most bishops were of a moderate disposition. They sought a middle-ground solution. This was especially true of the Italian bishops, who made up a third of the assembly. They had not participated in putting infallibility on the agenda. But Pius IX backed the conservative intransigents. As the Council moved to a vote on the matter and it became clear that infallibility would pass, sixty bishops went home rather than go on record against it. On July 18, 1870, 535 bishops approved the doctrine. The weather report for that day indicates a violent thunderstorm swept the Vatican.

By the end of summer the Franco-Prussian War began. Vatican I recessed, never to open again. France pulled its troops out of Rome. The soldiers of the United Italy moved in. Pius retreated to the Vatican property and became the "Prisoner of the Vatican." Not until Vatican II was Vatican I's unfinished business about the church and the bishops taken up. It may have been just as well. The mood of Vatican I did not seem to be one of readiness to speak of the church as the "People of God" or to take up the issue of the

Papal Infallibility
The majority of bishops at Vatican I (1869-1870) wanted a solemn proclamation that the pope, when he taught ex cathedra *(literally, "from the chair") on matters of faith and morals, was infallible due to the special grace of his office as the successor of Saint Peter. Henry Edward Cardinal Manning, Archbishop of Westminster in London, was the leader and articulate spokesman for this move.*

A number of bishops, however, believed that the time was not right for such a declaration. Most of them were not opposed to the teaching, but just to the wisdom of promulgating it then.

Even the great Father John Henry Newman of England, later a cardinal, held this position.

Nevertheless, the doctrine of papal infallibility was approved and proclaimed in Pastor Aeternus *on July 18, 1870. The several bishops who voted against it later submitted to the teaching. Vatican II clarified the bishops' role in defining infallible teachings in collegial communion with the pope.*

bishops' collegial relationship to the pope, let alone matters of religious freedom and ecumenical dialogue.

Pius IX died in 1878. He left behind him a church in siege as far as society was concerned: withdrawn, fearful, uninvolved. At the same time, life inside the church was vibrant. Hundreds of thousands of men and women packed the convents and monasteries. New hospitals, schools and missions sprang up all over the world. Mass attendance percentages were probably the highest in history and the devotional life of the church never had it so good. Catholicism became a world force to be reckoned with. The question was how anyone could open a dialogue. Ninety-two years later, John XXIII had an answer.

LOOKING BACK

. . . .

Liberalism

The eighteenth-century Enlightenment, the French Revolution of 1789 and the bloodbaths of the Napoleonic wars devastated the Catholic church, especially in France and its environs. Rationalist radicals oversaw the emptying of all the monasteries, the slaughter of priests and nuns, the pillaging of churches. Napoleon humiliated the pope and made puppets out of the bishops. People questioned the very existence of the church.

In 1815, only twenty-five years after the French Revolution, an astonishing turnabout took place. Thousands of new recruits flocked to the monasteries and seminaries. Missionary orders suddenly flourished again. Intellectuals reevaluated the thinking of the Enlightenment and declared it was not as impressive as it first seemed.

New thinkers judged the Enlightenment's view of human nature too shallow. They repudiated its mechanized vision of nature and renounced its dogma of progress. Was the "reign of terror" progress? Were the Napoleonic wars that drained the blood of Europe's youth progress? Some progress! The new thinkers sought once again the values of faith, mystery, reverence and regard for tradition.

Nevertheless, disenchantment with liberalism was not outright divorce. Many tenets of liberalism clearly were here to stay: The liberal agenda called for democratic government and the elimination of church control of marriage and education. Reaction to the violent results of liberal philosophy meant that liberals would lie low but not disappear.

Between 1815 and 1830 Europe was in no mood for liberalism or any of its revolutions. Kings returned to their thrones with self-confidence, supported by the conservative backlash. The church, accustomed to its traditional partnership of "throne and altar," was content.

Lammenais's Challenge

In 1831, new stirrings of liberalism were noted, this time inside the church. A brilliant priest named Lammenais became the founder of Catholic liberalism. Together with the eloquent preacher Lacordaire and the scholarly historian Montalembert, he fought for the acceptance of liberal concepts within the church.

His fundamental premise was that church and state should be separated. He counseled the church to examine more carefully the trends of history. He was convinced, correctly, that monarchies were dying. The church should cut its ties with moribund forms of government and back the democratic wave of the future. At the same time, Lammenais advocated the concept of a strong papacy.

He believed in freedom of education and freedom of the press: One must trust in the power of truth to overcome error. And fifty years ahead of his time, he preached the right of every human being to have a vote. One should trust in the common sense of the people and their reserve of popular wisdom. Said he, "Let us not tremble before liberalism. Let us Catholicize it."

He could hardly have preached a more unpopular message. By no standards of the time was the church ready for liberalism—even a Catholic one. The bishops preferred to tremble. They pointed out to him that such a plan would impoverish the church overnight. Lammenais thought that was a splendid idea. At last the church would be identified with the majority of humanity that was in fact poor, as well as with the Christ of Bethlehem and Calvary. He did not move them. Even the secular liberals repudiated him, especially his concept of universal suffrage. In 1831 they were not about to give the vote to the "ragged masses"—or to women.

Lammenais felt there was only one place to turn. Had he not supported the concept of a strong papacy? Surely the pope would listen to him. He misread Gregory XVI, the closed-minded authoritarian predecessor to Pius IX. Gregory probably felt he was, in fact, sufficiently strong. What more power did the papacy need? The papacy had survived the insulting behavior of Napoleon and lived to bury him.

But Lammenais and his two friends, Montalembert and Lacordaire, thought they could change Gregory's mind. They wrote a memorandum explaining their views and set out for Rome as "pilgrims for God and liberty." They gave the pope their memorandum on December 30, 1831. They waited for his reply. And waited...and waited. No answer. Disillusioned, they returned to France. The pope waited six months to give them his answer: a thundering no! His encyclical *Mirari Vos* totally rejected their plan.

Lammenais was crushed. Still, he spent a year trying to gain some concessions. In a series of letters with the Vatican he hoped to pry open some corner where a dialogue could begin. The pope would not listen; he demanded obedience. Lammenais despaired when the pope supported the Orthodox Russian Czar's suppression of Catholic Poland's rebellion. Bitter and exasperated, Lammenais left the church which had "divorced itself from Christ to fornicate with his torturers."

Why wouldn't the pope bend a little? Why was the church of the 1830s—and throughout most of the nineteenth century—so intransigent about liberalism? Perhaps a comparison with the twentieth-century church's attitude toward communism may help.

The Russian communist revolution was blatantly atheistic and overtly anti-church, not only in theory, but in practice. Communists used police-state methods to intimidate and destroy religion, however unsuccessfully. Pius XI and Pius XII were outspoken enemies of communism because of this atheism and hostility to religion. In the 1830's secularistic liberalism had attempted to destroy the church in much the same way, provoking the same reaction. Pope Gregory XVI raged against the liberalism of the French rationalist revolution for much the same reason that Pius XII would fume about the radicalism of the Russian communist revolution. Lammenais did not have a chance of being heard.

By extension, Gustavo Guttierrez, today's Latin American advocate of liberation theology which "Catholicizes" Marxism, would have had no hearing from Pius XI or Pius XII; neither did John Paul II enthusiastically endorse this approach. At the same time many of the liberal ideas advocated by Lammenais are now, a century later, accepted by the church. If history repeats itself, some of us may live to see elements of Marxism accepted by the church of the twenty-first century.

The story of Pius IX shows that Lammenais would have been no more successful with him. The events leading up to the election of Pius in 1846 reveal an uncompromising attitude within the church toward liberalism, whether of the secular kind or Lammenais' Catholic version. To their credit, liberals did not lie down and die. They stayed and fought, inside and outside the church. They have lived to see the church accept much of their agenda, modified by time and reflection and adapted to continuity with church tradition.

CONNECTING   TO   OUR   TIMES

. . . .

Today's Liberal Agenda

Liberalism means different things at different times. In this chapter we saw that nineteenth century liberalism in continental Europe had this agenda: (1) Get rid of kings and install democracies; (2) Call for separation of church and state; (3) Promote freedom of the press and free speech; (4) Remove the church's control of education and marriage. Churches could still have private schools and their own internal rules about marriage. That agenda eventually prevailed, as one can see in the nations of Europe and North America.

Liberalism today maintains vigilance over the agenda mentioned above. What are some of its new goals, especially in the United States? (1) Extend democracy to the developing nations. (2) Lobby for the empowerment of women. (3) Promote multiculturalism. (4) Advance the rights of such minorities as blacks, Hispanics and Native Americans. (5) Awaken nations to the importance of environmental concerns. (6) Increase the role of the courts in achieving social goals. (This is called judicial activism.)

Within the church, liberals call for decentralizing authority, shifting it from the Vatican to local churches. They advocate specific causes such as married clergy, women's ordination (despite Pope John Paul's letter denying its possibility), reinstatement of resigned married clergy and acceptance of artificial contraception as morally correct behavior. They also stress social justice causes.

The result is a division within our church today between liberals and conservatives. Father Avery Dulles, S.J., distinguished the extreme versions of these divisions (paleoconservatives and radical liberals) from more moderate forms of liberals and conservatives. He correctly believed that cooperation and mutual understanding is possible and desirable between the moderates of both persuasions. Civilized discussion and prayerful openness at this level can work. Responsiveness to the church tradition is necessary for all. Staying with the extremes only results in revolt and schism.

FOR REFLECTION AND DISCUSSION

. . . .

1. Respond to the following "forced choice" opinion sample. Discuss your answers:

   • Most Catholics are bothered by papal infallibility.
     Agree___ Disagree___

   • Most Catholics do not understand the limits of papal infallibility
     Agree___ Disagree___

   • It was unwise of Pius IX to encourage worldwide personal devotion to the pope, because this diminishes local loyalty to the bishop.
     Agree___ Disagree___

- Pius IX was right in rejecting Cavour's proposal about the Papal States and accompanying concessions. Pius XI should have similarly rejected Mussolini's proposal in 1929.

    Agree___ Disagree___

- It would not make much difference to us if the pope were still the ruler of the Papal States.

    Agree___ Disagree___

- Lammenais should have swallowed his pride, accepted defeat and stayed in the church.

    Agree___ Disagree___

- Just as the church finally accepted many of the liberal premises, so one day in the future the church will accept many Marxist premises.

    Agree___ Disagree___

- The study of the context of history excuses the decisions of people whom we think were wrong by our standards.

    Agree___ Disagree___

CHAPTER TWENTY-SIX

THE CHURCH'S SOCIAL TEACHINGS

> Once we begin not to
> worry about what kind
> of house we are living
> in, what kind of clothes
> we are wearing, once
> we give up the stupid
> recreation of the
> world; we have time—
> which is priceless—
> to remember that we
> are our brother's
> keepers and that we
> must not only care for
> his needs as far as we
> are immediately able,
> but we must try to
> build a better world.
> —Dorothy Day

Dorothy Day's challenging mission to assume the mantle of biblical prophets has raised her to the status of an icon in the modern church and may even lead one day to her canonization. She embraced a double ministry that moved her to address the symptoms of injustice as well as its structural causes. She lived with the poor and shared their lives while helping them with food, clothing and shelter. But at the same time, she was an ardent advocate for the poor with politicians and government, religious and cultural leaders to get them to eliminate laws and customs that hurt the poor and replace them with laws that are just. Her life's work took place within the centuries-old life of God's people from both the Old and New Testaments and the history of the church as well. This broad perspective is briefly reviewed here.

From the earliest times of salvation history there was a concern for the poor, the widows, orphans and strangers. God always called his people to a practical application of his command, "You shall love your neighbor as yourself" (Leviticus 19:18). The biblical prophets constantly challenged their people to develop a social concern for those in need. Amos and other prophets warned people against confining their religion to worship without applying its message and meaning to healing social ills. "If you would offer me holocausts, then let justice surge like water and goodness like an unfailing stream" (Amos 5:24).

One of the most memorable and powerful messages of Christ links salvation to practical love for the hungry, the thirsty, the naked, the sick, the prisoner and the stranger. He said that when he comes in glory, he will sit upon his throne and all the nations of the world will be gathered before him. Those who will be saved will told that they will inherit the kingdom God because they fed Christ, clothed him, cared for him when he was sick, visited him in jail and welcomed him when he was a stranger. "Whatever you did for one of these least brothers of mine, you did for me" (Matthew 25:40). The needy and oppressed of the world are Christ in disguise. One of the principles governing the people of faith is this: the universal destination of the goods of the earth. What God has given us is meant for the good of all and not just the favored few.

Throughout the history of the church various ways were developed to minister to human needs, especially those of the poor, widows, orphans, strangers and oppressed. Monasteries and parish churches provided food, clothing, medicine and shelter for the poor and homeless. Saint Francis founded an order to serve the poor. As the populations expanded in the seventeenth century, people like Saint Vincent de Paul and Saint Louise de Marillac founded religious congregations who devoted themselves to the well being and education of the poor.

However in the nineteenth century the Industrial Revolution created a new class of poverty. Thousands of people left the farms to work in the new factories. They crowded into cities, worked more than twelve hours a day for very low pay in unhealthy, dangerous conditions. Often their children were sent to work

*The Catholic
Worker Movement*
*Peter Maurin, the soul
of the Catholic
Worker movement,
was born to a farming
family in France in
1877. Though active
in his own country's
lay Catholic
movement, he
emigrated to the
United States in 1909
and worked as a
homesteader, teacher
and laborer. With
Dorothy Day, Peter
Maurin not only
founded* The Catholic
Worker, *but also
sparked a movement
based on nonviolent
social action and
human dignity. He
sought to create "a
new society within the
shell of the old."*

in these situations, deprived of education and mercilessly forced to do mind numbing tasks for tiny wages. Thousands of others went to the coal mines to slave away in even more desperate and dangerous underpaid work. Miserable living conditions, disease and early deaths were commonplace.

At first there were no unions to bargain for better salaries. There were no insurance plans for retirement. Governments paid little attention to the glaring injustices whose depths are only alluded to here. Gradually, the outcry for social reform began to be heard. Among these voices in the church was Pope Leo XIII who wrote an encyclical (*Rerum Novarum* [On the Condition of Labor]) in 1891 that initiated a vigorous tradition of social teachings. He called for the protection of the weak and the poor through the pursuit of justice. He affirmed the dignity of work, the right to private property and the right to form professional associations to lobby and negotiate for justice.

Private charity was always encouraged and good for both the recipient and the giver, but it was not sufficient to deal with the complex problems introduced by an industrialized economy that required a greater role for governments. Pope Leo wrote that the governments should have particular solicitude for the poor since the wealthy can take care of themselves: "For the nation of the rich is guarded by its own defenses and is in less need of government protection, whereas the suffering multitude without the means to protect itself, relies especially on the protection of the State" (#54).

Yet in the twentieth century, hunger and poverty in prosperous nations still existed especially during the Great Depression of the 1930s. In Europe this social discontent fostered the rise of dictators in Germany and Italy as had already happened in the triumph of communism in Russia. In the United States, nearly 25 percent of the workforce had no jobs. Hunger and poverty was widespread.

On the fortieth anniversary of Pope Leo's encyclical, Pope Pius XI wrote *Quadragesimo Anno* (After Forty Years) in 1931. He addressed the alarming concentration of wealth and power in rich nations and stressed the need for a principle of subsidiarity in which power and responsibility is shared at all levels of society. "Just as it is gravely wrong to take from individuals what they can accomplish by their own initiative and industry and give it to the community, so also it is an injustice...to assign to a greater and higher association what lesser and subordinate associations can do" (79).

While the prosperous nations recovered from the Great Depression and World War II, many of their citizens remained poor and some suffered from lack of proper education and malnutrition. A far greater gap existed between the rich countries and the developing ones. Pope John XXIII addressed this concern in his encyclical *Mater et Magistra* (Mother and Teacher), in 1961.

He wrote that the most pressing justice issue concerns the relationships between the economically advanced countries and those in the process of development. Nations that enjoy an abundance of everything may not overlook the plight of countries whose citizens are plagued with poverty and hunger.

Peter Maurin's program of action, voiced by Dorothy Day, focused upon reaching the people in the street with the social teachings of the church; reaching the masses through acts of voluntary poverty; building up a community of committed laypersons through roundtable discussions for "clarification of thought"; founding Houses of Hospitality where works of mercy would be practiced; establishing farming communes in an attempt to cure unemployment. Though he died in 1947, Peter Maurin's prophetic voice and spirit continue to guide the Catholic Worker Movement.

Pope John called for solidarity between the rich countries and the developing ones. He said:

> The solidarity that binds all people together as members of a common family makes it impossible for wealthy nations to look with indifference upon the hunger, misery and poverty of other nations who are unable to enjoy even elementary human rights. The nations of the world are becoming more dependent on one another and it will not be possible to preserve a lasting peace so long as glaring economic and social imbalances persist. (157)

Pope John also is remembered for his wise comment that there is no peace without justice.

Many other teachings on the need for justice and peace flowed from the pens of popes, bishops and lay leaders throughout the Catholic world. Their themes included the need for the church to understand its role as a servant to international needs. More attention was given to the needs of the developing countries. The Synod of Bishops in 1971 said that the pursuit of justice and peace was essential to the mission of the church.

Pope John Paul II wrote several encyclicals that reflected on the social and moral issues facing the church and the world, among which was his *Sollicitudo Rei Socialis* ("On Social Concern") in 1987. Throughout his papacy he upheld the dignity of every human person and the call for solidarity with all brothers and sisters on earth. This means that we commit ourselves to the common good of everyone. He was as strong as anyone in his attention to the poor. "A consistent theme of Catholic social teaching is the preferential option for the poor. Today this preference has to be expressed in worldwide terms, embracing the immense numbers of the hungry, the needy, the homeless, those without medical care, and those without hope" (42).

The passionate plea of Isaiah still resonates today:

> Trample my courts no more;
> bringing offerings is futile;
> incense is an abomination to me.
> …
> even though you make many prayers,
> I will not listen.
> your hands are full of blood.
> Wash yourselves; make yourselves clean;
> …
> cease to do evil,
> learn to do good;
> seek justice,
> rescue the oppressed,
> defend the orphan,
> plead for the widow.
> —Isaiah 1:12, 15–16

It was Dorothy Day who listened most closely to this call.[1]

FOR REFLECTION AND DISCUSSION

· ·

1. Dorothy Day was considered a radical. She took a stand and refused to back down. Is it possible to go against the tide and still keep one's faith? Can a person demonstrate against the government and still be a member in good standing in the church? What are the necessary ingredients to successful protest?
2. Even with the separation of church and state do the two sometimes seem intertwined? Are people's religious convictions brought out into the open? Is this more true of Catholics? Does the "public" expect more from Catholics? Why or why not?
3. Because something is legal, does that make it good? Are there some laws of the land which are contrary to the laws of God? Which ones? What is the difference between the law and the spirit of the law?

4. Consider specific teachings the church has concerning such things as:
   - The worker
   - A just wage
   - Working conditions
   - Civil disobedience
   - Bigotry
   - Racism

5. In your own town or city there must be many leaders in the fight for equal rights. Equal rights affects all of us. No one group or minority should be treated in a lesser way. Dorothy Day took a stand for the worker, Cesar Chavez of the United Farm Workers for the migrant worker, Jimmy Carter supports the poor in his work with Habitat for Humanity. Can you think of local persons who have made a difference?

6. How does the Catholic church measure up in the struggles for equality for all Americans? What programs in the church help? Is it the responsibility of all of us?

7. Throughout her life, Dorothy Day enthusiastically broke unjust federal laws. One time an IRS auditor met with her concerning delinquent tax payments. After some small talk she replied, "You figure out how much I owe you and I won't pay it. How's that?" Are there limits to civil disobedience?

CHAPTER TWENTY-SEVEN

. . . .

SOME LITERARY CONVERTS

> [T]he real purpose of asceticism is not cutting off one's relation to created things and other people, but normalizing and healing it. The contemplative life...is simply the restoration of man, in Christ, to the state in which he was originally intended to live.
>
> —Thomas Merton

. . . .

Thomas Merton ranks with a number of twentieth-century literary converts to the Catholic church whose writings conveyed a Catholic mindset through their poetry, novels and essays. Writers in the United Kingdom and the United States sometimes tended to be defenders of the faith to the Protestant ruling class, while in other cases they attacked the moral deficiencies of politics and culture and the errors of secularists. Several of them were closely linked to lifelong Catholic authors whose friendships enriched each other and will be mentioned in passing. No attempt is made here to be comprehensive, but rather to select several literary converts whose influence benefited the church much as Merton does today.

Thomas Merton

Thomas Merton belonged to the Trappists—the Order of Cistercians of the Strict Observance (O.C.S.O.). This expression of monasticism has its origins in the seventeenth century and was centered at the Abbey of la Trappe (hence the name) in France. This reform aimed to recover the austerity of the earlier Cistercians and their interpretation of Saint Benedict's Rule. La Trappe emphasized renewal in monastic enclosure, silence and manual labor, expressing a spirit of apartness from the world and dedication to prayer and penance.

The reform movement spread and was adopted by the Cistercian community of Melleray in Western France. That foundation's continued

G.K. Chesterton (1874–1936)

At the beginning of the twentieth century emerged a budding young literary genius, Gilbert Keith Chesterton, often fondly called "G.K." by his thousands of admirers and even his detractors. Early on he showed a talent for drawing and studied at the Slade School of Art and his first successes were as an illustrator. He married Frances Blogg in 1901. He claims to have been a pagan at the age of twelve and an agnostic teen, but Frances persuaded him to become an Anglican.

Eventually he found himself attracted to Catholicism and was received into the church in 1922 by a Father John O'Connor who became the model for Father Brown in Chesterton's detective stories. Around that time he became friends with Hilaire Belloc, a cradle Catholic who grew up to be a fierce advocate for Catholicism and wrote in a militant style that attracted, informed and consoled Catholics in need of ways to respond to their critics.

A tall man, G.K. became as round as Santa Claus and just as endearing and he draped himself in a full-length Edwardian cape that made him seem like the *HMS Victory* in full sail. Besides hundreds of columns and essays he wrote poems, one of which celebrated the Battle of Lepanto in which the Christian navy defeated the Turkish Armada. He filled the lines with martial rhythms to match the encounter. His two best-known and influential books are *Orthodoxy* and *The Everlasting Man*, both of which are creative explanations of Christian teachings and sometimes spectacular assaults on the emerging secularism of his times.

He used humor and an extraordinary ability with paradoxes to rebut the error of his opponents as when he said, "The whole modern world has divided itself into Conservatives and Progressives. The business of Progressives is to go one making mistakes. The business of the Conservatives is to prevent the mistakes from being corrected." In commenting on free thought, he wrote:

> Neither modern science nor ancient religion believes in completely free thought. Theology rebukes certain thoughts by calling them blasphemous. Science rebukes certain thoughts by calling them morbid. For example, some religious societies discouraged men more or less from thinking about sex. The new scientific society definitely discourages men from thinking about death: it is a fact, but it is considered a morbid fact.[1]

The closest he came to writing devotional works were his biographies of Saint Francis of Assisi and Saint Thomas Aquinas. In each case he unfurled the exuberance of these medieval saints such as his vignette of Aquinas brooding at a meal and suddenly straightening up and pounding the table and saying, "That settles the Manichees!"

C.S. Lewis (1898–1963)

Chesterton's *The Everlasting Man* influenced C.S. Lewis to become a Christian. Lewis converted to Anglican Church and became one of the greatest defenders of Christianity in modern times. He was born in Ulster in Northern Ireland to a strong Protestant family. His mother died when he was a young boy. His distress at her loss and the distant attitude of his father led him to

growth made the establishment of a new community necessary. Friendship with the aged American Bishop Flaget of Bardstown drew them to Kentucky. On December 21, 1848, forty-five men from Melleray founded the Abbey of Gethsemani, which Thomas Merton entered in 1941.

Trappists say of themselves: "This search for God is the goal of our monastic day, a day composed of the opus Dei, lectio divina and manual work. Our Cistercian life is simple and austere, truly poor and penitential in the joy of the Holy Spirit. Through the warmth of their welcome and hospitality our communities share the fruit of their contemplation and their work with others."

· · · · · · · · · · · · ·

Religious Life

"The teaching and example of Christ provide the foundation for the evangelical counsels of chaste self-dedication to God, of poverty and obedience. The Apostles and Fathers of the church commend them as an ideal of life. They constitute a gift of God which the church has received from her Lord and which by his grace she always safeguards....

withdraw from religion. After a few years in English boarding schools, he became an atheist, remaining that way during his student years at Oxford and his early years as a brilliant literature professor at Magdalen College.

Fortunately, he became friends with an ardent Catholic professor, J.R.R. Tolkien and other faith-oriented dons. They met weekly at a pub to read their writings to each other and discuss them. They called themselves *the inklings* probably because their fingers were smudged by their ink-filled pens. Tolkien seems to have been the strongest influence on his becoming a believing Christian. Both men wrote fantasy literature that cloaked Christian themes with fabulous characters and imaginary worlds. Tolkien wrote the *Lord of the Rings* trilogy and Lewis composed the tales of Narnia, stories still being read and even seen in the movies.

Lewis's most popular book is *Mere Christianity*, a lucid explanation of Christian teachings written in everyday language that stirred countless people to a life of faith. The book was based on a series of short radio talks commissioned by the BBC during World War II with the intention of lifting up the hearts of the British people during the bombings of their cities. Lewis also ventured into more spiritual matters in his meditation on his feelings after the death of his wife in *A Grief Observed* and his thoughts on prayer in *Letters to Malcolm* and *Reflections on the Psalms*. Though Lewis never became a Catholic, his high-church Anglican faith and orthodox writings perennially appeal to Catholics.

Robert Hugh Benson (1871–1914)

Another literary convert was Robert Hugh Benson praised in his own day as a leading figure in English literature, yet almost completely forgotten these days. Born to prominence as the youngest son of the Anglican Archbishop of Canterbury, he felt drawn to Catholicism early on. He joined the church in 1903 and became a priest several years later. Like his contemporary, G.K., he was an ardent writer on behalf of Catholicism, most notably in his historical novel *Come Rack, Come Rope.*

Biographer Joseph Pearce writes of this book that, "It leaps from the page with historical realism. The reader is transported to the time of persecution in England when priests were put to a slow, torturous death. The terror and tension of the tale describes the leading characters who courageously witness their faith." Benson was a best-selling author of fifteen novels and dozens of articles and sermons. He was more like a meteor than a star, shining briefly until blazing out in an untimely death in 1914.

The aggressive writing style of Chesterton, Belloc, Benson and C.S. Lewis belonged to the popular and acceptable debating techniques honed at the Oxford Union and still able to be witnessed in the Prime Minister's *Question Period* shown weekly in the United States on C-Span. Only Chesterton and Lewis seem to have become enduring Christian classics read eagerly today by a wide audience. The attack mode of Belloc and Benson has given way to an ecumenical mood that dwells on what unites rather than divides us from other Christians.

"From the God-given seed of the Councils a wonderful and wide-spreading tree has grown up in the field of the Lord, branching out into various forms of religious life lived in solitude or in community.... This sacred Council gives its support and praise to men and women, brothers and sisters, who in monasteries or in schools and hospitals or in missions adorn the Bride of Christ by the steadfast and humble fidelity of their consecrated lives and give generous service of the most varied kinds." (Constitution on the Church, 43, 46)

Walker Percy (1916–1990)

In the United States, the southern writer Walker Percy distinguished himself as a novelist. A descendant of a long line of southern gentry, his early life was marked by tragedies in which his father and grandfather committed suicide and his mother died when she accidentally drove her car into a river and drowned. An uncle raised him. Percy majored in chemistry at the University of North Carolina, Chapel Hill, and later graduated as a doctor from Columbia University medical school.

During his internship he contracted tuberculosis and recovered while at a sanitarium in upper New York State. Back home he wondered what to do. The life of a doctor had lost its appeal. Instead he decided to be a writer. He moved to Louisiana and, with his wife, he joined the Catholic church. At the sanitarium he had immersed himself in reading modern philosophy and the Russian novelists Tolstoy and Dostoevsky. He became convinced that Christianity had a better understanding of human nature than science and relativism.

Success took a while. After writing two unpublished novels, his third one was the charm. Titled *The Moviegoer*, it is the story of a stockbroker who wakes up one morning with the inner drive to become a searcher, though it is never clear what he is looking for. The people in the story are so ungrounded in their lives that they only feel real when they see something from their lives shown on a movie screen. His book won the National Book Award and has been selling ever since. In his acceptance speech he said that his book is a restatement of the Judeo-Christian notion that I am more than a blob in the universe, or even a well put together, mature person. I am a wayfarer and a pilgrim.

Percy illustrated this truth again in two comic, satirical novels, *Love Among the Ruins* and *The Thanatos Syndrome*. The pilgrim in each story is Dr. Thomas More, a small town unambitious psychiatrist who says, "I believe in God and the whole business, but I love women best, music and science next, whisky next and God fourth, and my fellow man hardly at all."

Through his novels, Percy criticized the shallowness of modern life where we amuse ourselves to death and scientists diagnose our ills in purely physical terms and social planners solve human problems by eliminating human beings. Percy tells us something has gone wrong with us. The cure begins by rediscovering who we are and why we were put here.

Like other good storytellers such as Flannery O'Connor, Percy uses a story to comment on the human condition and lead us to return to basics found in God's plan for human happiness and destiny.[2]

Other literary converts include Evelyn Waugh whose novel *Brideshead Revisited*, became a made-for-TV *Masterpiece Theater* series and, most recently (2008), a motion picture. It chronicles the decline of faith and morals in a superficially observant Catholic aristocratic family. Another example is Graham Greene, a hugely successful novelist who, after his conversion, wrote a few novels that had Catholic themes, such as *The Power and the Glory* about the injustices done to Catholics in the Mexican revolution. He eventually abandoned Catholic based stories, claiming, "I am not a Catholic novelist. I happen to be a Catholic who writes novels."

Thomas Merton's fellowship with these literary converts is slight. His most powerful writing began with his autobiography *The Seven Storey Mountain* and several spirituality books such as *New Seeds of Contemplation*. He also composed some religious poetry, especially in his slim volume, *The Tears of the Blind Lions*. His enormous output of letters, as well as books of essays against racism and for pacifism, won him a reputation as a perceptive social critic, similar to Chesterton and Percy, though not with G.K.'s playful language nor with the comic touch of Walker Percy's novels. His legacy, however, is influential and his spiritual and moral presence is widely felt today.

FOR REFLECTION AND DISCUSSION

. . . .

1. In his many writings on social activism, war and peace, Eastern and Western mysticism, Merton struggled with the reality of censorship. Is there a value to or need for censorship today?

2. Is there a lesson to be learned from Merton's acceptance of censorship even when he did not agree with the reasons for it?

3. Supposedly living apart from the world and its concerns, how do you think Merton was able to sensitize himself to speak out for the civil rights movement and against the Vietnam War? Why was he so respected in his lifetime? Why is he so respected today?

4. Have you learned something from another religion which served to strengthen your Christian faith?

5. How has literature informed your faith? What book has had the greatest impact on your life?

. . . .

CHAPTER TWENTY-EIGHT

NEW MOVEMENTS

> May God grant that
> all…participate even
> every day…in the
> divine sacrifice…
> receiving the body of
> Jesus Christ which has
> been offered for all to
> the eternal Father.
>
> —Pope Pius XII

. . . .

THE STATE OF THE CHURCH ON THE EVE OF VATICAN II: AN ANALYSIS
(1870–1962)

On October 11, 1962, an old stream bubbled its last as a new fountain of church life burst forth with the opening of Vatican II. For ninety-two years, Vatican I had cast a long shadow over the history of the church. Yet within its protective arms, new movements in liturgy, Scripture and ecumenism blossomed. We shall see how these three aspects of renewal fared on the eve of Vatican II. But we shall begin with a remembrance of things past: the devotional life of the Vatican I church.

Stations and Rosaries: The Devotional Church

Deprived of direct access to the Mass because it was in Latin and because the priest seemed so much in charge of it, Catholics developed a "people's religion." The Franciscans gave them the Stations of the Cross and the Christmas crib. The Dominicans countered with the rosary. Catholics fed on the cult of

253

the saints, the warmth of the Sacred Heart, the thrill of pilgrimages and the miracles at Lourdes. They showed enthusiasm for eucharistic processions, novenas, blessed medals, scapulars, holy water, relics, tuneful hymns, flowery personal prayers and similar forms of popular piety.

Many of these practices began in the Middle Ages; virtually all of them predated Vatican I. For the most part they were alive and well on the eve of Vatican II. Not everyone approved of this popular religion. Its critics judged the music too sentimental, the art tasteless and the emphasis on feeling vulgar. They hinted that such practices were barely a step away from superstition and deplored the excessive attention on Mary and the saints, claiming this diverted people from the proper attention to Christ.

The critics had a point, even if their judgments seemed snobbish at times and displayed too casual a judgment on the faith of the "people's religion." Vatican II heard the critics' complaints and did something. The Fathers put the liturgy in the vernacular and invited the laity to be active participants. Architects began to design spare, austere churches shorn of all those friendly statues and vigil lights. And when it was time to redecorate the old churches, a new, stripped-down look emerged.

Did popular religion die on the eve of the Council? Not quite. Millions of people a year still go as pilgrims to Lourdes, Rome and Jerusalem. Biblical rosaries and updated Stations hold their own. New books of saints are proving to be popular. And the music—ah, the music! While Catholics have begun to sing Protestant hymns of four hundred years' standing, they are also singing new songs, many of which are as sentimental as the old devotional ones.

Should popular religion die? Of course not. The liturgy has taken its proper place in the life of the church, but there is plenty of room for spontaneous, popular piety. Charismatic renewal, Marriage Encounter and small group sharing appear to be current forms of "people's religion."

LOOKING BACK

. . . .

The Liturgical Reform

In the beginning liturgies were celebrated at home. House Eucharists were the norm for over three centuries, until the move to basilicas in the fourth century (see chapter five).

In the Western church, the evangelization of the invading barbarians—non-Roman, non-Latin-speaking people—led to a situation where the majority of the new parishioners could not speak the language of the Mass. So the people watched and the priest did Eucharist. Then the people watched a little less and started doing things on their own. Celts developed penance prayers to keep themselves occupied. Gauls created prayers of affection to pass the time at Eucharist.

Sitting in silence, cut off from the altar and each other, the worshipers lost a sense of community at Mass. The "we" of community gave way to the "I" of personal devotion. The Protestants understood what was wrong and introduced vernacular liturgies and hymns that everyone could sing. Who knows but what the Council Fathers at Trent did look wistfully at the Protestants, but could not bring themselves to imitate them because that was tantamount to admitting their revolt was legitimate. What could one say then about their heretical teachings?

Trent reformed the liturgy by disciplining the priests to follow exact rubrics in a mechanical fashion. Trent put dignity into a liturgy that had grown sloppy. They froze an archaic form of worship that had stateliness and tradition going for it, but left no room for the pulse of the people.

Not until the nineteenth century did the seeds of liturgical reform really start growing. German researchers at Tübingen published studies about early church worship, showing it was a community affair that appreciated the liturgy's mysterious character. They remarked how the church

Popular Piety

"The religious sense of the Christian people has always found expression in various forms of piety surrounding the church's sacramental life, such as the veneration of relics, visits to sanctuaries, pilgrimages, processions, the Stations of the Cross, religious dances, the rosary, medals, etc.

"These expressions of piety extend the liturgical life of the Church, but do not replace it. They should be 'so drawn up that they harmonize with the liturgical seasons, accord with the sacred liturgy, are in some way derived from it and lead the people to it, since in fact the liturgy is by its very nature superior to any of them.'" (Catechism of the Catholic Church, #1674–1675)

255

Fathers insisted that the Body of Christ (Eucharist) builds up the body of Christ (church).

Benedictine monks at Germany's Maria Laach produced studies about Lent and Holy Week. There Dom Odo Casel developed the rites for the Easter Vigil that we substantially follow today. The French Benedictines at Solesmes rescued Gregorian chant from the archives and made it available—in Latin, of course—for popular usage. Benedictine Abbot Marmion wrote books that showed how one could have a spirituality based on Christ as its center and a liturgy as its expressive outlet.

Pius X encouraged the use of Gregorian chant and called for the writing of new church music in the spirit of the liturgy. He asked all Catholics to go to Communion frequently, thus drawing their attention to a sacrament as a major source of spiritual growth. Centuries of alienation from the Mass plus the false

The Church Before Vatican II

The understanding of the church before Vatican II could be described in three words: clerical, juridical and triumphalistic. Bishop Emile De Smedt said as much in his response to the first schema on the church at Vatican II, which was rejected and rewritten. The church was hierarchical because the clergy possessed all the power and initiative. A pyramidal structure predominated, with authority descending from the pope through the bishops and priests down to the faithful. The laity played a passive role, living out the teachings of the hierarchy.

The church was juridical because it placed great stress on law and penalty. Membership and its obligations were clearly defined. One knew who was or was not a "practicing" Catholic. Church ministry was also guided by the norms of canon law.

The triumphalistic church dramatized itself as a body set against the powers of evil, whether foreign culture or foreign religion. The church saw itself as alone having the fullness of the truth and discouraged contact with other religions. These were the days of Catholic isolationism, "ghetto Catholicism." This model of church would undergo radical reassessment at Vatican II as the Council Fathers reconsidered the church's understanding of authority, freedom and purpose in history.

. . . .

attitude developed by the Jansenists (who insisted one must go to confession before every Communion to be pure enough) had dulled the Catholic sense regarding the Mass. Mass attendance was reasonably good in many countries, but participation and reception of Communion was minimal. Pius X also lowered the First Communion age from twelve or thirteen to seven or eight so that young people could become accustomed to receiving the sacrament and its benefits from an early age.

Pius XII advanced the papal teaching on liturgy in his encyclical *Mediator Dei*, stating that active participation in the liturgy is the greatest source of the Christian spirit. He urged Catholics to go to Communion at Mass.

Little by little, in tentative ways, people were being drawn into the Mass. In the late 1950s many parishes had "recited Masses" in which the people communally recited parts of the Mass together. Simple chant arrangements of the Ordinary of the Mass made it possible for full congregational participation. Hymn singing increased.

National conventions dealing with liturgical reform and renewal became commonplace. St. John's Abbey of Collegeville published *Orate Fratres* (now *Worship*) magazine. A perusal of its old issues is a blow-by-blow account of how the liturgical movement gained momentum and final victory at Vatican II. In fact, the Council's first approved document was the one on the liturgy, and it was the least debated, criticized or opposed. Over a century of preparation, scholarship and hard work by farseeing and courageous people made that possible.

Catholics Open Their Bibles
Luther's attention to the importance of the Bible placed Protestants in the tradition of biblical faith. In reaction, Catholics concentrated on the tradition of doctrine, dogma and theology. Protestants knew their Bible; Catholics knew their catechism.

In the nineteenth century the new science of archaeology forced Protestant Bible scholars to take a new look at the Bible. Archaeologists had uncovered ancient pagan libraries, stories told by people who lived at the same time as Bible people. Scholars were astonished to find these stories similar to those in the Bible.

For example, the Babylonian epic of Gilgamesh has a flood story very much like Noah's. The Code of Hammurabi bore startling similarity to the Ten

Commandments. Armed with a better command of ancient languages and a more accurate appreciation of ancient literary styles and historical sense, the new scholars brought the Bible alive in an entirely new and fascinating way.

Previously most Bible studies had begun with the assumption that it is the Word of God. Divine inspiration was the starting point. The new scholars approached Scripture from the other end, the human side. Less concerned with the divine author, they wanted to see what the human author was doing. The Bible as a human word captured their attention.

This unlocked many mysteries. Why are there two creation stories, contradictory in detail and perspective? Why is John so different from Matthew, Mark and Luke? Scholars probed the minds of the writers, reconstructed their social milieu and gave us a clearer understanding of the purposes behind the authors' approaches. Some scholars emphasized the human side at the expense of the divine part of the process. This resulted in works like Renan's *Life of Christ* (1888), in which Jesus is only a human moral teacher, not Son of God and savior.

Catholic scholars developed interest in the Protestant work. Pope Leo XIII approved the opening of a Biblical Institute in Jerusalem under the leadership of Father Joseph LaGrange, a Dominican. But the pope was cautious. "The sense of Holy Scripture can nowhere be found incorrupt outside the church. One cannot expect to find it in faithless writers who only gnaw at the bark of Scripture and never attain its marrow."

The Catholic Scripture scholars had barely

gotten started when the Modernist crisis hit the church in the first ten years of the twentieth century. "Modernists" were the "modern" version of eighteenth-century Enlightenment rationalists who denied the reality of the supernatural or of divine inspiration. They viewed the Bible not as the Word of God, but as merely a human work inspired by human ingenuity. Its miracle stories were seen as myths, not historically true. The Bible was a human book pure and simple.

Pius X worried that such theories would affect Catholic theology and Bible studies and harm the faith of the people. His condemnation of Modernism in his encyclical *Pascendi* (1907) severely curtailed Catholic scholars, who lived under the constant threat of being called heretics. They carried on nonetheless, with patience and in obscurity.

Liberation finally came in 1943 when Pius XII issued their Magna Carta, his encyclical *Divino Afflante Spiritu*. He spoke positively about the new biblical studies, and cautioned scholars to be faithful to the church's teachings and have a pastoral concern for the Catholic people. He approved the research done on literary genres and called for fresh translations of the Bible.

Catholics could open their Bibles at last. Results of the new Scripture studies are much in evidence in the documents of Vatican II. The Bible ceased to be only a Protestant book and became a book for all believers.

Ecumenism: Church Unity Movement

The church lost the Orthodox in the twelfth century and the Protestants in the sixteenth. For that

Collegiality

The first session of Vatican II convened on October 11, 1962. Through the large bronze door of St. Peter's Basilica came Pope John XXIII, carried above the delegates on the sedia gestatoria, *the throne-like chair on which the pope sits. John soon left the chair, however, to walk through the ranks of the delegates to make his opening speech. John also wore a bishop's miter instead of the usual papal tiara—another sign of the equality and communion in which he held his fellow bishops. Today this attitude is termed* collegiality.

Aggiornamento

"The substance of the ancient doctrine of the deposit of faith is one thing, and the way in which it is presented is another." With these words, Pope John XXIII expressed the need for aggiornamento *(Italian for "updating"). Pope John's vision of aggiornamento stressed that the church's duty was "not only to guard this precious treasure, as if we were concerned only with antiquity," but to respond to the modern world and be open to serve it.*

matter, Christianity broke with Judaism in the first century and never had a chance to be in significant touch with the birth and burst of Mohammedanism in the eighth century. One God and so many divisions!

The Protestants who gave us the start on our biblical renewal also inspired us in matters of ecumenism. At the World Missionary Conference in 1910 they began the modern ecumenical movement, which came to flower in the World Council of Churches in 1948.

Inspired by this, Cardinal Mercier initiated ecumenical dialogue with the church of England in the 1920s. The Graymoor friars and nuns (a converted Anglican order of monks and nuns) made ecumenism one of their principal ministries. Little by little the ecumenical movement took a stronger foothold in the church until, on the eve of the Council, Pope John XXIII invited Orthodox, Protestant and Jewish observers to attend. John selected Augustin Bea, a German Jesuit biblical scholar, to oversee this development. Cardinal Bea gave ecumenism the visibility it needed. A Council document was written on the subject, as well as one on religious freedom prompted by Jesuit Father John Courtney Murray.

Since the Council there have been ongoing dialogues between Catholics and Anglicans, Lutherans and Orthodox, as well as special meetings with representatives of non-Christian religions. We are not at one yet. But at least we are talking with one another in a civil and faith-filled manner. We pray with Jesus "that all may be one" (see John 17:20–23).

The Time Was Ripe

Devotionalism, liturgical revival, biblical renewal and the ecumenical movement— these were the pieces simmering in the church on the eve of the Council. For over a century and a half, the church had fought off the liberal ideas of the eighteenth-century Enlightenment as well as the earlier positions of the sixteenth-century Protestants. But the time had come to stop debating, to start talking and to share legitimate common values. Vatican II provided the right platform at the right time.

Liberals and Protestants ceased to be seen as enemies of the church. In the friendly, nuanced conversation that ensued, a multitude of good ideas and practices were incorporated into the age-old tradition of Catholicism. John XXIII opened a window.

CONNECTING TO OUR TIMES

. . . .

Where Have All the Movements Gone?

New movements have a way of becoming old movements—or possibly no movement at all. This chapter takes a fond look at four movements bubbling at the eve of Vatican II in 1962: devotionalism, liturgical reform, new Scripture studies and ecumenism.

In a strict sense, devotionalism was never a movement, for popular piety is as old as the church itself, ever mutating in different cultures, always responsive to the faith tastes of a given age. The movements in liturgy, Scripture and ecumenism are no longer movements but established parts of church life. Liturgists continue to refine ritual. Scripture scholars will never be without

The term, which quickly became common Catholic parlance, means interior spiritual renewal or external adaptation of the church's teachings and structures to modern times. At the Council both meanings were applicable. Aggiornamento continues to be a process for a church that struggles for historical and cultural sensitivity.

. . . .

work to do. Ecumenists have a lengthy, unfinished agenda. Decades later we all realize that a movement, once accepted by the establishment, requires a long time and persistent effort to penetrate the faith-consciousness of millions.

Georgetown University's Father Larry Madden believes there should be a "second liturgical movement" so that its real meaning gets beyond the two hundred to two thousand parishes he believes are really in touch with all that liturgy is designed to do. (The United States has twenty thousand parishes.)

Many claim that ecumenism is presently at a standstill or plateau. The church of England's approval of women's ordination has set back Anglican-Catholic prospects of reunion. Theological dialogue continues at lofty levels, but movement to reunion among the Christian churches appears as far away as ever. In the United States Protestantism itself seems newly divided, as mainline churches weaken and evangelical-fundamentalist churches—the churches with whom there has been no significant dialogue—flourish.

Scripture study at the popular level is a real success story. Programs such as the Paulist's *Share the Word,* Liturgical Press's *Little Rock Bible Study,* St. Anthony Messenger Press's *Scripture from Scratch* and Our Sunday Visitor's *Popular Bible Study* proved that Catholics can have an enduring and active interest in faith building through prayer, study and meditation on the Bible.

Movements are a sign of life in the church. The Spirit will make sure we always have them. They are God's way of saying. "Wake up and put some energy into your faith commitment."

FOR REFLECTION AND DISCUSSION

. . . .

1. Is the church on the eve of a possible Vatican III? Do you see issues in the church and the world today that necessitate calling another ecumenical council? Or do you think Vatican II is yet unrealized, awaiting full implementation?

2. Prior to Vatican II, Catholicism could be described as having four central concerns: authority, sin, ritual and the miraculous. What concerns do you think are characteristic of Catholicism today? Can the above concerns still be seen in the church today?

CHAPTER TWENTY-NINE

JOHN XXIII AND VATICAN II

> Consult not your fears
> but your hopes and
> your dreams. Think not
> about your frustrations,
> but about your
> unfulfilled potential.
> Concern yourself not
> with what you tried
> and failed in, but with
> what it is still possible
> for you to do.
>
> —Pope John XXIII

The world into which Pope John XXIII came had plenty of kings and prophets. But what it needed most was a wise man. John was just such a man, rising up from a rich soil and a peasantry that gives birth to men who know reality and have deep faith. He never forgot that background and its wisdom.

This spirit was beautifully reflected on the night of his election in October, 1958. As *Time* magazine records the story:

In Sotto il Monte the three remaining Roncalli brothers, Zaverio, 75, Alfredo, 69, and Guiseppe, 64, were having supper after a hard day's work when the big news came over their old radio. The rice soup grew cold while they listened; then as excited neighbors poured from their houses, the brothers hurried upstairs to dress up for the occasion. And in Sesto San Giovanni, a little town near Milan, Angelo Roncalli's sister

Assunta was out buying bread when the news reached her. "My God, little Angelo!" she gasped. "What's the matter?" asked the baker, and Assunta explained: "My brother's just been elected pope. He will have to work so hard."[1]

He did indeed work hard. He strove to make real the Pentecostal prayer that the Spirit would "make new" the face of the earth. He faced this task with his favorite maxim of government:

> To see everything.
> To turn a blind eye on much of it.
> To correct a little.[2]

"I SEE THE LIGHT OF A NEW CREATION": A POPE FOR ALL PEOPLE
(1958)

It was the day after Christmas, 1958. Pope John astonished the people of Rome by paying a visit to Queen of Heaven Prison. In that gray light the first thing to catch his eye and visibly touch him was a beautiful crib made by the inmates.

A thousand prisoners, wearing their striped uniforms, stood before him. Pope John spoke to them as "dear sons and brothers." Then he was taken on a tour of the cell blocks. The prisoners were lined up to receive his blessing. He shook hands with each one until he came to one prisoner who drew back.

"I am a murderer, Holy Father," the man said.

John said nothing, but rather reached out and gave him a brotherly embrace.

Barely able to speak, the convict managed to say, "This is the happiest day of my life."

"Me, too," replied John simply.

The remarkable warmth of Pope John XXIII comes through constantly in the accounts of his life. For example, a few days after his coronation, Pope John held a special private audience for his family. The Roncallis entered the splendid papal apartments with feelings of discomfort, fear and hesitation. Quite a change from their farmhouse at Sotto il Monte!

Bashful and confused, they stood before the pope. They were so nervous that they dropped their presents. Homemade bread and wine and sun-cured ham, wrapped in colorful handkerchiefs, fell to the floor. They stood embarrassed and dismayed. John was not above smiling at the comedy of the situation, but he was quick to make them feel at home.

"Don't be afraid," he said. "It's only me."

An especially powerful example of John's genius with the common touch occurred about three months before he died. He received in audience the daughter of Nikita Khrushchev and her husband, the editor of the important Russian newspaper, *Pravda*.

The pope received them cordially and passed the time talking about their family. He asked how many children they had and what their names were. On finding out that the youngest was named Ivan, his eyes lit up and he said, "You must give my special love to Ivan, for I know that is the Russian name for John."

Before they were to leave, John asked if he might give them a blessing. The communist couple became a little embarrassed. "No, no, Holy Father. You see, we are unbelievers."

"Come now," said John, "won't you let an old man give you a blessing?"

They did so, and were deeply touched by this moving gesture from John. Just before they departed, John took into his own hands the hands of Khrushchev's daughter. He said: "When I look into your eyes, I think of the first chapter of Genesis where God said, 'Let there be light.' I know I see a light in you that speaks of a new creation."

That night John spent about forty-five minutes studying a Russian grammar book. Before he went to sleep he offered to God his life for the peace and conversion of "his dear people of Russia."

"I WILL CALL A COUNCIL"
(1959)

Pope John found plenty to think about as he read the Roman newspapers. He saw a picture of Russians in Red Square joyously celebrating a Sputnik triumph. He read of Charles de Gaulle's efforts to solve the Algerian crisis. Near the bottom of the page, he noticed an item about a bearded rebel, Fidel Castro, who stunned America by turning the island of Cuba into a communist fortress.

His diplomatic reports informed him of starvation in Asia, Africa and South America. If, indeed, the poor are always with us, never had so many been with us.

John looked at his world and wondered about the role of the church.

"Is my church a seed or pearl?

"Is it only the pearl of great price to be preserved from all possible contamination?

"Is the church also the seed that must burrow into the earth of the poor and bring them new hope? Should it not penetrate the soil of the rich and the mighty that their consciences might be touched by the gospel of Christ?"

John had heard critics complain that the church was irrelevant, that its pageantry and preoccupation with past glories obscured the message of Jesus. They claimed that people had stopped turning to the church for meaning. Instead of saving humanity the church seemed intent on saving itself.

John somewhat agreed with this criticism.

"Of course the gospel is precious. But if it is not allowed to take root in the lives of men, it will not be believed. If it is too protected, it will become like a

Church Councils

The first church council was held in the city of Jerusalem in or about the year 50. Peter himself was in attendance. There have been twenty-one councils since that time. They are generally named for the place that they were held. Vatican II was the second council held in the Vatican.

Each council was called for a specific reason:
- *Nicea I: to formulate a creed*
- *Ephesus: to deal with early church heresy*
- *Constantinople I, II, III, IV to reinforce the issues of faith*
- *Constance: to heal the Great Western Schism*
- *Trent: to deal with the Reformation*
- *Vatican I: to define papal infallibility*

In addition to the initiating reasons for calling these councils, many other things were accomplished. This was also true of Vatican II, which was called to bring the church into the modern era.

. . . .

museum piece—admired by tourists who give it a hasty glance. Men are saved by the living word of God, not by a lifeless trophy."

John decided that the church as God's seed must be generously poured forth in the world. He would call a council to bring this about.

"The idea came to me," he said, "like a ray of blinding light. A council!"

On January 25, 1959, Pope John went to the Basilica of St. Paul Outside the Walls of Rome to celebrate the nineteen-hundredth anniversary of the writing of Saint Paul's Letter to the Romans. After the service, John gathered the eighteen cardinals who were present and talked to them about the state of the church and the world.

"These problems must be faced. I intend to call a council of the universal church. I would like to have your advice."

The cardinals were so surprised that they sat in mute astonishment.

John recorded in his diary his disappointment that they did not show at least some enthusiasm. "Humanly speaking, I could have expected that after hearing what I had to say, they would have crowded around me to express approval and good wishes. Instead there was an unbroken and impressive silence."

In the days that followed, John's advisers offered many objections. When all else failed, they used the tactics of delay.

"It may take as long as twenty years to get ready for so vast a gathering."

John had no intention of waiting that long.

"I am an old man. [He was seventy-nine.] You get the council ready within two years."

He overcame their resistance and swept aside their objections.

The planning committee chose October 11, 1962, as the opening date. They picked this date with an eye to pleasing the members of the Eastern Orthodox churches: the feast of the Motherhood of Mary, recalling the fourth-century Council of Ephesus which declared that Mary is the Mother of God. Since this doctrine is held by the Orthodox churches, it serves as a point of unity between Rome and the East.

The choice of this date was a gentle invitation to the Christians of the Eastern churches to share in the new hopes of the council—and to reconsider the possibility of reunion.

In fact, the Russian church did send observers to the council, though the Greek Orthodox church was reluctant to do so. Several years later, Pope

Paul was to have a historic meeting with the Ecumenical Patriarch of Constantinople, Athenagoras. The "good seed" was already at work on the task of Christian unity.

The Second Vatican Council opened amid the pageantry and splendor of St. Peter's, as it played host to the church's leadership gathered from every corner of the world.

That evening, nearly a half million people poured into St. Peter's Square for a torchlight demonstration. John was overwhelmed.

"Dear children, dear children. I hear your voices. My voice is an isolated one, but it echoes the voice of the whole world. Here, in effect, the whole world is represented. You have come to open the Council, that God's treasures may be available to all men. He is on the wrong path who would limit himself to contemplating the luminous heavens and who keeps hidden the treasure that is the truth handed down by our forefathers. This Council will bring us to the right path."

LOOKING BACK
. . . .

Pope John XXIII

Few people expected a seventy-seven-year-old man to be such an ambitious changer of church history. The conventional opinion was that Angelo Roncalli would be a caretaker pope. Had they pondered more his unconventional career people might not have been so astonished. This most pastoral of popes had never had a parish. Virtually his entire life was spent in some form of administration. He was a desk priest, but one who never gave up his enjoyment of people.

His first ten years as a priest were spent in the service of Bishop Radini-Tedeschi, a first-rate diocesan planner. He worked with the bishop on the reorganization of the diocese while also teaching at the seminary. After a three-year service as an army chaplain in World War I, he took a post as national director for the Propagation of the Faith in Italy—a job similar to the one Archbishop Sheen held in the United States. He proved to be a successful fund-raiser, increasing annual contributions by 400 percent in just four years.

Ordained a bishop in 1925, he served as chief papal representative in Bulgaria for nine years. He felt lonely in that strange country where an unfriendly Orthodox church held sway. He also felt neglected, and recorded in his diary that he thought Rome was putting him on the shelf. Then one day a change came, an appointment as apostolic delegate to Turkey—further exile, in his opinion. For ten years he ministered to the tiny Catholic minority in a Muslim land.

None of this snuffed out his native love of people, regardless of religion or ethnic origin. In fact, his nineteen years in Bulgaria and Turkey broadened his outlook and fostered his sense of ecumenism. Finally, on his sixty-fifth birthday, just when many men plan on collecting their retirement benefits, he was offered a glamorous post: papal nuncio to Paris.

It was a nasty time to assume this distinguished post, for the anger of the French patriotic bishops was aflame against the cowardice of the Vichy collaborationist bishops. Roncalli used every wile he knew to put out the fire and heal the rifts in the French church. He did exceedingly well and was awarded the red hat as well as the affection of the French, who loved him shamelessly.

In his seventy-second year he was at last given a genuine pastoral assignment. The pope made him Patriarch of Venice in 1953. Age did not wither nor custom stale his infinite energies. Vigorously, he set about creating and implementing a pastoral plan for his archdiocese, much in the manner of his early tutor, Radini-Tedeschi.

When he arrived in Rome in October, 1958, his seventy-seventh year, to participate in electing Pius XII's successor, he brought with him years of administrative, diplomatic and ecumenical

Jewish-Catholic Relations
On October 17, 1960, Pope John XXIII received in Rome about two hundred delegates of the United Jewish Appeal, the great American Jewish welfare organization. He welcomed them with open arms as he quoted the biblical passage: "I am Joseph, your brother." (Joseph was the pope's baptismal name.)

experience. He also bore an ebullient love of people and a vision of what the church needed. On the third day of the conclave, two cardinals went to his cell and told him they were convinced he was about to be elected. One of them, Cardinal Ottaviani, urged him to think of calling a council.

John's immediate reaction is not recorded, but his ultimate one is. One hundred days after his election, John XXIII announced to the cardinals and worshipers assembled at the church of St. Paul Outside the Walls of Rome that he would call an ecumenical council for the renewal of the church. The old man, the so-called transitional pope, undertook the breathtaking challenge of changing the course of history in the Catholic church.

Pope Paul VI Completes and Implements Vatican II

From the early days of his priesthood, Father Montini (the future Paul VI) was introduced to the inside of Vatican affairs. His father was a prominent journalist involved in Italian politics—a fact that helped Montini gain a grasp of public affairs early on. With the election of Pius XII, Montini became one of two sub-secretaries of state. Before his death, Pius XII appointed Montini as archbishop of Milan. John XXIII included Montini among his first selection of cardinals.

During the first session of Vatican II, it became clear to Cardinals Montini and Suenens that an outline of a master plan was needed. Pope John had anticipated just one session and had not expected as much business as eventually arose. Montini and Suenens realized that the topics and positions for the Council were much more complex and open to debate than the preparatory committees envisioned. They approached Pope John and persuaded him to adopt their plan, at least in substance. As history would show, the acceptance of sixteen major documents on the topics actually discussed was virtually identical to their own plan.

Pope John died within six months after the close of the first session of the Council. Cardinal Montini was then elected pope and took the name Paul VI. He continued the work of the Council and was closely involved in its development over the next three sessions. If Pope John was the spiritual father of the Council, Pope Paul was its executor. His long years as secretary to Pius XII and his vast familiarity with church affairs, Vatican policy-making and a worldwide church served him well in his new ministry.

Paul's interest in world political and economic developments made him sympathetic to the thrust of the Pastoral Constitution on the Church in the Modern World *(Gaudium et Spes)*. The diplomatic and administrative skills acquired at the Vatican enabled him to move documents along. Experienced and bright, he knew more than most what was happening and why it would benefit the church.

The hard years lay ahead after the Council. The implementation of the Council documents introduced changes that had a vast immediate impact upon every Catholic. The Mass was now in the vernacular. Priests faced the people and a new lectionary was published. Thousands of priests, anticipating permission for a married clergy, were disappointed by Paul VI's *Sacredotalis Celibatus (On Priestly Celibacy)* in which he refused to change the discipline. Ten thousand priests resigned in the United States alone.

The most difficult challenge Pope Paul faced in the postconciliar years was the decision he had to make about artificial contraception. He appointed a commission to study the matter. The majority judgment of the committee was that taking the birth control pill was not contrary to the purposes of marriage or the laws of God. Pope Paul agonized over this. Many called him a "Hamlet," after the hesitant figure in the Shakespeare plays who found it hard to make up his mind.

But finally the pope did decide, going against the findings of his commission and publishing his encyclical *Humanae Vitae*. The negative reaction of a great number of theologians, the ambiguous support of some conferences of bishops and the resistance of many laity, especially in Europe and North America, remained a severe trial for him for the rest of his papacy. Yet many others pointed out the pastoral wisdom of the encyclical and his prescience as to what a "contraceptive mentality" would produce.

The first years after the Council produced a certain euphoria that misled many to think most traditions would disappear, even perennial truths of Tradition itself. This caused confusion about basic teachings and fundamental discipline. Pope Paul responded with a reaffirmation of Catholic faith in his *Credo of Paul VI*. He followed this with *Mysterium Fidei* (Mystery of Faith) to clarify and correct points of doctrine, especially on the Eucharist, that he believed were misleading in the widely popular *Dutch Catechism*.

Pope Paul VI had the unenviable task of holding the church together after the Council. It was as though his arms were stretched to the breaking point.

To his credit he succeeded with patience, calm and faith, intelligently illuminating what needed to be understood and peacefully addressing controversialists —or at least suffering in silence when he thought that was best.

All was not turmoil. He inaugurated the papal style of leadership fully embraced by John Paul II, making trips to Manila, Africa and Jerusalem. His embrace of the Ecumenical Patriarch Athenagoras signaled a new Catholic willingness to seek reunion with the Orthodox. He presided over the Holy Year of 1975, which brought millions of pilgrims to Rome. He piloted the church through rough waters and set it on a sure course. He left behind him one of the most distinguished papacies in history.

The Council

John XXIII set as the Council's immediate task the renewal of the religious life of Catholics, the updating of the church's teaching, discipline and organization. Its ultimate goal was the unity of all Christians.

The first period of the Council extended from October 11, 1962, to December 8, 1962. A number of the schemata were discussed but none was passed at this time. At the last general congregation, the already sick Pope John visited the Council to extend his thanks.

Pope John XXIII died on June 3, 1963. Shortly after his election, Pope Paul VI reactivated the Council proceedings, which had been suspended automatically at the death of the former pontiff.

The second period began on September 29, 1963, and lasted until December of that year. The fathers passed the Constitution on the Liturgy and the Decree on the Means of Social Communication.

The third period extended from September 14, 1964, to November 21, 1964. During this time, several parish priests were invited to participate in the general congregation as representatives of all parochial clergy. The fathers passed the Constitution on the Church, the Decree on Eastern Catholic Churches and the Decree on Ecumenism.

The final period extended from September 14, 1965, to December 8, 1965. The bulk of the schemata was passed during this period. It was also during this session that Pope Paul VI and Patriarch Athenagoras met and expressed their desire for unity between East and West.

On December 8, 1965, the last public session was held in the columned, majestic courtyard of St. Peter's Basilica. In solemn high pageantry, the leaders of the Catholic church, along with representatives from eighty-one governments and nine international organizations, celebrated the accomplishments of this great ecumenical council. Practical hard work had produced and issued four constitutions, nine decrees and three declarations. In effect, the Council had brought about a turning point in the history of the church.

CONNECTING TO OUR TIMES

What Do We Need, Reformers or Saints?

It has often been said that the church needs saints more than reformers. Of course, many saints have been reformers, such as Teresa of Avila and Ignatius of Loyola. What the saying really means is that reformers who lack sanctity seem to be crabbed and negative improvers of the church without the saving graces of love, holiness and persuasive witness. Pope John XXIII belongs to the saintly school of reform, a wise, holy, humorous and gentle pastor.

We could use a good dose of his approach again these days. Our church has become politicized by the wranglings of divided camps within the community. Much of the arguing is dominated by a humorless and strident tone. The merits of the opposing positions become submerged by failures in courtesy, resorting to caricature and a sense that the quest for holiness is on the back burner. Reformers without sanctity are oppressive. Pietists who pay no attention to people's needs are irrelevant.

Vatican II sent out a loud and clear call to every Catholic to reach for holiness. It is not meant to be the preserve of an elite corps within the church. The Holy Spirit excludes no one from this invitation. Actually, millions of Catholics are listening to the call.

Book publishers note that Scripture and spirituality are always at the top of their best-selling lists. The fact that so many people participate in daily liturgy, pray the Liturgy of the Hours (especially Morning and Evening prayer) and give themselves to regular sessions of centering prayer is a heartening and welcome sign that the search for holiness is alive and well.

John XXIII would be pleased. He prized the holy life above all else, as is evident from his diary, *Journal of a Soul*, and from Peter Hebblethwaite's wonderful biography of the pope. Those who wish to do something good for themselves, the church and the world could not choose a better goal than to respond to the Holy Spirit's call to holiness.

FOR REFLECTION AND DISCUSSION

1. Vatican II touched all Catholics' lives and still affects us today. Discuss the articles listed below and their value to your church.
   - Dialogue with other religions
   - The laity's involvement in the liturgy
   - A renewal of vocations
   - The role of women in the church
   - Active participation in the parish
   - Parish councils
   - Religious education programs
   - The support of parochial schools
   - The church's involvement in the "outside world"
   - The role of the pope in the world today
   - The role of the local bishop
2. How long did it take for the effects of Vatican II to become evident in the church? How did people react when these changes took place?

. . . .

CHAPTER THIRTY

MOVING FORWARD: THE FAITH ON FIRE

> [Y]ou are Peter, and on
> this rock I will build
> my church.
> (Matthew 16:18)

. . . .

"All of us, with unveiled faces, seeing the glory of the Lord as though reflected in a mirror, are being transformed into the same image from one degree of glory to another; for this comes from the Lord, the Spirit." (2 Corinthians 3:18)

When Pope John Paul II made his second pastoral visit to the United States in 1987, his first stop was the cathedral of Miami, where he met with the priests. Father Frank McNulty delivered an address on behalf of the priests. He opened with a story about a dinner party in an English country stately home. The guest of honor was a Shakespearean actor who was invited to recite some passages from the plays after supper. When finished his selections, he was asked to recite the Shepherd Psalm (Psalm 21). He said, "I will do so provided Father Reginald, your local pastor, would honor us by also reciting the psalm." Father agreed.

The actor declaimed the psalm with a dramatic touch and was greeted with warm applause. Then Father Reginald spoke its words in such a way that each phrase sounded like it came right from his heart. When he sat down the room was filled with meditative silence. The actor stood up again and said, "I hope you all understood what just happened. You applauded me and reacted with awesome silence to Father. We all then realized that I knew the psalm, but Father Reginald knew the Shepherd."

This final chapter will frame *The Story of the Church* in the last decades of the twentieth century and the first years of the new millennium through the lens of three figures who know the Shepherd psalm but who also know the Shepherd, Jesus Christ, to whom they have given their whole hearts.

We choose Mother Teresa, Pope John Paul II and Pope Benedict XVI, whose lives have affected most of the issues that touch the church today. Moreover they illuminate the verse quoted above from Saint Paul, by their journeying in faith and being transformed by God from glory to glory—an experience that should be the goal of every member of the church. In union with all the people of God they moved the church forward and ignited the communion of believers with a faith on fire.

> ### Philip Jenkins
> "We are currently living through one of the transforming moments in the history of religions worldwide…Over the past century the center of gravity in the Christian world has shifted inexorably southward to Asia, Africa and Latin America. Already the largest Christian communities on the planet are to be found in Africa and Latin America. If we want to visualize a 'typical' Christian, we should think of a woman living in a village in Nigeria or in a Brazilian favela…Christianity is doing very well in the global south—not just surviving but expanding…
>
> …Many of the fastest growing countries in the world are either predominantly Christian or else have very sizeable Christian minorities. Even if Christians just maintain their present share of the population in countries like Nigeria and Kenya, Mexico and Ethiopia, Brazil and the Philippines, there are soon going to be several hundred million more Christians in those areas alone…Christianity should enjoy a worldwide boom in the new century, but the vast majority of believers will be neither white nor European, nor Euro-American…. The fact of [this] change is itself undeniable: it has happened and will continue to happen.
>
> So little did we note this momentous change that it was barely mentioned in all the media hoopla surrounding the end of the second millennium" (Philip Jenkins, The Next Christendom, pp. 1–3).
>
> . . . .

Someone Beautiful for God

Who would believe that a small woman working in the slums of Calcutta would become the most famous and recognizable woman in the world? Who could expect a woman wearing a blue and white sari to have powers of persuasion with cardinals, bishops, mayors and heads of state eager to be seen with her and do what she wanted? Just when the church seemed stalled in debates about the meaning of Vatican II, a "living saint," as many named her, cut through the fog of competing ideologies and witnessed in the name of Christ a bare bones service to the poorest of the poor.

Mother Teresa was a refreshing example of the grace of God in a church yearning for saint. Born an Albanian in 1910, her name was Agnes Bojaxhui. Her father died when she was seven. Her mother sold embroidered cloth for a living. At eighteen, Agnes joined the Sisters of Loreto and went to India to teach at Saint Mary's school in Calcutta. Then in 1948 she heard a new call from God and left the sisters to work in Calcutta slums.

Soon she had a group of followers, many of them former students from her school. In 1950, the Vatican recognized her new community as the Missionaries of Charity. They looked for people dying in the streets and carried them to their home for the dying. The Hindus soon honored her as a living saint. Gradually she opened houses outside of India, including her first United States house in New York City in 1971.

Today her 4,500 nuns, 500 brothers and priests and thousands of volunteers run clinics, orphanages, soup kitchens and homes for the poor, the sick and the dying. Her work with AIDS patients changed negative attitudes toward them. British writer Malcolm Muggeridge went to Calcutta to interview her and do a film of her work. He named it *Something Beautiful for God*. She affected him so deeply that he abandoned his agnosticism and became a Catholic. His film brought her story to the wider world.

Teresa required a very simple life of her sisters—just three saris, a thin mattress to sleep on and the floor of chapel to sit on and pray. She claimed that luxury would spoil the spirit of her community and they must be poor in order to know and love the poor. She refused a steady salary for the work of her sisters and did no formal fundraising. She believed that God would provide—and God did.

When she was prevailed upon to give talks she emphasized the gospel teaching that in serving the poor we serve and love Christ in them. She also emphasized the sacredness of life and pointedly spoke against abortion at prominent settings such as a Harvard graduation, the Nobel Peace Prize gathering and the National Prayer Breakfast, where the audience gave her a standing ovation.

Nobel Peace Prize

In 1979 Mother Teresa received the Nobel Peace Prize. In accepting the honor she said:

> I choose the poverty of our poor people. But I am grateful to receive (the Nobel) in the name of the hungry, the naked, the homeless, of the crippled, of the blind, of the lepers, of all those people who feel unwanted, unloved, uncared-for throughout society, people that have become a burden to the society and are shunned by everyone.[1]

She invited the audience to join her in the prayer of Saint Francis:

> As we have gathered here together to thank God for the Nobel Peace Prize I think it will be beautiful that we pray the prayer of Saint Francis of Assisi....I think some of you already have got it—so we will pray together. Let us thank God for the opportunity that we all have together today, for this gift of peace that reminds us that we have been created to live that peace, and Jesus became man to bring that good news to the poor.[2]

The next excerpt from her speech reflects her opposition to abortion and the centrality of her mission in Jesus Christ:

> I believe the greatest destroyer of peace today is abortion because it is a direct war, a direct killing—direct murder by the mother herself. And we read in the Scripture, for God says very clearly, Even if a mother could forget her child—I will not forget you—I have carved you in the palm of my hand (cf. Isaiah 49:15–16). We are carved in the palm of his hand, so close to him that unborn child has been carved in the hand of God. That is what strikes me most, the beginning of that sentence, that even if a mother should forget her child—I will not forget you...
>
> ... It is not enough for us to say, "I love God but I do not love my neigh-

bor," since on dying on the Cross, God had made himself the hungry one, the naked one – the homeless one...[Christ is everywhere] Christ in our hearts, Christ in the poor we meet, Christ in the smile we give and in the smile we receive.[3]

Mass at Saint Patrick's

The world mourned the death of Mother Teresa in 1997. Her order, the Missionaries of Charity, operated six houses in New York City, including an AIDS hospice in Greenwich Village and a homeless shelter in the Bronx. She was no stranger to the city and thousands converged Saint Patrick's Cathedral to remember her in prayer and appreciation as noted in the *New York Times:*

> During the Mass, the upper reaches of the cavernous cathedral were suffused by the dark blue tones of the stained glass that let the day's subdued light through. The odor of burning incense reached the very back of the vast space, which seats 2,400 people but can hold more than 4,000. As Holy Communion was distributed, a mood of deep seriousness held sway, gripping those in blue jeans as well as the many in religious garb. The latter included a contingent in the front rows in the white and blue habits of Mother Teresa's order.
>
> In his sermon, Cardinal O'Connor used a story to summarize Mother Teresa's dedication. He recalled a diseased man, covered with maggots, whom he encountered on a tour led by Mother Teresa on one of his visits to Calcutta. He quoted the man as saying, "I have lived my life like an animal on the street, and I'm going to die like an angel, loved and cared for."
>
> The Cardinal asked what she had done for the poor man. She answered, "I cleaned him, and I knew I was touching the body of Christ." Because of his personal relationship with Mother Teresa, the Cardinal said the memorial Mass was very difficult for him. "I loved that woman very much," he said. "But even more, I was always astonished that she loved me."[4]

Beatification

October 19, 2003, Pope John Paul II beatified Mother Teresa. In his homily he made the following comment:

First and foremost a *missionary*: there is no doubt that the new Blessed was *one of the greatest missionaries of the 20th century.* The Lord made this simple woman who came from one of Europe's poorest regions a chosen instrument (cf. Acts 9:15) to proclaim the Gospel to the entire world, not by preaching but by daily acts of love towards the poorest of the poor. A missionary with the most universal language: the language of love that knows no bounds or exclusion and has no preferences other than for the most forsaken.

Come Be My Light

On the tenth anniversary of her death, a book was published, containing a collection of her letters to her confessors over a period of sixty-six years. In the book, titled, *Mother Teresa: Come Be My Light,* her letters reveal that for the last half of her life she endured spiritual darkness, felt no sense of the presence of God and endured a state of spiritual pain. She told a priest, "Inside it is all dark and feeling that I am totally cut off from God." This condition began with her ministry to the dying. This has surprised many of her admirers since her outward behavior was cheerful and marked by smiles. But the church expects these experiences in the lives of saints that have been recorded by her great spiritual masters such as Saint John of the Cross.

Despite the aridity in her soul, she arose every morning to be with Jesus before the Blessed Sacrament for contemplation, praying, "Jesus your happiness is all I want." She loved the Mass, the rosary and the other daily prayers. Without the inner feeling of God's affectionate presence, she strode forth to the streets lifting the dying with unfathomable love; she boarded countless jets and sped to the four corners of the earth to create new foundations and encourage the ones she founded; she visited the high and mighty but lived among the humblest people on earth. Remarkably, she brought joy to everyone she met while surrendering that inner joy she sought to the will of God.

Theologian and Lonergan scholar Father Matthew Lamb predicts that her letters will join spiritual classics such as the *Confessions of Saint Augustine* and Thomas Merton's *Seven Storey Mountain.* For a church coping with the spiritual aridity of a secular culture, Teresa's inner life may well become a ministry to a generation hungry for God, just as important as her public ministry was to the suffering humanity of the world. She often said the West suffers from starvation of the soul. It is well known that Princess Diana of Wales and Teresa liked each other and that Diana treasured a rosary Teresa gave her. It is said that one of Diana's sons insisted that the rosary be buried in the hands of his mother, who died the same week as Mother Teresa.

Certain of her sayings have become spiritual guidelines of numerous Catholics: "You do not need to do great things. You need to do small things with great love." "God did not call me to be successful but to be faithful." Mother Teresa summed up her life by often saying to Jesus: "If this brings you glory—if souls are brought to you—with joy I accept all to the end of my life."

The Pope Forgives His Assassin

In the 1983 Christmas season, Time magazine put a startling picture on its cover. It showed a prison cell where two men sat on plastic chairs. One wore a white cassock, a white cape and a white skullcap; the other, a blue sweater, jeans and running shoes. Time reported the story this way:

"Last week in an extraordinary moment of grace, the violence in St. Peter's Square was transformed. In a bare, white-walled cell in Rome's Rebbibia prison, John Paul tenderly held the hand that held the gun that was meant to kill him. For twenty-one minutes the pope sat with his would-be assassin, Mehmet Ali Agca. The two talked softly. Once or twice Agca laughed. The pope forgave him for the shooting. At the end of the meeting, Agca either kissed the pope's ring or pressed the pope's hand to his forehead in a gesture of respect."

"What did they talk about? 'That,' said the pope as he left the cell, 'will have to remain a secret between him and me. I spoke to him as a brother whom I have pardoned and who has my complete trust.'"

Did the pope's visit influence Ali Agca? One year later Agca proclaimed that he was renouncing terrorism to become a man of peace. He traced his conversion to the pope's visit. After extensive reading of the Koran, Agca said he had become a devout Muslim with profound respect for Christianity. He promised that if he were freed he would become a preacher to all nations, proclaiming goodness and truth to all peoples.

. . . .

Surprised by Cardinals
Pope John Paul II

A living church is always full of surprises, some of which are unfortunate and many of which are signs of vitality. On October 16, 1978, the cardinals surprised the world by electing a Polish Pope, Karol Wojtyla, who took the name, John Paul II. He was the first non-Italian in four centuries. It is said that some people just read history while others make history; such was the dynamic achievement of this vigorous new pope who made extraordinary history. The arc of his lengthy papacy of twenty-six years guided the church through the last two decades of the twentieth century and the first years of the third millennium.

He constantly preached the message, "Do not be afraid," an axiom he witnessed by his fearless life and teachings. He redefined the public ministry of the Bishop of Rome, roaming the world in over ninety trips as a living embodiment of the "New Evangelization." He showed everyone that we should not wait for people to come to Christ; we need to bring Christ to them. He broke the spell of ambiguity that beclouded the competing interpretations of Vatican II, a result of conflicts between the liberal and conservative wings of the church. He resolutely opposed those who saw the council as a revolutionary break with the past and instead insisted on its continuity with the church of the centuries.

In his journeys to Latin America he was outspoken in his opposition to the use of Marxist interpretations of Scripture in liberation theology. He was not opposed to needs of the oppressed and declared that the church should have a "preferential option for the poor." His own experience of Marxism in Poland and its furious hostility to the church stripped him of illusions about this philosophy. He often invoked the principles of the church's social teachings and the central theme of human dignity eloquently outlined in "The Church in the Modern World" [*Gaudium et Spes*]. For him the church's wisdom for coping with social problems was the best solution.

The New Evangelization

Since Vatican II, many Catholics have lost their interest in missionary efforts abroad. One outcome of this is the decline of missionary congregations. On the other hand the influence of missionaries of past years in places like India and Africa and Latin America have suddenly borne immense fruit. The largest province of the Jesuits is now in India. Social scientists have noted that Christianity is booming in the global south.

It's not a completely rosy picture for Catholics. Christian Pentecostals have made astonishing inroads in Latin America, mostly at the expense of Catholicism. The pervasive shortage of priests is a key factor in church's vulnerability to conversions to the Pentecostals. Also the prevalence of poverty, lack of economic opportunity, poor health care, absence of education for too many people imperils the church's existence and effectiveness.

The Latin American bishops who assembled in Aperecida, Brazil in 2007 acknowledged these problems but also resolved to commit themselves to a serious renewed evangelization of their peoples as well as working with the civil order to improve the lives of their flocks. In meeting with the bishops, Pope Benedict XVI enthusiastically supported the Latin American church's resolve to renew the faith of their people and to work with them to achieve a better way of life.

In Africa the rival to Catholicism is Islam, largely due to the huge investment of the Saudi Arabian government in planting thousands of mosques and Islamic schools in their towns and villages. One result of this intervention is a merciless civil war in Sudan where Islam is becoming the majority religion. But on the whole, Catholicism is flourishing in Africa and is the fastest growing part of the church. At the same time Africa faces immense social and economic problems.

The spread of AIDS is being checked, yet is still a grave health problem. The new governments that once were colonies continue to encounter political corruption, systems that are needed to help their people become self-sufficient and lack of investment from the rich nations of the world. Ferocious civil wars in Rwanda and Niger retarded the church's progress. As long as these conditions exist there will be a political and cultural instability that threatens the long range security and durability of the social structures that include the church. A mission of reconciliation, forgiveness and acceptance of repentance is essential for a new beginning.

Love, Sex and Responsibility
As a young priest Pope John Paul served as a chaplain to students at the Jagellonian University in Krakow. He liked young people and they liked him.

He hiked with them, went with them on camping trips, joined them on ski slopes and rowed boats with the best of them. In this he was always the pastor, the shepherd who heard their confessions, gave them Communion and desired to mentor them in Christ's spiritual and moral life.

Among the many questions they raised for him were issues related to sexuality. He listened to their difficulties in these areas and noted their hunger to know the truth and the best road to marriage and family. His famous Wednesday homilies on the first three chapters of Genesis during the first five years of his papacy were a fascinating reflection that was, in part, a result of his dialogues with the young in his early priesthood.

It was startling to hear him talking about the human body and its significance for love, sexuality, male-female relationships, family and responsibility. By asserting that God made our bodies and declared them good, he opposed hostility to the flesh as well as its exploitation. By teaching that God is the author of marriage and sexuality—man and woman shall be two in one flesh— he rescued sexuality from fears and disgust about it, but also from an idolatrous attitude that isolated sex from love and responsibility. In other contexts he noted the issues of temptations and sinfulness.

To hear a Pope talk this way from the very balcony of Saint Peter's basilica was unusual and perhaps a bit unsettling for some. In 1979 the sexualization of western culture was in full bloom—and it is even moreso today due to the extraordinary delivery system of the Internet that affords a contrary view of sex and marriage in endless variations. Most troubling of all is the trend to Internet pornography and its devastating effect on youth.

In these talks the pope was not tempted to issue thunderbolts of condemnation of the misuse of sex and its consequences, though he was fully capable of that on other occasions. Instead he sent forth to the world a calm, beautiful, desirable vision of the healthy role of the body as a gift from God, and how love, sex, responsibility and marriage are part of God's plan for the happiness of husbands and wives and their children. It took a few years before people began to realize the full meaning of John Paul's vision for them. Eventually it has been viewed in terms of the "theology of the body" and has proved to be a wholesome alternative to reckless sexual behavior.

The Gospel of Life and the Culture of Death

In the decade before the third millennium, Pope John Paul II aroused the world to confront the culture of death and stand up for the Gospel of Life—the title of one of his most powerful encyclicals published in March 1995. Many governments had legalized abortion. The United Nations lobbied other nations to follow suit. The state of Oregon passed a law supporting physician assisted suicide. Other states began to legislate funds for embryonic stem-cell research that required the destruction of human embryos. The innocent unborn and the frail elderly now are at risk everywhere. The lives of the most helpless among us are threatened. At the same time these powers that be did not lobby for funds for adult stem-cell research that has proved wonderfully effective in many cases and does not destroy human embryos.

The pope argued that democracies risked self-destruction if moral wrongs are defended as rights. "The state is no longer the common home where all can live together on the basis of fundamental equality, but is transformed into a tyrant state which arrogates to itself the right to dispose of the weakest and most defenseless of its members, from the unborn child to the elderly, in the name of public interest which is really nothing but the interest of one part [i.e., one group of voters and lawmakers]... How is it possible to speak of the dignity of every human person when the killing of the weakest and most innocent is permitted?" (Gospel of Life, 20, 2).

Quoting Cain after he murdered his brother Abel, "[O God] from your face I shall be hidden" (Genesis 4:14), John Paul declared that the deepest roots of this culture of death is the eclipse of the sense of God which leads to the loss of a sense of human dignity. Without a creator the creature would disappear. When we forget God our lives lose their real meaning. The pope stated that a person in this condition "no longer considers life as a splendid gift of God, something sacred entrusted to his responsibility and thus also to his loving care and veneration. Life itself becomes a mere thing...subject to his control and manipulation" (Gospel of Life, 22, 1).

"The Gospel of Life is the clearest, most impassioned and most outstanding encyclical of Pope John Paul and will be his signature statement in history" (Kenneth Woodward, quoted in George Weigel in Witness to Hope, p. 759).

. . . .

World Youth Days

Another contribution of Pope John Paul to the church was World Youth Days that are scheduled every three to four years. There was always a mysterious positive chemistry between the young and this pope, a fact that did not decline as he grew old and feeble, hands trembling and bent over with age. By the hundreds of thousands they came to him in Denver, Paris, Rome, Toronto and Krakow. And he brought them to confession, catechesis, prayer, affection for Christ and his Mother Mary, adoration of the Blessed Sacrament and the celebration of the Eucharist.

In each city where World Youth days are held, all the major churches are opened and crowded all morning with youth according to language backgrounds. Bishops lead their gatherings, giving them a catechesis related to the theme of the meeting. The youth are then invited to give witness to the power of Christ in their lives. The lines for confession are long. This is interspersed with prayer and meditation. The morning sessions conclude with Mass. Other religious events are scheduled for afternoons and evenings.

When World Youth Day was held in Denver in 1993, there was widespread worry that crowds of youth would not materialize. Denver was not near large populations of Catholics like Philadelphia, Chicago or Los Angeles. The bishops estimated that optimistically about 60,000 might come. Instead, early on, 250,000 from all over the world arrived—and thousands more came. The first two days were rainy—blunting their fervor.

By the time 90,000 young people crowded into Mile High Stadium on the third day, they were tired. But when the helicopter bearing the pope approached the stadium a roar arose from the stands: "John Paul Two, we love you!" The veteran pilot later said that the turbulence caused by the cheers buffeted the chopper and worried him about the instability, but he landed it safely.

Cardinal Stafford, then archbishop of Denver, noted that John Paul teaches us that young people can be affected by the language of presence. Being young is a time for searching. Our task is to be present for the search. At the final Mass, a half million people, the largest crowd ever assembled in the history of Colorado, gathered to pray. The sunset framed the majestic mountains in the distance. When the Mass was over, John Paul looked at his watch and said, "Good night. Make it a night of singing, of joy, of sacred joy. *Adios!*" For some months after that, guests at the pope's table in the Vatican noted that the only picture on his dining room side board showed the pope, rosary in hand, gazing from the window of his helicopter at a half million youth waiting for his closing Mass at Cherry Creek State Park.

Some of the positive results of these World Youth Days include a deepening faith in the participants. Many of them are converted from a self-destructive lifestyle. It is estimated that 25 percent of present vocations to the priesthood are alumni of these experiences. Most have resolved to become faithful in their marriages, committed to Christ, responsible as parents and willing to embrace the moral teachings of the church. They will have to battle with a culture that opposes them. They may need to struggle with their personal demons. They may fall and hope to rise

What makes today's young people more ardent churchgoers than their elders? For Gabi Zecha, 37, an official with Youth 2000, it's the age old search for meaning and communion. 'Young people are more actively looking for truth and credibility than their parents were. They want to experience that faith is alive, that it's fun and joyful. And they want to experience it in a community of like-minded people.'" (*Jeff Israely,* Time *magazine, August 15, 2005, pp. 34–35*)

. . . .

again. But they will never forget the cheers, prayers, love of thousands like themselves and an incredible father figure who seemed to understand them like no one they ever met.

Santo Santo! *Saint Saint!*
The Funeral of John Paul II

No one can remember a funeral like it. Nearly four million people flooded Rome to attend Pope John Paul's funeral. In Krakow a tearful 800,000 people watched it together on three TV's set up in a field. By radio and TV and other media the proceedings were transmitted to the globe. At one point three American presidents [George Bush Senior, Bill Clinton and George W. Bush] knelt before his body when it lay in state, a scene virtually unthinkable from Protestant America in years past. Dignitaries from 138 countries arrived. Leaders of all major faiths attended. Military planes patrolled the airspace over Rome and Italian police stood guard at all major intersections. Hundreds of thousands in an endless line filed past his body in Saint Peter's Basilica. This could have been a crowd control nightmare, yet it unfolded calmly and without incident.

When the great church bells tolled, Pope John Paul's coffin was carried from the basilica to the square. The plain cypress coffin adorned with an "M" for the Virgin Mary was set on a carpet in front of the altar. The book of the Gospels was placed on the coffin. The appearance of his coffin was acclaimed by applause and shouts of *Santo! Santo!* calling for his elevation to immediate sainthood.

Cardinal Ratzinger delivered the homily in which he traced the major steps in the late pope's life. The crowd interrupted him ten times with applause. Normally unemotional in public, the cardinal choked up with tears when mentioning one of John Paul's last public appearances to bless the people from his studio window. "We can be sure our beloved pope is standing today at the window of the Father's house, that he sees and blesses us." As he said those words, he pointed to the third floor window of the pope's apartment above the square.

The Mass ended with everyone singing, "May the angels accompany you into heaven, may the martyrs welcome you when you arrive and lead you to Holy Jerusalem." When the pall bearers brought his coffin to the doors of

Saint Peter's they turned it around to give John Paul one last farewell to the church he loved. To rhythmic applause thousands chanted, *"Giovanni Paulo Santo"* or "Saint John Paul." Their acclamation occurred just before the chanting of the Litany of the Saints. John Paul asked that he be buried on the bare earth near the tomb of Saint Peter and that is where he rests now. Thousands of people visit his tomb every day.

The popular desire to make John Paul a saint had an appropriate echo in the fact that he loved to canonize saints. Matthew Bunson writes:

> John Paul declared 1,338 blesseds in 147 ceremonies and 482 saints in 51 liturgical celebrations. His seventeen predecessors, from Pope Clement VIII to Pope Paul VI, canonized a total of 302 people. The stress he placed on universal holiness and the recognition of sanctity as deeply relevant to the modern world are all well known and will be the source of fruitful reflection for many years—even centuries—to come.[6]

The Sex Abuse Crisis

For some years Catholic social critics warned the American bishops that a severe crisis connected to the issues of the sexual abuse of children and teens by priests and some bishops would explode unless they took radical action. They waited too long, The predicted firestorm appeared in Boston in 2002, spearheaded by an extended series of articles and programs in the Boston news media about priests molesting children and young people. Hundreds of victims came forward and told their stories to the public. Their lawyers mounted expensive lawsuits.

Many bishops were charged with irresponsibility for moving priests around to other parishes after they had molested youth in a given parish. The accusations spread to all the dioceses with unanticipated rapidity. Cardinal Law of Boston was so overwhelmed by the problems that he resigned from his post and was reassigned to oversee Saint Mary Major Basilica in Rome.

Sometimes there were false accusations as in the case of Cardinal Joseph Bernardin of Chicago who was charged with molestation by a former Cincinnati seminarian during the time Bernardin was archbishop there. He immediately called a press conference and denied the charges and called for a committee to investigate the charges. Eventually, the accuser retracted his words and was hospitalized with a fatal case of AIDS. Bernardin flew to his bedside in Philadelphia where he personally forgave the man, offered Mass in his sickroom and gave him Communion and the sacrament of Anointing.

The national response of the bishops occurred in Dallas at their annual spring meeting June 12–14, 2002. Led capably by their president, Bishop Wilton Gregory, they forged the Charter of Rights for the protection of Children and the Young. The Charter called for training of all priests and laity, involved in teaching or supervising children and the young, in behavior that assured their safety, identifying boundaries to make it happen. Independent agencies were formed to accredit dioceses and religious orders to see that the Charter's rules were being followed.

Over the next five years hundreds of lawsuits were filed and over two billion dollars were paid out to victims. The Charter was updated in 2005. Its pastoral goals aim: (1) To promote healings and reconciliation with victims/survivors of sexual abuse of minors. (2) To guarantee effective responses to allegations of sexual abuse of minors. (3) To ensure the accountability of the procedures. (4) To protect the faithful. The effects of the crisis will last for some years to come. It is often stressed, rightly so, that the large majority of priests were faithful to their celibacy and committed to chastity.

God Is Love
Pope Benedict XVI
On April 19, 2005, white smoke floated over the Vatican signaling the election of a new pope. The cardinals elected a German, Cardinal Joseph Ratzinger. He took the name Benedict XVI. The name echoed admiration for one of his predecessors, Benedict XV, who reigned during World War I and who worked ceaselessly for peace. Another reason the pope chose this name was his affection for Saint Benedict whose monks played a major role in the Christian cultural development of Europe. The new pope wants to continue John Paul's vision for a new evangelization of Europe.

Already the best known of the cardinals due to his twenty years as head of the office of the Doctrine of the Faith, his critics called him the pope's Rottweiler especially for his opposition to certain liberal theologians. On the other hand his admirers saw him as a German shepherd protecting the flock. Clearly he has a quieter public style than John Paul, rarely using large gestures in his speeches and adopting a simple, direct preaching style that puts attention on the text rather than the speaker. His audience talks have been brief biographies, first of the apostles and next of the Fathers of the church—or sometimes the saint of the day. He weaves into these stories applications to the faith life of his listeners. He is at heart the professor of theology that was his early career, but by framing truth in the context of the lived experience of saints he makes the truth more accessible.

Pope Benedict's first encyclical, *God is Love,* is meant to be the signature theme of his papacy. His view of love always includes the reality of truth and the role of reason in the life of faith, hence his vision of love is far more than just emotion. At one point he tells us that while love is a matter of the gift of self, there is also a need to receive love.

> Man cannot live by oblative, descending love alone [that is, love as giving of self], he must also receive. Anyone who wishes to give love must also receive love as a gift. Certainly, as the Lord tells us, one can be a source from which living waters flow (John 7:37–38). Yet to become such a source, one must constantly drink anew from the original source which is Jesus Christ, from whose pierced heart flows the love of God (cf. John 19:34).[7]

The pope often returns to the theme of God as love in his numerous talks. When he created his first group of cardinals he emphasized love:

> I am counting on you, venerable brothers…to proclaim to the world that "Deus caritas est," and to do so through the witness of sincere communion among Christians…I am counting on you to ensure that the principle of love will spread far and wide and will give new life to the church…I am counting on you to see to it that our common endeavor to fix our gaze on Christ's open heart will hasten and secure our path toward full unity of Christians.[8]

Islam

Since 9/11 the world has become newly conscious of militant Islam, but this does not mean that all Muslims are involved in hostility to the West. Millions of Muslims in Europe and the United States live in peace with their neighbors and go about their daily tasks fulfilling their responsibilities to their families, their faith and their civic duties. The Vatican seeks friendly relations with Muslim states. Pope Benedict is concerned that Catholics be treated fairly in

Muslim countries. Catholic scholars in dialogue with Muslim religious leaders are addressing issues that are meant to promote mutual understanding and respect for one another. As always, political pressures, threats of war and memories of clashes in earlier history often impede progress and peaceful exchange. Love of neighbor still abides as a common ground for making headway.

Ecumenism

Relationships between the Catholic church and other Christian faiths have come a long way since Vatican II opened the door to dialogue. But the path to unity has faced bumps in the road. Issues such as women's ordination, same sex marriages and abortion are not only dividing Protestant denominations, but imperiling the dream of unity with Rome. Nonetheless, the progress in ecumenical relations continues as all participants continue to struggle with theological differences and cooperate in charitable endeavors to alleviate the causes and symptoms of poverty and injustice. The Holy Spirit is the ultimate cause of unity and cooperation with and trust in the Spirit must never be lost.

Pope Benedict has followed John Paul's special desire for union with the Orthodox churches. Relations with the Ecumenical Patriarch Bartholomew I, in Istanbul have been cordial for some years. John Paul made progress with the Greek Orthodox church, even to the point of a joint prayer service with their bishops in Athens in the forum where Saint Paul preached to the gentiles. Benedict hopes to build a firmer bridge to Moscow with their patriarch Alexei by appointing a new Catholic archbishop acceptable to him. The primacy and jurisdiction of the pope is the major dividing issue between the churches and will not be easily solved, but should not deter an increasing need to seek union.

Catholic Identity

For about fifteen years after the Council there some confusion about what it meant to be a Catholic. So many changes in the liturgy, so many new ways of talking about our beliefs produced ambiguity in what we hold as members of the church. With the election of John Paul II in 1978, the leadership of the church gradually became more and more sure of itself. Little by little this settled into the diocesan and parish life. A key moment in this development was the publication of the *Catechism of the Catholic Church* in 1992. Speaking of it as a systematic, comprehensive presentation of the truths of the faith, John

Paul wrote, "I declare the catechism to be a sure norm for teaching the faith."

Pope Benedict has continued this quest in a dramatic way by restoring the Latin Mass as it was celebrated just before Vatican II whenever a stable group of Catholics request it. He has approved a brief statement of the Congregation of the Faith that the church of Christ, the true church endures in Catholicism alone, though elements of salvation can be found in other ecclesial communities. The popes are defining the limits of what theologians can teach, curbing the authority of national bishops' conferences and asserting supervision of liturgical practices. They seek a strong Catholic identity that eliminates unnecessary confusion or vagueness about the truths of faith.

Benn…e…detto!

In August 2005, another World Youth Day assembled in Cologne where they would greet a new Pope. The centerpiece was the grand medieval cathedral of Cologne in the heart of the city and by banks of Rhine River. The theme for the meeting was, "We have come to adore him," words spoken by the Magi in the birth of Christ narrative of Matthew's Gospel. The words were linked to the shrine of the "Three Kings" inside the cathedral, the golden chests believed to contain the bones of the Magi.

Once again a million youth flocked to the event. The opening day was sunny and cloudless. Hundreds of thousands lined the banks of the Rhine to see Pope Benedict on the deck of midsized ship sail to the dock outside the cathedral. At his arrival he walked up steps and across a section paved with stones from Roman times. He entered the cathedral for a visit to the Blessed Sacrament. When he emerged from doors he saw a sea of young humanity in all directions ready to greet him with the chant: *Benn…e…detto!* interspersed with applause.

Formerly a very private man, he discouraged display, but by this time he had become accustomed to it and he raised his arms many times in grateful appreciation. Archbishop Timothy Dolan of Milwaukee was there and said later to friends, "They loved John Paul, but they also instinctively love the papacy. Their cheers were as much about that as for the man." The ice was broken and Benedict and his legions of youth spent the week in prayer, testimony, Eucharist, song and faith.

A number of Catholic lay movements have grown up Europe that have a strong appeal to the young. Communion and Liberation claim 50,000 members and Opus Dei counts 80,000. Other growing groups include the Neocatechumenal Way, Saint Egidio and the Focolare. Pope John Paul was a strong supporter of these groups and Pope Benedict wants to build upon this legacy. They may be just what the church in Europe needs. Church attendance is plummeting with Ireland dropping from 91 to 65 percent, Italy from 48 to 39 percent and France from 19 to 5 percent. The number of candidates for the priesthood has fallen dramatically.

Pope Benedict has a special affection for the United States and this was returned to him by the enthusiasm American Catholics demonstrated to him during his pastoral visit. Among his memorable words are the following:

> Dear brothers and sisters, in the finest traditions of the Church in this country, may you also be the first friend of the poor, the homeless, the stranger, the sick and all who suffer. Act as beacons of hope, casting the light of Christ upon the world.... The spires of Saint Patrick's Cathedral are dwarfed by the skyscrapers of the Manhattan skyline, yet in the heart of this busy metropolis, they are a vivid reminder of the constant yearning of the human spirit to rise to God.... [W]hen we leave this great church, let us go forth as heralds of hope in the midst of this city and all those places where God's grace has placed us. In this way the Church in America will know a new springtime in the Spirit, and point the way to that other, greater city, the new Jerusalem, whose light is the Lamb (*Rev* 21:23).[9]

A Closing Meditation

Ave Maria

In concluding our reflections on church history we return to the dawn of the church. After Christ's Ascension into heaven, the disciples who followed Christ assembled in the Upper Room to pray for the coming of the Holy Spirit. Scripture tells us the Mother of Jesus was there (see Acts 1:14), and the icons of this scene always depict Mary in the center of the gathering. One might have thought that Peter would hold the central spot.

The faith of the artists runs deeper. No one knew Jesus better that his mother. For at least thirty years she lived in communion with her Son and this relationship continued throughout his public life. When the 120 followers of Christ in the Upper Room gazed on her, they remembered that she was their earthly link to Jesus. Through her they reached her Son and urged her to lead them in prayer that he would send them the promised Spirit. She was their leader in prayer for this historic moment when the Spirit manifested the church. Just as Mary was the mother who gave birth to physical body of Christ, so she is filled with contemplative prayer, longing for the birth of the Mystical Body of Christ. From that scene we can observe the connection between deep prayer and the birth and continuity of the church.

Just as she prayed for the coming the Spirit who would manifest the church at Pentecost, she still prays for the Spirit to come and make ever new the church in which we receive the Eucharist to journey from "glory unto glory" being thereby transformed into the likeness of Christ.

Mother of Christ, star of the sea,

Pray for the wanderer, pray for me.

FOR REFLECTION AND DISCUSSION

· ·

1. The church has become increasingly involved in environmental issues. It seeks to promote all forms of life, including the whole of creation. To this end Pope John Paul II has said that "in many parts of the world society is given to instant gratification and consumerism while remaining indifferent to the damage which these cause." Do you see the church helping to promote an attitude of ecological responsibility? Do you? What concrete acts can be done at the institutional and individual levels to protect the environment?

2. In the political realm, the church traditionally has sought to avoid becoming identified with any particular government, political party or social movement. Has this always been successfully achieved? How should Catholic politicians balance their religious beliefs with their civic duty? Is there an essential link?

3. In the wake of Vatican II, the Catholic church has attested to the positive value of culture. Do you see any tension between American culture and Catholicism? What gifts does American culture offer the church? Where is American culture challenged by the gospel message?

4. According to theologian Avery Dulles, the richness of the church's reality is expressed by a series of images or models: mystical communion, sacrament, herald, servant and community of disciples. *The Catechism of the Catholic Church* adds Temple of the Holy Spirit, body of Christ and people of God. None of these models or images exhausts the mystery of the church. Taken together, they form a lovely tapestry that engages our contemplation and deepens our relationship to the church. How many of these models and images touch you? How can you come to appreciate all of them individually and combined into one overview?

5. After a long period of a shortage of vocations, a number of dioceses are beginning to show a turnaround. In all cases the bishop is taking active leadership in recruitment. Parishioners offer prayer and adoration of the Eucharist. Younger priests and seminarians preach the call to priesthood as well as make personal contact with potential candidates. Several dioceses have established houses for college-age candidates who continue their education while becoming part of a priestly formation program on a residential basis. One diocese with eighty parishes already has forty-five seminarians. Continue to pray for an increase in vocations.

6. How do you see the role of women in the church? How has the church benefited from women's contributions? How, as a member of the church, have you?

7. "Bishops, with priests as coworkers,…are heralds of faith who draw new disciples to Christ; they are authentic teachers of the apostolic faith, endowed with the authority of Christ" (*Catechism of the Catholic Church*, #888). Name some ways this teaching office strengthens our faith.

8. As the twentieth century drew to a close, Pope John Paul II saw the West embracing a "culture of death" with its emphasis on abortion, euthanasia and violence. He challenged the church and the world to support a "culture of life." What spiritual, moral and political means should we espouse to enhance human dignity and protect human life from conception to the natural end of earthly life?

9. As the church begins the third millenium, what pressing issues must it address? What challenges will it face in the years to come?

Notes

Chapter Four

1. Justin Martyr, *First Apology*, 66.

Chapter Seven

1. Thomas Bokenkotter, *A Concise History of the Catholic Church*, (Garden City, N.J.: Doubleday, 1977), p. 51.

Chapter Ten

1. Bokenkotter, p. 100.

Chapter Sixteen

1. *Declaration on Religious Freedom*, 2.

Chapter Seventeen

1. *Proslogion*, 1, 97, LH, Vol. I, p. 184.
2. Bonaventure, *The Journey of the Mind into God*, LH Vol. 3, p. 1536.
3. Thomas Aquinas, *Exposition on John*, Chapter 14, lecture 2, LH, Vol. 3, p. 316.
4. From Dame Julian's "Revelations of Divine Love," Chapter 24 in Elizabeth Ruth Obbard, Josef Pichler, trans., *Introducing Julian, Woman of Norwich* (London: New City, 1995), p.71.
5. Thomas à Kempis, *Imitation of Christ*, Leo Shirley-Price, trans. (London: Penguin, 1952), p. 192.

Chapter Twenty-Six

1. Note: This brief survey of papal teachings on social justice was adapted from the Web site Catholic Social Teaching issued from the Office for Social Justice by the Archdiocese of Saint Paul-Minneapolis, Minnesota. Their office offers a clear and thorough catechesis of this important topic. Available at www.osjspm.org.

Chapter Twenty-Seven

1. G.K. Chesterton, *Orthodoxy* (New York: Image, 1959), p. 21.
2. Adapted from Amy Wellborn's Web site, section on Flannery O'Connor and other Catholic writers. Available at www.AmyWellborn.com

Chapter Twenty Nine

1. *Time* magazine, "I Choose John…," November 10, 1958.
2. *Time* magazine.

Chapter Thirty

1. Quoted from Mother Teresa's Acceptance Speech at the Nobel Ceremony.
2. Quoted from Mother Teresa's Acceptance Speech at the Nobel Ceremony.
3. Quoted from Mother Teresa's Acceptance Speech at the Nobel Ceremony.
4. *New York Times*, September 9, 1997.
5. Pope John Paul II, homily, October 19, 2003
6. Matthew and Margaret Bunson, *John Paul II's Book of Saints* (Huntington, Ind.: Our Sunday Visitor, 2007), p. 554.
7. Benedict XVI, *God Is Love*, 7.
8. Benedict XVI, homily, March 24, 2006.
9. Pope Benedict XVI, homily at St. Patrick's Cathedral, New York, April 19, 2008.

Bibliography

Abbott, Walter J., s.j., ed. chapter one of the *Declaration on Religious Freedom* in *The Documents of Vatican II*, New York: Herder and Herder, 1966.

———. *Decree on Oriental Catholic Churches* and *Decree on Ecumenism*, in *The Documents of Vatican II*, New York: Herder and Herder, 1966.

Allaire, James and Rosemary Broughton. *Praying with Dorothy Day*. Winona, Minn.: St. Mary's, 1995.

Allegri, Renzo, Marsha Daigle-Williamson, Ph.D., trans., *John Paul II: A Life of Grace*. Cincinnati: Servant, 2007.

Augustine, Saint, Marcus Dods, trans. *The City of God*, New York: Modern Library, 1950.

Bainton, Roland. *Christendom: A Short History of Christianity and Its Impact on Civilization* (two vols.). New York: Harper Torchbook, 1966.

Baldwin, Anne B. *Catherine of Siena: Biography*. Huntington, Ind.: Our Sunday Visitor, 1987.

Barr, Gladys. *The Master of Geneva*. New York: Holt, Rinehart and Winston, 1961.

Baus, Karl. *Handbook of Church History: From the Apostolic Community to Constantine*. New York: Herder and Herder, 1965.

Becker, Jurgen. *Paul: Apostle to the Gentiles*. Louisville, Ky.: Westminster/John Knox, 1993.

Beckwith, Barbara. *Joan of Arc: God's Warrior*. Cincinnati: St. Anthony Messenger Press, 2007.

Bergan, Jacqueline Syrup and Marie Schwan. *Praying with Ignatius of Loyola*. Winona, Minn.: St. Mary's, 1991.

Bernard, Saint, Marie Bernard Said. trans. *Sermons on Conversion*, Kalamazoo, Mich.: Cistercian, 1981.

Bodo, Murray, o.f.m., and Susan Saint Sing. *A Retreat With Francis and Clare of Assisi*. Cincinnati: St. Anthony Messenger Press, 1996.

Bokenkotter, Thomas. *A Concise History of the Catholic Church*. New York: Image, 1977.

Brown, Peter. *Augustine of Hippo*. Berkeley, Calif.: The University of California Press, 1975.

Brown, Robert McAfee. *The Ecumenical Revolution*. New York: Doubleday, 1967.

Chadwick, Owen. *The Reformation*. New York: Penguin, 1972.

Chesterton, G.K. *St. Francis of Assisi*. New York: Image, 1957.

———. *St. Thomas Aquinas*. Kansas City, Mo.: Sheed and Ward, 1933.

Clark, Kenneth. *Civilization*. New York: Harper and Row, 1969.

Crews, Clyde F. *American and Catholic: A Popular History of Catholicism in the United States*. Cincinnati: St. Anthony Messenger Press, 1994.

Crowe, Jerome. *The Acts*. Wilmington, Del.: Michael Glazier, 1979.

Cunningham, Lawrence S., ed. *Thomas Merton: Spiritual Master*. Mahwah, N.J.: Paulist, 1992.

Cwiekowski, Frederick J., s.s. *The Beginnings of the Church*. Mahwah, N.J.: Paulist, 1988.

Danielou, Jean. *The Bible and the Liturgy*. Notre Dame, Ind.: University of Notre Dame Press, 1966.

Daniel-Rops, Henri. *Cathedral and Crusade*. New York: E.P. Dutton, 1957.

Dawson, Christopher. *The Making of Europe*. Kansas City, Mo.: Sheed and Ward, 1945.

Day, Dorothy. *The Long Loneliness*. Chicago: Thomas More, 1989.

Deedy, John. *The Catholic Fact Book*. Chicago: Thomas More, 1986.

Dolan. Jay P., ed. *The American Catholic Parish: A History from 1850 to the Present*. Mahwah, N.J.: Paulist, 1987.

Donaghy, Rev. Thomas J. *Lives of the Saints II*. New York: Catholic Book, 1990.

Ellis, John Tracy. *American Catholicism*. Chicago: University of Chicago Press, 1969.

Empie, Paul C., T. Austin Murphy and Joseph A. Burgess, eds. *Teaching Authority and Infallibility in the Church*. Minneapolis: Augsburg, 1978.

Erikson, Erik. *Young Man Luther*. New York: W.W. Norton, 1958.

Farra, Harry. *The Little Monk*. Mahwah, N.J.: Paulist, 1994.

Fitzpatrick, Joseph P., s.j. *Paul, Saint of the Inner City*. Mahwah, N.J.: Paulist, 1990.

Foley, Leonard, o.f.m. *Believing in Jesus: A Popular Overview of the Catholic Faith*. Cincinnati: St. Anthony Messenger Press, 2009.

Freze, Michael, s.f.o. *They Bore the Wounds of Christ: The Mystery of the Sacred Stigmata*. Huntington, Ind.: Our Sunday Visitor, 1989.

Ganshof, Francois Louis, Philip Grierson, trans. *Feudalism*. New York: Longmans, Green, 1952.

Gies, Frances. *Joan of Arc: The Legend and the Reality*. New York: Harper & Row, 1981.

Gilmore, Myron. *The World of Humanism*. New York: Harper and Row, 1952.

Gjerghi, Lush. *Mother Teresa: Her Life, Her Works*. Maryknoll, N.Y.: Orbis, 1991.

Gonfried, Robert S. *The Black Death: Natural and Human Disaster in Medieval Europe*. New York: Free Press, 1983.

Grana, Janice, ed. *Images: Women in Transition*, Nashville, Tenn.: Upper Room, 1976.

Granfield, Patrick. *The Limits of the Papacy*. New York: Crossroad, 1987.

Grave, Leif, John Rasmussen, trans. *The Augsburg Confession*. Minneapolis: Augsburg, 1987.

Hahnenberg, Edward P. *A Concise Guide to the Documents of Vatican II*. Cincinnati: St. Anthony Messenger Press, 2007.

Haile, H.G. *Luther: An Experiment in Biography*. New York: Doubleday, 1980.

Hamman, A. *Early Christian Prayers*. Kansas City, Mo.: Sheed and Ward, 1961.

Harrington, Daniel J., s.j. *Jesus: A Historical Portrait*. Cincinnati: St. Anthony Messenger Press, 2007.

Harris, Marguerite, ed. *Brigitta of Sweden: Life and Selected Writings*. Mahwah, N.J.: Paulist, 1989.

Hebblethwaite, Peter. *Paul VI: The First Modern Pope*. Mahwah, N.J.: Paulist, 1993.

————. *Pope John XXIII: Shepherd of the Modern World*. New York: Doubleday, 1985.

Hennesey, James J. *American Catholics*. New York: Oxford University Press, 1981.

Hill, Brennan R. *8 Spiritual Heroes: Their Search for God*. Cincinnati: St. Anthony Messenger Press, 2004.

Hinson, Glenn, ed. *Spirituality in Ecumenical Perspective*. Louisville, Ky.: Westminster/John Knox, 1993.

Hoever, Rev. H., S.O., *Lives of the Saints*. New York: Catholic Book, 1990.

Hollis, Christopher. *The Jesuits: A History*. New York: Macmillan, 1968.

Hughes, John Jay. *Pontiffs: Popes Who Shaped History*. Huntington, Ind.: Our Sunday Visitor, 1994.

Jedin, Hubert, ed. *The Imperial Church From Constantine to the Middle Ages* in *History of the Church*, Vol. II, New York: Seabury, 1980.

Johnson, Paul. *History of Christianity*. New York: Macmillan, 1976.

Koenig-Bricker, Woodeene. *Meet Dorothy Day: Champion of the Poor*. Cincinnati: Servant, 2001.

Latourelle, Rene, ed. *Vatican II: Assessment and Perspectives*, Mahwah, N.J.: Paulist, 1988.

Marthaler, Berard L. *The Creed*. Mystic, Conn.: Twenty-Third, 1987.

Matura, Thaddee, O.F.M. Paul Lachance, O.F.M., trans. *Francis of Assisi: Writer and Spiritual Master*. Cincinnati: St. Anthony Messenger Press, 2007.

McBride, Alfred, O. PRAEM. *The Gospel of the Holy Spirit*. Huntington, Ind.: Our Sunday Visitor, 1993.

————. *Saints Are People*. Dubuque, Iowa: W.C. Brown, 1980.

————. *A Short History of the Mass*. Cincinnati: St. Anthony Messenger Press, 2008.

Merton, Thomas. *The Seven Storey Mountain*. New York: Harcourt, Brace and Company, 1948.

Miller, Arthur. *The Crucible*. New York: Viking, 1957.

Monshau, Michael. *Praying With Dominic*. Winona, Minn.: St. Mary's, 1993.

Monti, Dominic V., O.F.M., *Francis and His Brothers: A Popular History of the Franciscan Friars*. Cincinnati: St. Anthony Messenger Press, 2009.

Nardone, Richard M. *The Story of the Christian Year*. Mahwah, N.J.: Paulist, 1991.

Noflke, Suzanne, P.O., trans. *Catherine of Siena: The Dialogue*. Mahwah, N.J.: Paulist, 1980.

Penock, Michael Francis. *This is Our Faith*. Notre Dame, Ind.: Ave Maria, 1989.

Pope John Paul II. *Crossing the Threshold of Hope*. New York: Alfred A. Knopf, 1994.

Schreck, Alan, Ph.D. *The Compact History of the Catholic Church*. Cincinnati: Servant, 2009.

————. *Vatican II: The Crisis and the Promise*. Cincinnati: Servant, 2005.

Seward, Desmond. *The Hundred Years' War*. New York: Atheneum, 1978.

Simsic, Wayne. *Praying with Thomas Merton*. Winona, Minn.: St. Mary's, 1994.

Stone, Irving. *The Agony and the Ecstasy*. New York: Doubleday, 1961.

Sullivan, Francis A., s.j. *Magisterium: Teaching Authority of the Catholic Church.* Mahwah, N.J.: Paulist, 1983.

The Rite of Christian Initiation of Adults in *Rites of the Catholic Church.* Collegeville, Minn.: Liturgical, 1990.

Tillard, J.M.R. *The Bishop of Rome.* Wilmington, Del.: Michael Glazier, 1983.

Treece, Patricia. *Meet John XXIII: Joyful Pope and Father to All.* Cincinnati: Servant, 2008.

Tuchman, Barbara. *A Distant Mirror: The Calamitous 14th Century.* New York: Alfred A. Knopf, 1978.

Turpin, Joanne. *Catholic Treasures New and Old.* Cincinnati: St. Anthony Messenger Press, 1994.

Undset, Sigrid. *Catherine of Siena.* Kansas City, Mo.: Sheed and Ward, 1954.

United States Conference of Catholic Bishops. *The Challenge of Peace: God's Promise and Our Response.* Washington, D.C.: USCCB, 1983.

Van der Meer, F. *Augustine the Bishop.* Kansas City, Mo.: Sheed and Ward, 1961.

Vinje, Patricia. *Praying With Catherine of Siena.* Winona, Minn.: St. Mary's, 1990.

Waldron, Robert. *Thomas Merton: In Search of His Soul.* Notre Dame, Ind.: Ave Maria, 1994.

Witherup, Ronald D. *Saint Paul: Called to Conversion.* Cincinnati: St. Anthony Messenger Press, 2007.

Williams, Marty and Anne Nichols. *Women in the Medieval Ages: Between Pit and Pedestal.* Princeton, N.J.: Markus Wiener, 1994.

Ziegler, Phillip. *The Black Death.* New York: John Day, 1969.

AUDIO

Acts of the Apostles, by Eugene LaVerdiere. Credence Cassettes.

Authentic Spirituality, by Michael Downey. Ave Maria Press.

The Confessions of Saint Augustine. Distributed by Ignatius Press.

Developing a Conscience, by Thomas Merton. Credence Cassettes.

Dialogue of St. Catherine of Siena. Distributed by Ignatius Press.

In the Image of God, by Thomas Merton. Credence Cassettes.

Joan of Arc. Ignatius Press.

Life and Holiness, by Thomas Merton. Distributed by Ignatius Press.

The Life of Saint Catherine of Siena, by Raymond of Capua. Distributed by Ignatius Press.

Love Casts Out Fear, by Thomas Merton. Credence Cassettes.

Meaning of Monastic Spirituality, by Thomas Merton. Credence Cassettes.

Monastic Spirituality, Part II, by Thomas Merton Credence Cassettes.

Monastic Spirituality/Citeaux, by Thomas MertonCredence Cassettes.

The New Catechism: A Comprehensive Overview, by Alfred McBride, O. Praem. Alba House Communications.

Praying with Paul, by Eugene LaVerdiere. Credence Cassettes.

Pure Love, by Thomas Merton. Credence Cassettes.

The Sacred Feather, narrated by Waylon Jennings. Our Sunday Visitor.

The Search for Wholeness, by Thomas Merton. Credence Cassettes.

Seeds of Contemplation, by Thomas Merton. Distributed by Ignatius Press.

Signposts for Pilgrims: An Inspirational Collection of Papal Quotes, narrated by Rev. Owen Campion. Our Sunday Visitor.

St. Augustine (Rome: 354-430 A.D.), The Giants of Philosophy: The Audio Classics Series, narrated by Charlton Heston. Knowledge Products.

Tales from the Catholic Worker, by Dorothy Day. Credence Cassettes.

The Thirst for God, by Thomas Merton. Credence Cassettes.

True Freedom, by Thomas Merton. Credence Cassettes.

VIDEO

A.D.: History of the Early Church. Distributed by Ignatius Press (three two-hour videos).

Adult Baptism: Exploring Its Meaning. Catholic Update Video, St. Anthony Messenger Press (31 minutes).

The Agony and the Ecstasy. UA/MGM (120 minutes).

Art Shapes Faith Shapes Art, by Jean Morman Unsworth. ACTA Publications (two 50-minute videos).

Brother Felix and the Virgin Saint. Films for the Humanities (75 minutes).

Byzantium: From Splendor to Ruin. Films for the Humanities (52 minutes).

Castle. Unicorn Products (60 minutes).

The Catacombs—A Walk Through the Past. Vatican Press Release (15 minutes).

Cathedral. Unicorn Projects (60 minutes).

Catholics/Americans. Paulist Press (twenty-two 15-minute sections on six videocassettes).

Charlemagne. Series for the Humanities (60 minutes).

The City of God. Films for the Humanities (52 minutes).

The Company: Inigo and His Jesuits, produced and directed by Joseph D. Fenton, S.M. Credence Cassettes (52 minutes).

The Crusaders: Saints and Sinners. Brown-ROA (28 minutes).

An Empire Conquered. Brown-Roa (three 16-minute segments about six early martyrs: Clement, Cecilia, Apollonius, Agnes, John and Paul).

Exeter. International Films (29 minutes).

The Greek Orthodox Church. Films for the Humanities (30 minutes).

How to Pray as a Family, by Gaynell Cronin. Ikonographics (20 minutes).

Jerusalem. Educational Video Network (19 minutes).

Jesus in My Life Today. Brown-ROA (15 minutes).

Jesus of Nazareth. 20th Century Fox (three videos, 371 minutes total).

Joan of Arc. Educational Video Network (36 minutes).

Joan of Arc: Portrait of a Legend. America (100 minutes).

John Paul II: Biography of a Statesman of Faith. A & E Productions (50 minutes).

Julian. Paulist Press. (60-minute video with study guide).

Late Have I Loved Thee, written and narrated by James J. O'Donnell, Ph.D. Santa Fe Della Productions.

Let Us Pray, by Gaynell Cronin. Ikonographics (two 25-minute segments).

A Man for All Seasons. United Artists (120 minutes).

Maximilian Kolbe. Daughters of Saint Paul (21 minutes).

Merton. Mass Media Ministries (60 minutes).

Michelangelo: Artist and Man. A & E Biography (50 minutes).

My Father's House. Teleketics, Franciscan Communications (10 minutes).

The Mystery of Faith: An Introduction to Catholicism, by Michael Himes. Distributed by St. Anthony Messenger Press (ten 25-minute videos).

On This Rock: A Look Inside the Vatican, produced by Daniel White. Cineco-Centrill Media Productions (30 minutes).

Orient/Occident. Films for the Humanities (30 minutes).

Paul, Apostle to the Church Today. Teleketics, Franciscan Communications (six 30-minute segments).

Pippin. 20th Century (120 minutes).

Quo Vadis. MGM (122 minutes).

RCIA: The Journey Through Easter. ROA (31 minutes).

The Reformation. Encyclopedia Brittanica (42 minutes).

Return to Glory: Michelangelo Revealed. Ignatius Press (52 minutes).

Rome—In the Footsteps of Peter and Paul, Part One. Brown-ROA (50 minutes).

Rome—Iin the Footsteps of Peter and Paul. Part Three. Brown-ROA (20 minutes).

Roses in December. Ave Maria Press (56 minutes).

Saint! Don Bosco Multimedia (30 minutes).

The Scarlet and the Black. 20th Century (156 minutes).

Sister Thea: Her Own Story. USCC Publishing Services.

The Sleep of Reason. Films for the Humanities (53 minutes).

The Story of the Cross. Doko (26 minutes).

A Time to Build. United States Catholic Conference (60 minutes).

The Vatican: Fortress of Christianity. Films for the Humanities (39 minutes).

Thine Is the Kingdom. Films for the Humanities (52 minutes).

Third Millennium: Vatican II. Credence Cassettes (ten 25-minute videos).

This Land of God. Our Sunday Visitor (60 minutes).

Where Luther Walked, by Roland Bainton. Vision Video (30 minutes).

Work of Love. Our Sunday Visitor (30 minutes).

Zwingli and Calvin. Vision Video (28 minutes).

INDEX